P9-DWK-416

THE FBI IN OUR OPEN SOCIETY

THE FBI
IN
OUR OPEN SOCIETY

HARRY AND BONARO OVERSTREET

W · W · NORTON & COMPANY · INC ·
NEW YORK

CONTENTS

PART THREE

THIS CONTROVERSIAL BUREAU

PART FOUR

UNFINISHED BUSINESS

FOREWORD

THE MORE federal laws multiply, the greater becomes our need to understand and evaluate federal law enforcement. The research which gradually moved us toward the writing of this book began, random-wise, in the early 1950's, as a project in self-education.

It developed by a process which we can perhaps best indicate by quoting a question E. B. White asks in his *Quo Vadimus?*: "Did it ever occur to you that there's no limit to how complicated things can get, on account of one thing always leading to another?" Every facet of the FBI's work to which we gave attention, every criticism of its policies or practices, every case that enlisted our interest led us further into the complexities of federal law and its enforcement than we had realized at the outset that we wanted to go.

By the early 1960's, our file of materials about the Bureau had assumed fairly substantial proportions. But not until the fall of 1964, when we read J. Edgar Hoover's testimony before the Warren Commission, did we recognize that we wanted to put into a book what our personal interest had moved us to learn.

When we started to write, it quickly became evident that our learning had, in fact, scarcely begun. At that point, our research stopped being desultory.

There would be no way for us to give individual credit to the many persons who have helped us along the way; so we will simply voice our thanks to them all.

HARRY AND BONARO OVERSTREET

Falls Church, Virginia

PART ONE

INTRODUCTION
TO COMPLEXITY

ONE

THE PAST THAT WAS PROLOGUE

NOTHING AKIN to the Federal Bureau of Investigation
would have been thought necessary or tolerable when
our Government was founded. The FBI is a by-product of
the growth of federal law—which is itself a by-product of
changes that no one at the outset could have foreseen.

The Attorney Generalship was created by Act of Congress
in 1789. The first man to hold that office, Edmund Randolph, was appointed by President Washington. But his conduct of it must have been somewhat casual; and his successors under Presidents Adams, Jefferson, and Madison must
have emulated his casualness.

Drawing on the Justice Department's "first letter book,"
Cummings and MacFarland report in their *Federal Justice*
that when William Wirt took office under President Monroe,
in 1817, he was amazed to find "no scratch of the pen indicating the duties of his position or preserving the work of his
predecessors." He forthwith established a record system.[1]

---

[1] Homer Cummings and Carl MacFarland, *Federal Justice*, Introduction
(New York: Macmillan, 1937), p. v.

In 1861, the Attorney General was given administrative control over United States district attorneys and marshals. Not until June 22, 1870, however, did Congress create the Department of Justice, with the Attorney General as its head.

The enabling act transferred to Justice prosecutive tasks previously handled by the solicitors of Treasury, Navy, and Internal Revenue, and the "law officer" of State; the "duties enjoined upon the auditor of the Post Office Department"; and "supervisory powers now exercised by the Secretary of the Interior over the accounts of district attorneys, marshals, clerks, and other officers of the courts of the United States."

Section 6 of the act was designed to insure—for the first time—consistency of legal interpretation throughout the executive branch. It specified that each department head might "require the opinion of the Attorney General on all questions of law," and it made his interpretation binding, subject to court review.

Section 8 empowered the Attorney General "to make all necessary rules and regulations for the government of said Department of Justice, and for the management and distribution of its business." Under this section, President Grant's Attorney General, Amos T. Akerman, gave the department its original structure; and under it, later Attorneys General have made such organizational changes as their workloads have dictated.

To take one example, when Attorney General Frank Murphy decided in 1939 to establish, within the department's Criminal Division, a Civil Liberties Unit—forerunner of today's Civil Rights Division—he did not need to ask Congress for enabling legislation. Acting under *Section 8,* he simply issued *Order of the Attorney General No. 3204.*

Section 14 instructed the Justice Department "to procure the proper evidence for, and conduct, prosecute, and defend all suits and proceedings in the Supreme Court of the United States and in the Court of Claims, in which the

United States or any officer thereof is a party or may be interested."[2]

In 1871, Congress voted $50,000 for the "detection and prosecution of crimes against the United States": the first federal funds ever earmarked for such a purpose. Since then, such moneys have, in differing amounts, been voted annually.

Attorney General Akerman promptly organized the department for its prosecutive work. On the "detection" side, however, he appointed only one agent—later designated as a Special Agent—to conduct certain limited types of investigation for him. Otherwise, he farmed out the department's investigative work, added it to the already heavy assignments of United States attorneys and marshals, or hired detectives by the day.

For the story of how the Justice Department handled its investigations prior to 1908, when the Bureau of Investigation was formed, we are again indebted to *Federal Justice*. This book was based on a "huge mass of undigested papers for the years since 1870" which Attorney General Homer Cummings found to exist in the department when he took office in 1933. Our quotations in the section that follows will be from its Chapter XVIII, pp. 366 ff.

The essence of the story is that the "detection" of crimes against the United States began on the level of makeshift; and there it stayed, year after year. It would appear that Attorney General Akerman had no wish to create a detective unit within the department. But had he tried to do so, he would have encountered formidable opposition.

Some of it would have come from Justice's own law officers, a number of whom would have preferred to limit the department's activities "to proceedings in court, leaving the investigation of facts and the apprehension of offenders to other departments or to interested private citizens." But

---

[2] *An Act to Establish the Department of Justice: United States Statutes at Large*, 41st Congress, Vol. 16, pp. 162–165.

more potent opposition would have come from Congress. It would have been spearheaded by the House Appropriations Committee; and to judge by later events, it would have been made effective by strings attached to funds granted.

Congress' attitude toward federal investigations was then, and for several decades remained, strikingly ambivalent. The legislators wanted violations of federal law to be brought to light. But they did not want the very department to which they had assigned the task of bringing them to light to have an investigative capability equal to this assignment—lest States' rights be infringed or police-state procedures develop; and they did not want either members of Congress or those who financed their campaigns to be investigated.

So the story begins: "Attorney General Akerman in 1871 called upon the Secret Service of the Treasury Department to employ 'capable and trusty persons' to operate in the South and unearth violations of the enforcement acts." Elsewhere, United States attorneys were given lump sums to spend on investigations.

In 1875, Attorney General Williams appointed four regional "special detectives"; and from that time on "a few 'agents' or 'special agents' were employed . . . ." Chiefly, however, the department hired detectives only when United States attorneys requested them for specific tasks.

Beginning in 1878, a few "examiners" were hired to "investigate the records and accounts of clerks of court, marshals, commissioners, and district attorneys." But such appointments soon became matters of patronage; and while the examiners were ostensibly supervised by a "General Agent," they were prone to render "desultory service."

In 1878, Attorney General Devens "reminded Congress that the Department of Justice was without the means of investigating infractions of the law"—but without results. "His successors faced the same condition."

Attorney General Brewster, 1881–1884, declared himself to be "averse" to hiring detectives at all, and said that he "disposed" of them as quickly as possible. Yet it was he who introduced the hiring of men from the Pinkerton agency—with results that moved Congress, in 1892, to forbid the use of detectives from any source outside the Government.

After this prohibition was established, Justice—having to get its work done somehow—began "to obtain the assistance of customhouse inspectors, agents of the Interior, bank examiners, and particularly the Secret Service operatives of the Treasury." As time went on, not only Justice but various other departments came to rely upon these operatives for the conduct of investigations—so that the Secret Service became, in effect, a central pool of detective manpower.

In 1896, Attorney General Harmon, stressing the "time, care and skill" required to obtain legal proof of conspiracies in antitrust cases, told Congress that he did not have the men to do the job. If the department was not to be given an adequate investigative force, it ought, he felt, to limit itself to prosecutive work; the task of "detecting" crimes should be assigned to some other agency. But his words produced no results.

By 1906, Congress was authorizing Justice's use of as many as 32 Secret Service operatives for temporary assignments. But even this provision was a makeshift. It was not written into law but depended upon the will of the House Appropriations Committee to continue it from year to year—by the granting of funds. The only established functions of the Secret Service were to investigate counterfeiting "and similar related outrages" and, after 1907, to protect the person of the President of the United States.

Those who took the brunt of things, out in the field, during all these years, were the United States attorneys and marshals. In an ever-more-populated land, and under ever-more-complex conditions, they were required—with never enough resources—to do everything that their counter-parts had done in early America, plus various chores not assigned to anyone else.

As soon as the Justice Department was created, the attor-neys were instructed "to follow upon the heels of rumor, to investigate, and to reach the truth of complaints." The mar-shals were told to "spare no effort" to uncover violations of the federal laws—although Acting Attorney General Phillips stated in 1881 that he could find no statute which required marshals to perform "the service of detectives."

When the department was asked by United States attor-neys to provide detectives for special cases, it hired them by a process so deliberate as to make impossible a swift response to an emergency. But when the attorneys and mar-shals requested permission to hire detectives on the spot, they were told that there was "no precedent" for their doing so.

Often, particularly in the South and West, the duties of the attorneys and marshals "brought them into conflict with the prejudices and passions of whole communities." The attorneys found walls of silence between them and the evi-dence they sought. Marshals and their deputies lived precar-ious lives.

In 1889, Attorney General Miller reported that deputies were being killed in the Indian Territory at the rate of 20 a year. A like number of marshals were killed during one 36-month period in the state of Arkansas alone. Yet in spite of the urgings of successive Attorneys General, Congress refused to make the killing of a federal officer a federal crime. It did not do so, in fact, until May 18, 1934.

By the turn of the century, Justice had given up trying to handle any cases save those that involved conspicuous frauds and scandals. "Even where public and industrial interest was sharply focused—cases of monopoly and railroad rate discrimination—the small, unorganized forces of the Department of Justice were utterly insufficient."

Attorney General Moody, in his *Annual Report* for fiscal 1905 (p. 16), said that evil would have to be allowed to flourish, with the occasional punishment of a detected criminal, or some remedy "deeper than any law now upon the statute books" would have to be found.

Yet the record which we have summarized suggests that the "deeper" remedy needed was a determined will to equip Justice to enforce the laws already on the books. The man who brought such a will to bear was Moody's successor, Attorney General Charles Joseph Bonaparte—the American-born grandson of Napoleon's youngest brother, Jerome.

In a double sense, Bonaparte was a Theodore Roosevelt man. Only a reformer of the Roosevelt type would, in the atmosphere of that time, have wanted him in the Cabinet; and he would not have accepted an appointment from a President who would have held back from doing battle with the entrenched forces of corruption.

Even as a student at Harvard, Bonaparte had viewed with contempt, and fought with a gay fervor, those who corrupted the political process. As a senior, he had, in 1870, helped to found the Signet Society, to fight the domination and manipulation of campus elections by the secret fraternities.

Later, as a lawyer of independent wealth, practicing in his native city of Baltimore, he had been a cofounder of both the National and the Maryland Civil Service Reform leagues. Also, he had initiated—and sustained for 20 years, until success was achieved—a campaign to oust the corrupt Gorham machine, which controlled both elections and political appointments throughout the state of Maryland.

Writing in the *Forum* of March, 1892, he had bluntly stated the case against "the big and little 'bosses' and members of 'rings' of various diameters" who comprised this machine. They had all, he said, been implicated in election scandals. Many had criminal records: "...those who have not are indebted for immunity, not to the public belief in their innocence, or even, in most cases, to the want of tangible evidence against them, but simply to their 'pull.' "

As an attorney, he became, often at his own expense, the courtroom champion of those who were being pushed around: intimidated Negroes, bewildered immigrants, those whom poverty made helpless before the law. Meanwhile, his sheer capability insured his having all the wealthy clients he wanted.

Unperturbed by the fact that his political foes called him "friend of the nigger," he urged Negroes to equip themselves to compete on equal terms with the white man. And he fought to a finish a proposed amendment to the Maryland constitution which would have disfranchised most of the state's Negroes by means of a "grandfather clause."

When Theodore Roosevelt, in September 1901, was made President by the shot that killed William McKinley, he at once put Bonaparte on the Board of Indian Commissioners and sent him down to look into corruption in the Indian Territory. The report which Bonaparte and his co-workers submitted in March 1904, persuaded Congress to revise the Government's Indian policy.

He was next assigned to prosecute postal frauds. Then, in May 1905, over the protests of old-line politicians in both parties, he became Secretary of the Navy. Roosevelt, however—as he later told Bonaparte in a letter dated May 31, 1906—saw this appointment as a "stop-gap" means of keeping him in the Government until the Attorney Generalship became open.[3] It did so before the end of 1906, with the resignation of Attorney General Moody. Bonaparte succeeded him on December 17th.

Congress was not, of course, all of one mind about how federal investigations should be manned. Two factors, in

[3] This letter appears in facsimile opposite p. 130 of Joseph Buchlin Bishop's *Charles Joseph Bonaparte* (New York, Scribner's, 1922).

addition to the intense anti-federalism which had prevailed throughout the whole life of the Justice Department, made for wariness with respect to the Government's investigative work.

One factor was an overgeneralized but not unwarranted contempt for detectives and their practices. Many persons who then went into such work were recommended for it by their own criminal records and what these had taught them about the underworld, not by any respect for the law.

To Attorney General Bonaparte, the fact that detectives tended not to be of a "high type" signified that Justice should have its own force of carefully chosen and rigorously supervised investigators. But to many members of Congress—among them Chairman James A. Tawney of the House Appropriations Committee—it signified that detectives should, to the greatest possible extent, be kept out of the Federal Government.

The other factor was a state of tension between Congress and the President. Its basic cause was the fact that a Congress still rooted in the McKinley–Mark Hanna tradition of politics had no taste for Roosevelt's many-sided reform program—or for his "trust-busting" fervor.

Speaker Joe Cannon, for example—the most powerful man in the House—broke with the President and became one of his arch-foes because of the Government's antitrust action against Standard Oil. This and other actions of like type had, Cannon contended, shaken the confidence of the business community and brought on financial panic.[4]

Secondary causes of tension were, however, soon added to the primary cause. In 1905, Senator John Mitchell and Representative John Williamson, both of Oregon, were indicted in land-fraud cases. When Roosevelt said, in terms that sounded like a blanket charge of wrongdoing, that he would order as many more investigations of members of Congress

[4] Henry F. Pringle, *Theodore Roosevelt* (Harvest Books; New York, Harcourt, Brace & World, 1962), p. 339.

as seemed warranted, that body went on the defensive. It was kept there by rumormongers, some of whom were indubitably in the pay of elements that wanted to goad Congress into halting Justice's use of Secret Service operatives.

The Secret Service—so the rumors went—had become a mammoth secret-police force. President Roosevelt—so the rumors went—was using its operatives to "get something" on members of Congress who opposed his legislative program.

All in all, the atmosphere within which Attorney General Bonaparte took office was not exactly hospitable to Federal investigations. Nonetheless, he undertook to organize for maximum efficiency and accountability Justice's small force of "eight examiners and twelve special agents."[5] And when the first opportunity offered itself, he initiated a tenacious campaign to get the department's investigative work, once for all, off the level of makeshift.

[5] Cummings and MacFarland, p. 386.

TWO

CHALLENGE AND DECISION

A 1907 HEARING on a Deficiency Appropriations Bill gave Bonaparte his first chance to ask that Congress authorize a small permanent detective force for the Justice Department.[1] He did not ask for the legal right to create it: that was his by virtue of the Department of Justice Act of 1870. He asked that certain strings attached to Justice's appropriation be cut—strings that held him, as they had held his predecessors, to the practice of temporary hiring of investigative personnel.

The Attorney General, he said, should have under his own control some detectives who would be always on call, for whom he could plan appropriate training, who could be made subject to strict supervision and discipline, and who could be deployed as a mobile unit, to go wherever they were needed.

His quarrel was not with the Secret Service: "I do not want to be understood as in any wise criticizing that force . . . ." It was with a policy that made him entrust even "deli-

[1] *Hearings of the House Appropriations Committee on Deficiency Appropriations Bill for 1908*, pp. 202–203.

cate and highly confidential" investigations to temporary employees who were answerable not to him but to the Secretary of the Treasury.

Moreover, because the process of temporary hiring was slow and cumbersome, many investigations were tardily begun—and were thus made needlessly difficult and expensive. The Assistant Chief of the Secret Service, W. H. Moran, described this process to the Committee at a later hearing:

The Attorney General writes a letter to the Secretary of the Treasury stating that he has a certain matter that he wants investigated . . . . In reply to that they are told that Mr. So-and-so is a person who is probably able to meet the requirements, and if they want him he will expect a certain per diem and expenses.

Sometimes the recommended person proved to be on a higher salary scale than Justice could afford. Sometimes no operative was available. In the latter case, Treasury might report to this effect. Or it might put temporarily on its payroll someone from its eligibility list, and then hire him out to Justice—adding its clerical expenses to the fee charged for his work.[2]

Since Treasury had to know how its operatives were being used, they were never hired out for a span of time, but only for designated assignments. Thus, Justice could not pull a man off the case for which he had been hired and put him on a more important one that suddenly developed.

It was in terms of such considerations that Attorney General Bonaparte asked permission to use some of his appropriation to create and maintain "a small permanent detective force." His request was not granted. At this 1907 hearing, Chairman Tawney *was*, in effect, the Committee; and he

---

[2] *Hearings of the House Appropriations Subcommittee on Sundry Civil Appropriations Bill for 1909*, pp. 185 ff.

was strongly opposed to the creation of any new federal investigative body.

The Attorney General, "beaten to fight better," discussed the problem in his *Annual Report*, and renewed his request on April 2, 1908, at a hearing on the Sundry Civil Appropriations Bill for 1909. Further, he suggested that when Justice's force had been authorized and was functioning, and when provision had been made for the needs of other departments, the Secret Service should be relieved of its manpower-lending role, an ambiguous one for which it had no affection.

At this April 2nd hearing, Chairman Tawney proposed as a compromise that the Attorney General be empowered to hire men from "the eligible list in Treasury." Such men, he urged, would be wholly under the Attorney General's control while they were on his payroll. But he could so word their contracts that he could let them go when their assignments were finished. If Bonaparte would accept this plan, he, the Chairman, would ask Congress for enabling legislation.

Bonaparte said *No*: men on such contracts would be, in fact and in their own minds, temporary employees. He needed a force that could be welded into a working unit and encouraged to develop the type of competence, loyalty, and morale by which federal investigations should be safeguarded.

Few of the opinions expressed by Committee members touched, in any practical sense, upon the problems of federal law enforcement. Most of them stemmed from anxiety about the rumored police-state practices of the Secret Service and from a general distaste for detective work. The tenor of the discussion can be illustrated by the following exchange.

There had been, said Congressman Sherley of Kentucky, "much talk" about Secret Service probings into private

affairs "to determine whether or not a crime had been committed." Too many detectives tried to make work for themselves by ferreting out some crime to investigate. Bonaparte
replied that the practice of temporary hiring encouraged
this evil. It was, on the other hand, discouraged where

. . . you have a man who is permanently employed in the Department and whose retention depends upon the faithful discharge of
his duty, and not on the fact of his making work for himself.
Congressman Sherley: I think there may be some force in that
argument.
Mr. Bonaparte: If you pay him by the job and make his continued employment dependent on his finding more jobs, you run the
danger . . . of making him what they call abroad an "agent provocateur," a person who creates the crime in order that he may get
the credit for detecting and punishing the criminal.

Here, Congressman Walter I. Smith of Iowa broke in to
say that he had read somewhere—"I do not know how true it
is"—that the Government of the United States had far more
secret agents than had Czarist Russia. Bonaparte voiced his
skepticism about the writer's having had access to reliable
facts on which to base such a comparison. Then he returned
to the subject of the *agent provocateur*, saying that nothing
is "more open to abuse than the employment of men of that
type."

"Nothing," said Congressman Smith, "is more opposed to
our race than a belief that a general system of espionage is
being conducted by the General Government." Bonaparte
replied that he did not think there was need for "apprehension" on that score so far as the Justice Department was concerned. On this note the hearing ended.[3]

A spectator at this hearing might have felt it to be a
toss-up whether Congress would authorize Bonaparte's
detective force or hold him to the going practice. It did
neither. Implausibly, it put an end to the use of Secret Serv-

[3] *op. cit.*, pp. 773–780.

ice operatives by Justice and other departments and *author-*
ized no alternative source of investigative manpower.

The key to this extraordinary action lay in the fact that
the quarrel of Congress with President Roosevelt was
mounting to a climax. As Henry F. Pringle reports in his
Theodore Roosevelt, pp. 339–340, the President, in
April–May 1908, became increasingly peremptory in his
demands for Congressional action on his reform program;
and Congress—pressing toward adjournment, "so that its
members could hurry to their home districts for the coming
campaign"—turned an increasingly deaf ear to his messages.

Then, just as the Appropriations Bill came up for debate
in the House, Congressional anger was raised to a new pitch
by rumors of "a Secret Service system similar to that of the
hated Black Cabinet in St. Petersburg." Roosevelt was said
to be using the Secret Service "to obtain interesting data
when the gentlemen of Congress trod, heavily and rashly,
the Primrose Path"—his alleged purpose being to secure
"damaging evidence" with which to coerce opponents of his
program into supporting it.

Congress' credulity with respect to such rumors—none of
which it could ever substantiate—recalls Horace's definition
of anger as "a short madness." But when the Bill was passed,
it carried a hastily conceived amendment:

No part of any money appropriated by this act shall be used in
the payment of compensation or expense for any person detailed
or transferred from the Secret Service of the Treasury Department or (and) who may at any time during the fiscal year 1909
have been employed by and under said Secret Service Division.[4]

The New York Times of May 6, 1908, responded to the
House vote by saying in a blunt editorial, "The Representatives have, however unwittingly, become the tools of thieves.
The Senators are duly warned." United States attorneys
begged Bonaparte to find some way to keep the Senate from

---

[4] *Senate Report 970; 43 Congressional Record,* p. 2181.

confirming the vote of the House. But on May 27th, the Senate passed the Bill as amended.

Three days later, Congress adjourned, not to reconvene until after the November elections. It had voted Justice's appropriation for the "detection and prosecution of crime against the United States." But it had walked out on the question of how, with the Secret Service out of the picture, and no force authorized to take its place, such crimes were to be "detected."

The Appropriations Bill was slated to go into effect on July 1st, when fiscal 1909 would begin. Thus, Bonaparte had one month in which to make some provision for Justice's investigative work that would let him use the funds granted and yet not violate the terms of the amendment.

It was Henry L. Stimson, then United States attorney in New York, who suggested in a letter dated June 5, 1908, that the Attorney General hire as permanent employees some of the Secret Service men who had worked well for the Department. To do so, he said, would provide a core of good men for the new force that must be created and would prevent appointments to this force from becoming matters of patronage.[5] After a swift round of consultations, Bonaparte acted on the proposal.

Later, on January 27, 1909, Chief John E. Wilkie of the Secret Service told the House Appropriations Committee how the transfer of men had been conducted.[6] He had provided a list of available men—some of whom had worked more constantly for Justice than for the Treasury. The Attorney General had wanted to hire twelve or eighteen; but the cost had proved to be "more than he could handle." Also, he had been forced to pass over some of those whom he most wanted because they were "on a higher salary scale than Justice could afford." In the end, Bonaparte had selected

[5] Cummings and MacFarland, p. 378.

[6] *Hearings of the House Appropriations Committee on Sundry Civil Appropriations Bill for 1910*, pp. 235–236.

nine men. On June 30th, these nine were separated from Treasury. Before fiscal 1909 began, they were on Justice's payroll.

There had been, Wilkie emphasized, no infringement of the law or of the terms of the May amendment: "What the Justice Department is doing is what it was thought they would have to do . . . ." Furthermore:

That is where investigative forces really belong, in my opinion. They should be in the Department of Justice. The cases have to go there eventually. All our cases go to that department for prosecution.

To the embarrassment of the Committee, Wilkie also pointed out that the amendment was, in practice, discriminatory. Congress did not outlaw the hiring of Secret Service men but merely forbade their being paid out of the 1909 appropriation. Some departments, among them Justice and Agriculture, were wholly dependent upon their current appropriations. But others, such as State and Navy, had been able to divert moneys from reserve funds and go on hiring Secret Service operatives.

On July 1, 1908, Attorney General Bonaparte put his nine new detectives and such special agents and examiners as were already on his payroll under the supervision of his Chief Examiner, Stanley W. Finch—and thus gave himself a force of twenty-three men. On July 26th, acting on Presidential instructions, he issued the order which made this force a permanent subdivision of the Department, with Finch as its Chief.

It remained for his successor, Attorney General George W. Wickersham, to christen the new unit. In March 1909, he named it the Bureau of Investigation. In 1935, it was renamed the Federal Bureau of Investigation: the FBI.

The drama of Congress' authorization of the new force began on December 8, 1908, when Theodore Roosevelt delivered to the Sixtieth Congress, Second Session, a message in which he declared that the May amendment to the 1909 Appropriations Bill had been of benefit only to criminals:

The chief argument in favor of the provision was that Congressmen did not themselves want to be investigated . . . . I do not believe that it is in the public interest to protect criminals in any branch of the public service . . . .[7]

Compounding the insult resident in these words, he went on to suggest that if the legislative body felt that the conduct of its members would not stand examination, it might vote to let Secret Service operatives be used to investigate any suspects who were not in the House or the Senate.

Congress was already touchy on the subject of the amendment. It had been made so by editorials like the one in *The New York Times*, and by press reports, some of them considerably exaggerated, about key investigations' having had to be dropped.

Moreover, some of its members, particularly in the Senate, had come to realize that they had been duped by rumormongers in the pay of vested interests. A lengthy exchange of letters, for example, between the President and Senator Frederick Hale indicates that the latter had been grossly misled about the size of the Secret Service, and that he had been moved to support the amendment by "sordid confidential information," or alleged information, that had been pressed upon him.[8]

Further, Congress was clearly vulnerable on two counts. It had, in 1907, held the Attorney General against his will to a hiring practice which, a year later, it had rated as so nefarious that it must be halted *at once*. And it had adjourned in

[7] *Senate Report 970; 43 Congressional Record*, p. 2181.

[8] Cummings and MacFarland, p. 378.

such haste, to spend five months campaigning, that it had failed to authorize any means by which crimes against the United States could be detected.

Yet in long-range terms, Congress was not so much guilty of doing the wrong thing as of doing the right thing in the wrong way for the wrong reasons. It stood on firm ground when it held the existence of *any* centralized police or detective force to be incompatible with our free system.

Assistant Chief Moran, we would recall, testified on March 24, 1908, that, when its own operatives were all busy, the Secret Service often satisfied requests—from Justice and other departments—by putting temporarily on its own payroll men from its eligibility list. Questioned by Chairman Tawney, he had said that it could, by this means, if it had enough eligible applicants, "satisfy" the needs of the whole executive branch.

The Secret Service's annual appropriation was supposed to provide for the number of men it needed to perform its work. But the appropriation provided, in fact, no reliable clue to how many operatives were on its payroll—since those whom it hired expressly *to hire out* to the departments were paid out of the budgets of the requesting departments.

There is nothing to suggest that Chief Wilkie had exploited this situation in any way. There was no emergency reason why the use of Secret Service men could not have been phased out at a pace that matched the development of alternative resources. But Congress was not just seeing ghosts when it saw the lending practice—which it had itself continued and condoned—as a potential threat to our liberties.

A power-hungry and ruthless Chief could have planted his own henchmen in sensitive positions throughout the executive departments by simply recommending them when operatives were requested. During the six months prior to the hearing at which Moran testified, Justice, War, Navy, Commerce and Labor, and various other departments had hired Secret Service men.

To ready itself to answer the President's charges, the Senate, on December 16, 1908, instructed its Appropriations Committee to study and report on the original intent of Congress in creating the Secret Service. The House, in response to a second message from the President on January 4, 1909, appointed a Select Committee on Appropriations for Prevention of Frauds upon and Depredations in the Public Service. Its task was to investigate both the history and the current practices of all the Federal investigative bodies.

Both committees held hearings and studied documents in workmanlike fashion. Related issues were debated, meanwhile, on the floors of both houses. In brief, the type of thinking that should have preceded action in May 1908—and that had never really been done since the Justice Department was formed—was belatedly undertaken in January– February 1909.

To judge by the texts of hearings, debates, and committee reports, there was never any real doubt about the acceptance of Justice's new detective force. What was more and more decisively ruled out was any return to the practice of using the Secret Service as a central pool of investigative manpower. The view which prevailed can be illustrated by passages from a speech which Congressman Smith of Iowa made on the floor of the House on January 8, 1909, and from the report of the Senate Appropriations Committee—*Senate Report 970*—which was submitted on February 11th.

Congressman Smith, reviewing the history of the Secret Service, brought out the fact that it had originally been established by the same process as had Bonaparte's detective force. "There never was any law, as I understand it, creating the Secret Service . . . ." It was brought into being by administrative order of the Secretary of the Treasury.

Prior to the Civil War, Smith said, Congress had made "trifling appropriations . . . for the detection and punish-

ment of counterfeiters." But the war "caused a vast issue of
greenbacks, national-bank notes, and bonds...." Counterfeiting swiftly increased; and Congress, in 1864, "commenced making regular appropriations for its suppression."
The Treasury Department created "what it called the
'Secret Service Division' to administer these annual appropriations."

The issue before the House, Congressman Smith emphasized, was not whether Bonaparte had been justified in
establishing his force, but whether Congress "was subject to
just criticism" for having ended the hiring out of Secret
Service operatives.

I may say, however, that as there never was any special creation by act of Congress of the detective force now known as the
"Secret Service," except by the appropriation of funds for the
detection of counterfeiting, I am wholly at a loss to know why
the Attorney General has not the power to organize a detective
force under the numerous appropriations now at his disposal,
and his last report shows he has already done so.[9]

The final consensus was that he did, indeed, have that
power; and a supportive appropriation was voted accordingly.

Senate Report 970, in accord with the usage then
common, treats the uncapitalized term secret service agent
as synonymous with detective or investigator. In this Report,
we read:

Congress has made an appropriation for the employment of
secret service agents by the Department of Justice, and that
department has at present such a force organized; and it is the
opinion of your committee, that with the exception of a small
force in the Treasury Department for use in investigating counterfeiting and protecting the person of the President of the
United States the Department of Justice is the proper place for
the employment of secret service agents, as it is the department

---

[9] 43 Congressional Record, p. 672.

on which all violations of the law must be reported and which must conduct the prosecutions and trials.[10]

The Select Committee, in *House Report 2320*, drew Congress' attention to the fact that both the Secret Service and Justice's new force still depended for their existence upon appropriation acts. It recommended their being given permanent legal status, with their duties defined and limited by law.[11]

This *Report* was submitted on March 3, 1909. The next day, Theodore Roosevelt and Charles Joseph Bonaparte left office, to be succeeded by William Howard Taft and George W. Wickersham.

Testifying before the House Appropriations Committee on February 8–9, 1909, Bonaparte neither apologized for his new force nor made extravagant claims. He said, "I think they are fairly efficient men, and on the whole the work is done as well as I think could reasonably be expected under the circumstances."[12]

His contribution was not limited, however, to what he had been able to convert into organization during the brief period from July 1, 1908, to March 4, 1909. Rather it lay in his having been—so far as we can determine—the first Attorney General categorically to reject the view that investigative work is, by its nature, on a lower plane than prosecutive; and the first to specify in detail what would constitute professional standards for an investigative body.

Repeatedly, he had defined these standards. Such a body must be able to provide permanent positions, not just piecemeal assignments, for those who render it loyal and competent service. Its special agents must be chosen with the utmost care, given appropriate training, and imbued with

---

[10] *Senate Report 970; 43 Congressional Record*, p. 2183.

[11] *House Report 2320; 43 Congressional Record*, pp. 2181–2183.

[12] *Hearings of House Appropriations Committee on Sundry Civil Appropriations Bill for 1910*, p. 1007.

the conviction that all federal statutes are to be impartially enforced.

Under date of January 14, 1909, he had written to President Roosevelt, "The difficulties encountered in recruiting a trustworthy and efficient detective force are serious." Very few first-rate men, he said, were available in the field; and such men were discouraged from going into it by the low esteem in which it was generally held.

To overcome public prejudice, he continued, Justice's force should be on a salary scale that would be attractive to well educated men of good character, and its agents should be subject to extremely strict discipline and supervision. Responsibility for its conduct should rest with the Attorney General, "so that, if any ground for reasonable complaint . . . shall be found to exist, he shall be the person justly to be called to account."[13]

At the hearing on February 8–9, 1909, he had discussed the "inherent dangers of abuse" that exist in any police or detective system, and the need to provide safeguards against them. Asked by Congressman Sherley what could best be done to make such a force useful and yet keep it within bounds, he replied:

My opinion is that there are two essential elements in all good administration upon which one must rely as a safeguard against abuse; first a centralized and accurately ascertained authority and responsibility; and second, such a system of record as will enable the legislative branches of the Government, the head executive, and possibly the courts to fix responsibility for anything that goes wrong.[14]

Attorney General Wickersham's aims and policies formed a natural sequence with those of Bonaparte—even to the extent of his keeping Stanley W. Finch on as Chief of the

[13] Quoted by Cummings and MacFarland, p. 379, from Department of Justice File, 44-3-11-3.
[14] *Hearings of the House Appropriations Committee on Sundry Civil Appropriations Bill for 1910*, p. 1932.

Bureau of Investigation. Moreover, because Wickersham held office for four years, he could tackle problems for which his predecessor had not had time during the 8-month segment of his term that followed the creation of his "small permanent detective force."

He laid down rules, for example, to govern the relationship of Justice's Special Agents to the investigative forces of other departments. They could offer such help as did not involve the spending of the Department's funds for tasks outside its domain. They should transmit any data relevant to the work of other departments that came to their attention. But they must not "concern themselves with investigations specifically assigned by law to other federal agencies."[15]

Thus, by the time Wickersham left office in 1913, the Bureau of Investigation appeared to be set for a healthy development. No problem of manpower, training, or organization had been conclusively disposed of; but what had been done had been geared to durably sound standards.

Yet dark years lay ahead: years in which these standards would suffer a tragic decline. *"Facilis descensus Averno,"* wrote Virgil: "Easy is the descent to Hell." What took place between 1918 and 1924 underscores this insight. Given either a situation that makes even reasonably good men see the *intolerable* as the *necessary* or one that propels corrupt men into key policy-making posts, it is all too easy for an open society to descend into the hell of lawless law enforcement.

[15] Cummings and MacFarland, p. 318.

THREE

THE MAKING OF DARK YEARS

THOMAS W. GREGORY was Attorney General during World War I. He was neither callous nor corrupt. He was a determined foe of profiteering, which he called a "capitalization of misfortune." In matters relating to enemy aliens, he tried to prevent the innocent majority's being rendered suspect by the enemy-serving activities of a small minority. Together with President Wilson, he successfully opposed a move, supported by the Senate Military Affairs Committee, to make civilian offenders against our war effort subject to court-martial. The proposal, he said, was "subversive of fundamental principles of justice."[1]

Yet under Attorney General Gregory there took place three intolerable departures from sound standards of federal law enforcement. Two of them he authorized. The third followed from these. The persuasive voice to which he listened was that of A. Bruce Bielaski, whom Attorney General

[1] *The New York Times*, April 23, 1918.

McReynolds had appointed as Chief of the Bureau of Investigation and whom Gregory kept on in that post.

First, at the urging of Bielaski, Gregory welcomed the help offered by a private self-designated patriotic organization, the American Protective League (APL), which indicated its wish to investigate and report disloyal acts and utterances.

"Complaints of even the most informal and confidential nature are welcome," said Gregory. "Citizens should feel free to bring their information and suspicions to the attention of the nearest representative of the Department of Justice."

So far so good. But he did not stop with encouraging members of the APL to exercise this common privilege. He sanctioned their having badges and identifying cards which bore the words *Secret Service Division*.

Secretary of the Treasury William McAdoo strongly protested this use of the phrase "Secret Service." Also, he recalled the "grave abuses and injustices" which a group similar to the APL, the Sons of Liberty, had perpetrated during the American Revolution. But Gregory refused to concede that any danger resided in his policy with respect to the APL.

He did propose a new badge: one that declared the League to be "cooperating with" Justice. The APL rejected the phrase as too weak; and many of its members refused to give up their old badges. Still unwarned, Gregory let the APL designate itself as "Auxiliary to the Department of Justice."[2]

In brief, he bestowed a highly exploitable, quasi-official status upon a body of untrained, self-appointed "investigators" over whom he could exercise no control; and he appears to have been honestly amazed and shocked at the

---

[2] Cummings and MacFarland, pp. 421–422.

consequences. Don Whitehead sums these up in *The FBI Story*:

The good work which many responsible and sober citizens performed, with full regard to the law, was buried under the violations of civil rights perpetrated by the army of amateur sleuths. APL operatives made illegal arrests and searches, and in many cases they encouraged the impression that they were federal officers.[3]

By way of contrast, we might note that J. Edgar Hoover has never allowed volunteers to invade the FBI's area of responsibility. After the outbreak of World War II, the Bureau was deluged with investigative tasks related to espionage and sabotage. But Hoover told the House Appropriations Subcommittee that the FBI was not accepting help from "self-designated groups . . . some of them super-patriotic in character, some very well-meaning, and again some selfish in that they have a desire to secure personal aggrandizement or financial gain."[4]

Like Attorney General Gregory, Hoover has encouraged citizens to communicate freely with the Bureau. But he made clear his concept of their proper relationship to its work in an editorial called "Internal Security" in the *FBI Law Enforcement Bulletin* for April 17, 1962: "Refrain from making private investigations. Report the information you have to the FBI and leave the checking of data to trained investigators."

In the second place, Attorney General Gregory sanctioned the use of dragnet methods to locate "draft-dodgers"—and again Bielaski was the persuader. Having used the dragnet

[3] Don Whitehead, *The FBI Story* (New York, Random House, 1956), pp. 35–36.

[4] *Hearings of the House Appropriations Subcommittee on Justice Department's Appropriation for 1941*, p. 155.

in Pittsburgh, with the help of the local police, Bielaski urged it upon Gregory as "highly successful"; and the latter authorized its further use. Bielaski forthwith employed it in Chicago and Boston—letting the APL in on the act.

The climactic roundup, arranged by Bielaski and presided over by the Bureau's District Superintendent Charles De Woody, was staged on September 3–5, 1918, two months before the war ended. It covered New York City, Jersey City, and Newark.

The press had been asked to remind men of draft age that the law required their having their draft classification cards with them at all times; and to advise men outside this age group to carry "properly attested evidence of the date of their birth." But the public was not warned that a checkup was pending. We again quote Don Whitehead, pp. 37–38:

Regional armories were designated as detention points . . . . A fleet of automobiles was provided for transporting the suspects. Draft board members and APL volunteers were alerted to be prepared to check on the military eligibility of those brought in.

When zero hour arrived, De Woody had his task force organized for the sweep: 35 special agents from the Bureau of Investigation, 2,000 operatives from the APL; 1,350 soldiers and National Guardsmen; 1,000 sailors; and several hundred policemen. . . .

Out of a force of more than 4,500 persons, in short, there were only 35 over whom the Attorney General had authority. Yet Justice was responsible for the conduct of the operation.

At the close of the three-day raid, some 50,000 men had been hustled from theaters, restaurants, street cars, railway stations, pool halls and street corners. Soldiers with bayonets fixed on their rifles halted men on the street and demanded proof of registration. APL operatives "arrested" suspects . . . . Workers were seized when they left their jobs. Men were forced to stand for hours without food, unable to telephone for help in establishing their innocence.

Hoover has never sanctioned the use of dragnet methods. But the future is long, and the emotion-arousing crises which it may contain are unforeseeable. Hence, we must take stock both of how these methods work and of what can induce a resort to their employment.

For as decent a man as Gregory to accept as *necessary* so indecent a method as the dragnet, he must be under heavy pressure to apprehend in haste, in the public interest, far more persons than his agent force could possibly handle by standard investigative means. When the United States entered World War I, the Bureau had 300 special agents. In the following June, the number was raised to 400. But the workload was increased throughout the war by one massive assignment after another.

Critics of today's FBI call it dangerously "huge." But what happened in 1918 illustrates the danger which resides in a law enforcement body's being so much too small for the work it has to perform that it is tempted to resort to short-cut methods.

A certain type of official, however, can see the dragnet as *desirable*. If a man is politically on the make at a time when an emotionally charged public is clamoring for action against some particular category of offender, he may opt for the spectacular show which the dragnet makes possible.

For the method to be applied, the persons sought must all be covered by some common label: in the above case, that of "draft-dodger." Further, they must be "lost" within some larger body of persons that can be distinguished from the rest of the public. In the above case, the category was that of men who were, or appeared to be, of draft age and who were not in uniform.

The method consists of rounding up all reachable members of this larger category and *then* sorting out the wanted from the unwanted—with the latter presumed to be guilty until proved innocent. "Sentence first—verdict afterward," screamed the Red Queen at the trial in *Alice in Wonderland*. The dragnet method would have been right up her alley.

On May 16, 1918, the *New York Evening World* had demanded an inquiry into the methods used to locate "draft-dodgers." The President had asked the Attorney General to clarify the situation. Cummings and MacFarland, pp. 426–427, quote Mr. Gregory's reply.

He assumed full responsibility for the use of the dragnet. Then he went on to say:

Contrary to my express instructions, however, instructions which I have repeated over and over again, and contrary to law, certain members of the investigating force of this Department, without consultation with me or with any law officer of the Department, used soldiers and sailors and certain members of the American Protective League, I am satisfied, in making arrests.

The fact that what the Attorney General called "contrary to law" in May 1918 could take place on an unprecedented scale in September of that year points to the third of the *intolerables* that developed under Gregory. The Bureau of Investigation got wholly out of hand.

Gregory's successor, A. Mitchell Palmer (1919–1921) was a man who, it would appear, hoped to ride into the White House on the tide of postwar xenophobia and anti-radicalism, but whose personal makeup also led him to use extremist methods. His name and that of his Bureau Chief, William J. Flynn, are inseparable from the phenomenon of the "Red raids."

On October 16, 1918, Congress passed a law, since replaced, which was designated as *An Act to exclude and expel from the United States aliens who are members of the anarchistic classes*. Section 1 named the categories to be excluded. *Section 2* made subject to deportation aliens already here who belonged to any of these categories. It was under *Section 2* that Attorney General Palmer conducted his dragnet operations.

The categories were "aliens who believe in or advocate the overthrow by force or violence of the United States or all forms of law; aliens who advocate or teach the assassination of public officials; aliens who advocate the unlawful destruction of property"; and "aliens who are members of or affiliated with" any organization that believes in, advocates, or teaches such views and actions.

This was not a criminal statute. It defined certain bases on which aliens could be excluded or deported; but it did not outlaw the specified beliefs and actions. No citizen could be prosecuted under it. We stress this because a criminal statute which outlawed *beliefs* could scarcely have survived a constitutional test. But while aliens—being "persons"—have, under the Constitution, certain guaranteed rights of due process, there is no basis on which they can challenge the authority of the United States to open or close its doors to outsiders.

The atmosphere which prevailed after World War I was such that anti-radicalism and xenophobia became inseparably fused. Thus, the deportation statute was made to order for an Attorney General who combined within his own person an overdose of the spirit of the times and a will to propel himself into the limelight as the very model of a modern anti-radical.

The anti-radicalism of that period was not much ado about nothing. Rather, it was much too much ado about something: a gross over-reaction. For a host of Americans, a real problem had assumed fictional proportions.

Radical violence existed. Its advocates were, for the most part, members of the Industrial Workers of the World, Bolsheviks, or members of one wing of the anarchist movement—the other wing being pacifist. The hopes to which the revolutionary radicals geared their actions were wildly unrealistic. There was no danger of their overthrowing the Government. But there was danger of their causing an intolerable destruction of life and property.

In May–June 1919, thirty-eight actual and attempted bombings were aimed at high officials of federal, state, and city governments and at wealthy private citizens. The Attorney General was among the intended victims. On the night of June 2nd, the front was blown out of his house in Washington.

Moreover, advocates of revolutionary violence were chiefly aliens. Theodore Draper writes of the original Communist party in this country that "East Europeans made up over 75 per cent of the total membership; the Russians almost 25 per cent, and the English-speaking members only 4 per cent."[5]

Between 1900 and 1920, the great tide of immigration brought in 14,531,000 persons, of whom 9,605,000 came from southern and eastern Europe. As Morison and Commager report in *The Growth of the American Republic* (Vol. II, pp. 180ff), the newcomers from these areas did not spread out over the continent as had earlier groups of immigrants. They formed enclaves in cities and industrial areas, crowding into whatever space was available for the poorest of the poor. Neither did they spread out across the vocational spectrum: they became, for the most part, unskilled laborers in mines and factories and on the railroads.

Most revolutionary radicals came out of these enclaves. They formed only the tiniest percentage of the alien population. But the whole body of unassimilated newcomers began to look like a seething "mass" to those who viewed it through the lens of xenophobic fear.

Distorted vision, in short, began at the point where aliens, *because they were aliens*, took on the lineaments of violent revolutionaries. The record would suggest that Attorney General Palmer was afflicted with this type of distorted vision.

The Labor Department had jurisdiction over the deportation statute. Secretary of Labor Wilson was responsible for

[5] Theodore Draper, *American Communism and Soviet Russia* (New York, Viking Press, 1960), pp. 19–20.

deciding which bodies, by reason of their beliefs and practices, so clearly fitted the terms of the statute that membership in them would be sufficient basis for an alien's being deported. He named the Communist Party; and the Department's Solicitor, called upon to make a decision when the Secretary was absent, named the Communist Labor Party—a decision which Mr. Wilson reversed some months later. These two parties were the prime targets of Palmer's "Red raids."

Arrest warrants had to be issued by Labor; but Justice, in a cooperating capacity, could request their issuance—and did so in wholesale lots. After arrests were made, the evidence was turned over to the Secretary of Labor. The Assistant Secretary, Louis B. Post, had the task of evaluating the evidence to determine whether or not it justified, in individual cases, the signing of deportation orders.

These details may seem academic. But one factor which led, in the end, to Congressional hearings and an aroused public interest was a collision between the Attorney General's policy of mass arrests and Post's policy of judging cases on an individual basis—and cancelling a host of warrants.

The first deportation raids took place in November 1919. On the night of January 2, 1920, massive dragnet operations were carried out in thirty-three cities—with the aim, declared later, of clearing the country, in one sweep, of alien members of the Communist and Communist Labor Parties. All persons present at places where members of these Parties were known, or presumed, to gather were taken into custody. They were searched and detained for however long it took the Justice Department's agents to determine their status.

The number who had later to be released—either because they were citizens, or for lack of evidence that they had any connection with any radical body—constituted a clear indictment of the dragnet method. But nothing in the record suggests that the Attorney General even glimpsed this fact.

When Louis B. Post cancelled hundreds of warrants from among those turned in with accompanying evidence, Palmer was outraged. As Cummings and MacFarland report, pp. 430–431, he charged that Post had "utterly nullified the purpose of Congress in passing the deportation statute" and had "set at large among the people the very enemies whom it was the desire and intention of Congress to be rid of."

To summarize what followed, the House Rules Committee held hearings to determine whether or not Post should be impeached; but the impeachment proceedings collapsed, in the end, of their own absurdity. Finally, in January–March 1921, a five-man Subcommittee of the Senate Judiciary Committee, headed by Senator Thomas Walsh of Montana, conducted hearings on *Charges of Illegal Practices in the Department of Justice*. Testimony and evidential items fill a volume of 788 pages.

No criticism that we have read of Palmer's conduct of his office is, to our minds, as damning as his defense of it before this Subcommittee. On count after count, he seemed to lack a firm grasp of either the letter or the spirit of the law.

When, for example, the Subcommittee challenged the legality of certain departmental orders with respect to searches and seizures, he was unable to say under what statute they had been issued. Further, he expressed doubt that the Fourth Amendment protected the person or property of an alien.

Asked by Senator Walsh whether he had "contemplated" that the raids would lead to the arrest of innocent persons as well as guilty, he answered, "We contemplated that it might happen that the proof would establish that the Government was mistaken in some cases, yes." The injustices suffered by the innocent seemed to cause him no concern. The state of disorder in the country, he said, called for strong measures. Then: "The reason that the arrests were made simultaneously, however, was purely a matter of administrative convenience."[6]

---

[6] *Hearings*, p. 644.

Whole stretches of his testimony were impassioned detours around the questions put to him. But in the end, two facts stood out with a kind of absolute clarity.

One was that his thinking was far too simplistic to match the nuances of legal—or human—problems. Both Senator Walsh and Assistant Secretary Post, for example, recognized that illiterate aliens could easily be drawn into groups the real purposes of which they did not understand; and that no individual case, therefore, could justly be closed at the point where membership in the Communist Party or Communist Labor Party was proved. It was necessary in each case to search out the meaning which such membership had for the person involved.

No such considerations troubled Attorney General Palmer. He seemed unable, indeed, to think of *an alien*. He could think only of *aliens*—in the mass. Moreover, when Senator Walsh asked about the qualifications of certain inspectors who had passed judgment upon the evidence, Palmer said:

It is a very simple question whether a person is within this deportation statute or not. Is he an anarchist. Is he a member of the Communist society. Does he believe in the principles of or is he affiliated with any of these associations.

It would not, he declared, "take a man of great learning" to know whether or not an alien was answering questions truthfully.

The other fact was that illegality practiced in a "good cause" left him unshocked. If a few agents, "overzealous or perhaps outraged as patriotic American citizens," had "stepped over the bounds and treated [(the aliens)] a little roughly, or too roughly," he would, he said, "forgive them." He would not "raise any row about it." Finally, p. 582:

I apologize for nothing that the Department of Justice has done in this matter. I glory in it .... and if, as I said before, some of my agents out in the field ... were a little rough or unkind, or short and curt, with these alien agitators whom they observed seeking to destroy their homes, their religion, and their country, I think it might well be overlooked . . . . That is all I have to say.

Conspicuously, he said nothing about the host of persons who had not been seeking to destroy anything but who had been treated as though they were.

The stygian darkness of the 1921–1924 period was that of outright political corruption. President Warren G. Harding was himself not, it would appear, a dishonest man. Also, some of his appointments were above reproach. Secretary of State Charles Evans Hughes and Secretary of Commerce Herbert Hoover were, for example, rocks of integrity in a sea of corruption. But in exaggerated measure, Harding established a *crony* administration; and his taste in cronies was almost unbelievably bad.

Secretary of the Navy Edwin Denby; Secretary of the Interior Albert B. Fall; Colonel Charles R. Forbes, Director of the Veterans' Bureau; Colonel Thomas W. Miller, Alien Property Custodian; and, as a first among equals, Attorney General Harry M. Daugherty: these were the men whom Harding appointed to high office because he liked to have them around. And these were the men whose self-serving "deals" or outright criminality reduced his administration to a shambles.

Attorney General Daugherty, supported by Bureau Chief William J. Burns, specialized in three enterprises; and in no one of them did he let himself be inhibited by the law. He made war on the "Reds"—and on those whom it pleased him and his friends to have thus catalogued—with slight regard for rules of evidence or constitutional rights. He made "deals"—conducting, for example, an illegal but highly lucrative traffic in pardons and liquor permits. And he saw to it that those who might threaten his hold on the Attorney Generalship had reason to fear him. This last enterprise enabled him and Burns to hold on for months after Harding died and Coolidge became President.

Alpheus T. Mason, in his biography of Harlan Fiske Stone, Daugherty's successor, describes the Bureau that Burns left behind him. It "had become a private secret service for corrupt forces within the government . . . . Included among the special agents were some with criminal records. Bureau badges and property had been issued to persons not employed by the government": persons who worked "as confidential agents and informers to 'frame' evidence against personal enemies of the Harding administration . . . ."[7]

Attorney General Stone was, as Mason says, a "pillar of the law." He knew the type of Bureau with which wanted to replace the Burns-made caricature, and the type of man he wanted as its Director.

An odd element of drama resides in his choosing J. Edgar Hoover, then 29 years old, who had been in the Department throughout the dark years. He had entered it in 1917 as an Assistant Attorney General. He had stayed on under Palmer and had headed up the General Intelligence Division (GID) created by Flynn—but without control over its field work, which Flynn kept in his own hands. He had stayed on under Daugherty, and was, at the end, working directly under William J. Burns.

He had, in short, been operating for seven years in posts close to the nerve-centers of illegality and corruption. Yet he was recommended to Stone—for his intelligence, integrity, and devotion to law and duty—by that uncorrupted fellow veteran of the Harding debacle, Herbert Hoover, who was in no way related to him.

The Attorney General was in no hurry to make a choice. He was prepared to wait as long as need be for the right man. But every inquiry which he directed to persons who knew the young Hoover and who had worked with him brought a response which confirmed the rating given him by Herbert Hoover; and various fellow workers credited him also with remarkable executive ability. Stone decided to try

[7] Alpheus T. Mason, *Harlan Fiske Stone: Pillar of the Law* (New York, Viking Press, 1956), p. 149.

him out. Thus, in 1924—first as Acting Director, and then as Director—J. Edgar Hoover undertook to reconstruct the Bureau, adhering to standards worked out in multiple talks with the Attorney General.

Nine years later, Stone—who had been elevated to the Supreme Court in 1925, but who had kept in close touch with the activities of his young appointee—summed up in a letter to Felix Frankfurter his reasons for believing that he had chosen the right Director. Hoover, he said, had

... removed from the Bureau every man as to whose character there was any ground for suspicion. He refused to yield to any kind of political pressure; he appointed to the Bureau men of intelligence and education, and strove to build up a morale such as should control such an organization. He withdrew it wholly from extra-legal activities and made it an efficient organization for investigation of criminal offenses against the United States.[8]

This letter was not written as an idle gesture. In 1933, Hoover was under bitter attack by elements that were in nowise reconciled to having the Bureau removed from the spoils system and put beyond the reach of "any kind of political pressure." Much as Attorney General Bonaparte had done a quarter of a century earlier, Attorney General Stone was spelling out what he took to be the minimum requirements for a Federal investigative bureau in our open society.

Later, in 1937, Stone expressed regret about the extent to which the Bureau was having to be enlarged; and also about the publicity which had attended its war on the gangs. But to the end of his life, he felt that his initial judgment of Hoover had been sound; and he never wavered in his respect for the law-bound efficiency of the FBI.

The body of Federal law is enormously larger today than it was in 1908, or 1924, or 1937. Inevitably, therefore, the Federal Bureau of Investigation is also larger. This fact makes all the more imperative a widespread appreciation of

[8] Quoted by Mason in *Harlan Fiske Stone*, p. 152.

the standards which alone can make this indispensable but always potentially dangerous bureau safe to have around.

It would be naive to think that no politician would now want a spoils-system right to have favored individuals appointed as special agents; and that no pressure group would now want to have the FBI function as a servant of its purposes. It would be equally naive to think that the post of Attorney General will always be held by men who share the concern of Bonaparte and Stone about the maintaining of Bureau standards. To safeguard the FBI's standards *by an informed public opinion* must be counted, then, as part of freedom's enterprise of "eternal vigilance."

PART TWO

MEN AT WORK

FOUR

THE SEARCHLIGHT OF TRAGEDY

I DON'T THINK you can get absolute security without almost establishing a police state, and we don't want that," said J. Edgar Hoover, testifying before the Warren Commission on May 14, 1964. "You can't put security in a black groove or a white groove. It is in a gray groove, and certain chances have to be taken."[1]

The subject under discussion was the extent to which our open society can defend against harm the person of the President. Within this lay a more specific question: namely, by what criteria should the FBI rate individuals as "risks" and transmit their names to the Secret Service for inclusion in the files of its Protective Research Section (PRS)?

Prior to the assassination of President Kennedy, the FBI *Handbook* had carried the following directive to Bureau personnel:

Any information indicating the possibility of an attempt against the person or safety of the President, members of the immediate

[1] *Hearings Before the President's Commission on the Assassination of President Kennedy*, Vol. V (U.S. Govt. Printing Office, 1964), p. 102.

family of the President, the President-Elect or Vice-President must be referred immediately by the most expeditious means of communication to the nearest office of the U.S. Secret Service.

The FBI had not been wont to regard political opinions or affiliations—even those which it rated as subversive for purposes of its own domestic security assignment—as a sufficient reason to label anyone as a potential assassin; and the Secret Service had neither expected nor wanted it to do so. The Dallas tragedy, however, opened wide the question of who should be counted as likely enough to make an attempt upon the life of the President to be singled out for surveillance.

Oswald had been a defector and a self-designated Marxist. He had claimed to represent a New Orleans chapter of the Fair Play for Cuba Committee—although a checkup made by the FBI after his arrest in that city for distributing leaflets without a permit seemed to establish the fact that he constituted the whole "chapter" in his own person.

Thus, after the assassination, the Bureau was subjected to insistent demands that it treat *an affirmed belief in Marxism or Communism*, particularly if coupled with activity in a Communist front, as equivalent to *a tendency to commit acts of violence*. Equally insistent were demands that the life of the President be made virtually invulnerable to attack.

Within an atmosphere charged with such demands, the Warren Commission undertook to explore the question of whether or not the Dallas tragedy could be attributed to remediable shortcomings in our machinery—or philosophy—of protection. Director J. Edgar Hoover and Assistant to the Director Alan H. Belmont of the FBI and Chief James J. Rowley of the Secret Service all discussed this question. What they put on record, each from the angle of his own experience and responsibility, was the fact that, for a free people, the maintaining of security, including the security of the President, is—like politics—"the art of the possible"; not the art of the perfect.

In the wake of the assassination, all government agencies re-examined their standards for the referral of "risk" names; and a broadening of criteria took place all across the board. Thus, on December 23, 1963, the FBI instructed its agents to report immediately to the Secret Service information concerning:

Subversives, ultrarightists, racists and fascists (a) possessing emotional instability and irrational behavior, (b) who have made threats of bodily harm against officials or employees of Federal, state or local governments or officials of a foreign government, (c) who express or have expressed strong or violent anti-U.S. sentiment or who have been involved in bombing or bomb-making or whose past conduct indicates propensity for violence and hatred toward organized government.[2]

In its voluntary working out of criteria, the FBI had made them as inclusive as it had felt it could in the light of other values to be preserved: namely, those inherent in the civil and constitutional rights of individuals. Were the new criteria what they should be, or too broad, or too narrow?

They had been in effect for over four months when Belmont and Hoover testified, on May 6 and 14, 1964, respectively; and for almost six months when Rowley testified on June 18th. During these months, the FBI had transmitted to the Secret Service more than 5,000 additional names, including those of all known defectors. Hence, all three men could appraise the new criteria in terms of how they had, so far, worked out in practice.

Belmont declared the FBI to be "not entirely comfortable" about them; for under them "we are furnishing names of people who have not made a threat against the President, people who expressed beliefs, who have belonged or do belong to organizations which believe in violent revolution or taking things into their own hands. Unless such informa-

[2] op. cit., p. 18.

tion is handled with judgment and care, it can be dangerous."

In response to a question as to whether or not the
expanded criteria had created or were likely to create, "any
problem or difficulty" for the FBI or any individual, Belmont
explained why both he and Hoover were uneasy about
them:

It seems to me that there is a necessity to balance security
against the freedom of the individual . . . . It is a simple matter to
increase security. But every time you increase security you
diminish the area of the rights of the individual . . . .

We have been asked many times why we don't pick up and jail
all Communists. The very people who ask these questions don't
realize that if action, unrestrained action, is taken against a particular group of people, a precedent is set which can be seized
upon in the future by power-hungry or unscrupulous
authorities . . . , and which will inevitably gnaw away at this free
society we have . . . .[3]

Hoover's statement about security's being in a "gray
groove" supported this analysis. He was worried, he told the
Commission, lest we "become hysterical" and go too far in
restricting the citizens of our country from exercising their
civil and constitutional rights. "The mere fact that a person
disagrees with you in a matter on Communism doesn't mean
he should be arrested . . . ."

If our zeal to protect the President made us lose sight of
the basic principles of our society, the result could be injustice on a grand scale—"because in New York City alone, you
run into maybe three or four thousand such individuals who
would be members of subversive organizations, and then
you get into the twilight zone of subversive fronts . . . ."

In one case at least the danger inherent in the broadening
of the criteria had been made evident. When President
Johnson had visited Chicago on April 23, 1964, the Secret

[3] *op. cit.*, pp. 18–19.

Service had done what it had to do in the light of its limited manpower and the multiplication of "risk" names, a multiplication to which all transmitting agencies had contributed. It had sought help from the local police. It had been forced, in short, *to delegate federal investigative work—that of checking on the persons designated as "risks"—to non-federal workers.*

In such a case, the policemen assigned as helpers are not, of course, just given a list of names and turned loose to operate as they see fit. To the limit of its power to do so, the Secret Services maintains control. But in the final analysis, it cannot exert over local policemen the degree of authority and discipline appropriate to so delicate a task.

"Many local police departments," Hoover said, "are capable and efficient; some are not. Many have good judgment and some have not. Wherever you have a police department of 10,000, 15,000, 20,000 men you are bound to find a few who will barge in and do something which better judgment would dictate should not be done."

To make "doubly sure" that the President suffers no harm from any "risk" person for whom they are responsible, such men may resort to types of surveillance that constitute an infringement of rights. They may be tempted to resort to virtual house arrests. "That is what you would call totalitarian security."

The burden of the Director's testimony was that the "enforcement of security and the enforcement of laws dealing with subversion ought to be handled in the American manner." To protect the President *in the American manner* requires that weight be given to certain factors which a dictator can ignore. The Secret Service must work within an open society the citizens of which want as intimate a contact as possible with their President; and it must respect the civil and constitutional rights of individuals—which do not lose their importance because the President is in town.

Again, the President, as titular head of his party, must weigh the risks of mingling with the people against the political advantages. If he is buoyed up by the presence of American crowds, or feels that he would invite political death by seeming to fear them, no multiplying of "risk" names and no amount of dedicated effort by the Secret Service can guarantee his safety.

At one point, Allen Dulles, a member of the Commission, broke in to ask, "How many names, Mr. Director, could the Secret Service process? Aren't their facilities limited . . .?"

They were, Hoover said, "extremely limited." At Chief Rowley's request, the FBI had been lending such agents as it could spare to help carry the burden of security at the sites of Presidential visits. But the Chief's own force should be "enlarged considerably." Otherwise, with the multiplying of "risk" names, he would have to depend upon local police forces.[4]

Chief Rowley saw the problem of criteria as that of working out categories that would cover the "Oswald-type" individual—with no explicit way to define this type—and yet not lead to the transmission of an unmanageable number of names. ". . . if every agency forwards and inundates us with many reports—say we expand to 3 million names, obviously the whole intelligence family could not cope with that . . . . On the other hand, if you restrict the categories too much, then you find yourself in a position where you may miss another Oswald . . . ."

Interpreting the new criteria for the Commission, he said, "The interest must be toward the President, or others named, or other high Government official in the nature of a complaint, coupled with an expressed or implied determination to use means other than legal and peaceful to satisfy any grievance, real or imagined." Only where this condition was met would such elements as "mental instability" and "history of violence" justify the referral of a name to the Secret Service.

To turn the Secret Service's Protective Research Section into a general depository for the names of social malcontents

[4] *op. cit.*, pp. 102, 113–114.

and unstable personalities—or of "subversives, ultrarightists, racists and fascists"—would be to render it useless for the purpose for which it was set up. Of the names transmitted so far by reason of the broadening of the criteria only a "small percentage" had been of interest.[5]

If the Secret Service is flooded with more names than it can possibly check at the site of a Presidential visit, it is trapped between unhappy alternatives. It can confine its surveillance to the more likely trouble-makers named in its files—and thus become guilty of indefensible "negligence" if an "Oswald" appears among those on whom it has not checked. Or it can enlist the help of the local police.

If it does the latter, it cannot limit the impact of its security measures upon the reputations of persons who have no designs upon the President's life. The President may be in town for a few hours. But names brought to the notice of the police because of his visit are almost certain to remain on file. Even if the persons named suffer from no overt police action, they are, in effect, *blacklisted*: the fact of their names' having been put on a "risk" list casts them in the role of *potential assassins*.

Thus, Belmont, Hoover, and Rowley spelled out the practical problems involved in protecting the President. Each of them in turn emphasized the folly of adding a small and questionable cubit to his security at the risk of large trespass upon rights.

In contrast, the Commission felt the broadened standards of referral to be still too narrow: "While these tentative criteria are a step in the right direction, they seem unduly restrictive in continuing to require some manifestaton of animus against a government official. It is questionable whether such criteria would have resulted in the referral of Oswald to the Secret Service."[6]

[5] *op. cit.*, pp. 446, 465–466.

[6] *Report of the President's Commission on the Assassination of President Kennedy* (U.S. Govt. Printing Office, 1964), p. 462.

This appeared to be the crux of the matter so far as the Commission was concerned. It felt that, somehow, the "Oswald-type" individual must be identified and covered. In line with this feeling, it concluded that only "an unduly restrictive view of its own responsibilities" had kept the FBI from transmitting Oswald's name to the Secret Service.

The Commission did not say, however, where it felt the line should be drawn—if the standard of "manifestation of animus against a government official" was discarded—in order to include an "Oswald" and yet not inundate the PRS files with irrelevant names or inflict grave injustice upon persons who intended no harm to the President. It stopped at the point of recommending further exploration of the problem.

Oswald had been a defector. "Have you any notion," Representative Hale Boggs asked Chief Rowley, "as to why the names of defectors were not provided to you prior to November 22nd?"

Chief Rowley replied, "Yes; under the broad picture, Mr. Congressman, there was no indication that they had made any threat toward the President or members of his family. Wherever there was a threat made, we were furnished promptly by the different agencies with the information on the individual's name. All this was done in voluminous reports by the FBI and the other agencies."

Boggs was still puzzled: "This fellow was interviewed by the FBI several times . . . . I agree that there had been no indication of a threat on the President's life. But obviously he was a person in the FBI files who was under some degree of surveillance. It would seem strange to me that the FBI did not transmit this information to the Secret Service."

"The FBI, Mr. Congressman," Chief Rowley replied, "are concerned with domestic security." Its agents had sought to determine whether Oswald "was a potential recruit for espionage, intelligence, or something like that." During the FBI's talks with Oswald, "there was no indication that he bore malice toward anyone, and particularly the President . . . ."[7]

The FBI has a broad and general assignment, the Secret Service a narrow and a specific one. The latter's task, beyond the investigation of counterfeiting and forgery of Government securities, is, in Chief Rowley's words, to protect

the President, members of his immediate family, the Vice-President, President-Elect, Vice President-Elect, and the former President for a reasonable period of time after he leaves office.[8]

To perform its broad assignment, the FBI must interview and, often, keep "under some measure of surveillance" a wide assortment of unsavory and subversive characters. But if it transmitted to the Secret Service any sizeable fraction of these, it would deluge the PRS files with the irrelevant.

"How effective are you going to be then?" Chief Rowley asked, in his exchange with Representative Boggs. And besides, "you get into the area of civil rights . . . ."

The Commission agreed that the task of defending our President differs in kind from that of defending a dictator. But it stressed only one element of difference: namely, that the President's "position as representative of the people prevents him from effectively shielding himself from the people." Thus: "Under our system measures must be sought to afford security without impeding the President's performance of his functions."[9]

Belmont, Hoover, and Rowley all stressed a wider imperative. They all emphasized that measures must be sought that will not impede the President's performance of his functions; make the work of the Secret Service unmanageable; infringe civil and constitutional rights; or lead, however inadvertently, to the blacklisting of persons who intend no harm to the President.

[7] *Hearings*, Vol. V, pp. 471–472.

[8] *op. cit.*, p. 450.

[9] *op. cit.*, p. 450.

While the Commission was convinced that Oswald's name should have been transmitted, it did not come to grips with the task of defining the "Oswald-type" individual. Thus, it left unanswered a question that stood out ever more clearly as the discussion went on: *If Oswald's name should have been transmitted, on the basis of what was known about him prior to the assassination, how many other names, in how many categories, should likewise have been transmitted?*

If, in short, the line is not to be drawn between persons who have voiced threats or exhibited some will to achieve their ends by violent means and those who have not, where is it to be drawn? The Commission did not attempt to say. Acknowledging that its criticisms were "tinged with hindsight," it recommended further study of the problem.

The persons most ready to condemn the FBI in unqualified terms for its failure to transmit Oswald's name were ones not involved with what Samuel Lubell, in *Revolt of the Moderates*, calls "the arts of governing day by day, and problem by problem." They were persons who did not have to deal with the complex problem of defining the "risk" type of human being and who could, therefore, treat it as simple.

Thus, Drew Pearson, in his "Washington Merry-Go-Round" of December 14, 1963, declared it to have been a

shocking oversight to permit an unstable, irrational young man who had lived in Russia, had passed out circulars favoring Fidel Castro, and quite recently had taken a trip to Mexico to contact the Cuban Embassy, to remain unwatched and unreported to the Secret Service when the President of the United States passed through the city where he lived and past the building in which he worked.

To Pearson it was obvious—as it was not to Chief Rowley—that "the FBI had either fallen down on its part of the job in Dallas or else was not cooperating with the Secret Service." It was obvious, also, to Harold Feldman, as he made plain in an article in *The Nation* of January 24, 1964, "Oswald and the FBI:"

Lee Oswald, the twice-court-martialed marine who defected to Russia and renounced his American citizenship, the pro-Cuba activist who had been arrested a few months earlier for distributing leaflets, this erratic "Marxist" who was employed on the route of the President's motorcade—Lee Oswald did not qualify for the FBI's exclusive "risk" list. And why? Because the FBI's "statutory responsibility" was limited to suspected spies and saboteurs!

It was no less obvious to William W. Turner—an ex-FBI agent turned critic. In an article called "The FBI Could Have Saved President Kennedy's Life!", in the March 1964 issue of *Saga*, Turner asked, "What did the FBI have on Oswald?"—and answered his own question by saying, "Plenty." He then listed items which, we must conclude, represented to him *plenty of evidence* that Oswald might be a potential assassin:

In its thick file on Oswald, the FBI had all the pertinent information on his erratic behavior; his attempted defection to the Soviet Union; his record in the U.S. Marines (including his marksmanship); his correspondence with the New York headquarters of the pro-Castro Fair Play for Cuba Committee, and his overt left-wing activities in New Orleans.

Said Turner, "The Secret Service is trained to recognize exactly such danger flags as flew over Oswald." But which of the "danger flags" catalogued above would have warned the Secret Service that Oswald should be watched?

Chief Rowley's testimony gives the answer: *None of them.* Rowley had been no more inclined than had Hoover to regard political affiliations, front activities, defection, Marxist views, a wish to visit Cuba, or personal erraticisms not expressed in threats or violence as a reason to pinpoint an individual as likely to make an attempt on the life of the President.

The only item which Rowley felt that he might have singled out as a warning, had Oswald's full record been before him, was one that the Navy Department, not the FBI, would have had to transmit. This was Oswald's letter to Governor John B. Connally—former Secretary of the Navy—"intimating that he would use whatever means were necessary to obtain the change in his undesirable, or as he called it, dishonorable discharge."

The reason Rowley thought that this letter might have caught his attention was that "[a]ll legal means had been used in [Oswald's] case, where the Navy Review Board had examined it and come to a decision."[10] But he did not condemn the Navy's failure to transmit the item. Oswald might have been just emphasizing the fact that he would continue to try to get his status changed. And as Allen Dulles remarked, the letter "was not a threat against the President."

"In my opinion," said Turner, "only one course of action could have been indicated: on November 22, when President Kennedy was in Dallas, Lee Harvey Oswald should have been under the strictest surveillance—*if not locked up.*" The italics are ours. To quote Hoover, "That is what you would call totalitarian security."

The items listed by Pearson, Feldman, and Turner would seem to indicate that they would all favor far broader criteria of name-referral than any that have been officially proposed. No one of them, apparently, would feel an expression of "animus" or a demonstrated tendency toward violence to be an essential factor. They would all give far more weight than would either Hoover or Rowley to personal erraticisms, a professed belief in Marxism, and overt, but nonviolent, manifestations of pro-Communism.

It is hard to see how their criteria could fail, in practice, to flood the PRS files with the irrelevant and to create a considerable danger that innocent persons would be "blacklisted." Yet since no one of the three acknowledged any

---

[10] *op. cit.*, p. 368.

slightest tinge of doubt or "hindsight" in his judgment, the listed items must be taken to represent their pre-assassination, as well as their post-assassination, concept of how a "risk" personality can be identified.

Thus, we are confronted by an "if of history." *If* the FBI had transmitted Oswald's name, and *if* the Secret Service had kept him under surveillance, so that no tragedy occurred, what then? What stand would Pearson, Feldman, and Turner have taken if Oswald had protested that the FBI had branded him as a *potential assassin* and initiated an infringement of his rights just because he was a defector, had been court-martialed, had distributed Fair Play for Cuba leaflets without a permit, was a Marxist, and had tried to visit Cuba?

Would these critics of the FBI have told Oswald flatly that, in view of his record, the Bureau had done what was obviously called for? Or would they have taken up his cause—as that of a dissenter persecuted by the FBI?

Only the former course would be consistent with their unequivocal denunciations of the Bureau for not transmitting Oswald's name. But the latter would be far more consistent with the general body of their expressed views.

More than a few prominent persons executed strange gyrations under the searchlight of tragedy. And the shadows cast by a fair number of them fell obliquely across their own records of professed commitment to civil and constitutional rights.

Those charged with the safety of the President can aspire to practice "the art of the possible" with ever greater skill and insight. But limits are set by factors as commonplace as the unwatchable number of windows that overlook the route of a motorcade—windows of private buildings from which no federal authority could oust private citizens. Also, they are set by the President's reluctance to seem cautious, and often by his positive pleasure in mingling with American crowds.

They are further set by the problems of the host city. How far in advance should the route of a motorcade be publicized? An early announcement could benefit a would-be assassin. But a too late one could mean citizen anger, sparse crowds along the route, and a mammoth traffic jam.

Again, limits are set by our imperfect capacity to recognize danger signs in human conduct or to predict the course of irrational behavior. "Now, I remember a situation," said Chief Rowley, "involving a member of Truman's staff, where a fellow stalked this man to his house . . . . We satisfied ourselves that he wasn't a real threat—but we picked up a paper a year later and found out that he had shot an assemblyman in Staten Island." Precisely *because* the Secret Service is trained to recognize "danger flags," it knows that its ability, or anyone's ability, to do so falls short of perfection.

Then there are the limitations of manpower: "Well, we never have enough agents for the activities that the President today is engaged in," said Chief Rowley.

But the most important factor that limits the possible in all security matters is our will to preserve an open society. It is this which dictates that we must "maintain a balance."

The Secret Service, not the FBI, has the task of protecting the President. All Federal agencies, not just the FBI, have the task of setting proper standards for the referral of "risk" names. Yet the Commission's exploration of these matters opened up issues that are similar in kind to those with which the FBI must reckon every day of the year.

National security can no more be put into "a black groove or a white groove" than can the security of the President; and neither can federal law enforcement. The FBI's job is to enforce laws passed by Congress and to perform its domestic intelligence function without infringing on civil and constitutional rights; and to respect and uphold these rights without letting the exercise of them tear apart the structure of liberty under law.

FIVE

THE BUREAU'S LICENSE TO ACT

IF THE FBI's area of jurisdiction is broad, and becoming broader with each session of Congress, it is also limited. Only as we get the feel of both its scope and its limits can we develop a kind of sixth sense as to what we can rightly expect of the Bureau; what we must never demand of it, what we must not let others demand without being challenged; and what we must not let it do on its own initiative.

Obviously, no lay citizen needs to be able to tot up a full list of the statutes which the FBI is responsible for enforcing. No national danger would be signalled, for example, by a pollster's having to stop a host of men on the street before he found one, if he ever did, who knew that Public Law 88-200, approved December 13, 1963, amends the Peace Corps Act to make it a violation to misuse the Peace Corps "name, seal or emblem."

Yet this law embodies, in capsule form, the story of FBI jurisdiction. In the beginning is some type of action which is judged to be inimical to the common welfare, to be a matter of legitimate federal concern, and to be unreachable by any existing statute. When, and only when, Congress has made it a federal crime to commit the designated act—or to commit it interstate—can the FBI, under proper instructions, investigate alleged instances of its commission.

There can be a further chapter, one not likely to be written with respect to Public Law 88-200. A person convicted under the statute may appeal; and the Supreme Court may reverse his conviction on constitutional grounds. It may declare the law to be a trespass upon states' rights or individual rights; or it may declare its wording to be too vague to meet constitutional standards.

If this happens, the Justice Department halts all prosecutions, and the FBI all investigations, that are in process solely by reason of the law or section of that law that has been invalidated. Most of the key provisions of the McCarran Act—the Internal Security Act of 1950—have been thus set aside.

This does not signify, however, that the FBI was guilty of infringing constitutional rights when it tried to enforce, for as long a time as they were on the federal books, these now obsolete provisions. To rate it as thus guilty would be tantamount to saying that it should have arrogated to itself the right to anticipate Supreme Court rulings and have refused, on the basis of its own anticipation, to enforce a law passed by Congress.

The McCarran Act is an interesting case in point because its passage expressed what a majority in Congress took to be expedient in an election year—and at a time when many of the States were enacting hastily conceived anti-Communist laws. The debate which preceded its passage was long and heated. In the end, however, on September 17, 1950—with congressional elections just six weeks away—many Congressmen who had expressed strong opposition to it joined in voting it into law.

Most key persons in the executive branch, including

Hoover, were opposed to the Act. Cabinet members almost unanimously urged President Truman to veto it. He would have done so in any case—and in spite of the contrary pressure put upon him by Democratic Party leaders, including Vice-President Barkley. The "political climate," these leaders said, demanded that he sign the bill.

In one of the strongest and most prescient veto messages ever penned, the President stated his conviction that the McCarran Act was probably unconstitutional and certainly unenforceable. It would contribute nothing, he said, to national security; its trouble-making potentialities were enormous; and it would force the Justice Department to spend a vast amount of time and energy to no good purpose.

It took the House less than an hour to pass the measure over his veto—by a vote of 286 to 48. It came up for reconsideration in the Senate just twenty-four hours before the time set for adjournment. Thus, there was a possibility, the President felt—albeit a remote one—that a filibuster might still prevent the bill's becoming law. He took up the question with Hubert Humphrey, then a young first-termer. A bare handful of Senators—with Humphrey, Paul Douglas, Herbert Lehman, and William Langer chief among them— were willing to run the political risks involved in opposing the measure.

The filibuster was initiated, with a few committed Senators spelling one another throughout a long night. As Cabell Phillips reports in *The Truman Presidency*, p. 377:

Langer collapsed from exhaustion shortly before daylight . . . . Humphrey and the others pushed doggedly on, but with diminishing hopes, until midafternoon. After twenty-two hours of valiant futility, President Truman gave them permission to throw in the towel. At 4 o'clock the Senate voted 57 to 10 to override, and the Internal Security Act of 1950 became law.

It became law—and it became a long headache for the Justice Department and the FBI. But the point we wish to make is simply that once Congress had put the law on the books, the effort to enforce it, however fruitless, had to be made. The FBI Director has no type of veto power that lets him decide not to bother about a statute just because he is personally convinced, or even because the President is personally convinced, that it should not have been enacted in the first place.

Ill-considered laws are certain to be passed from time to time. All too often in our history such laws have been a Congressional response to public hysteria. But not even the worst type of statute that Congress could bring itself to pass in the name of political expediency would, in the interval before it could be declared unconstitutional, do a fraction of the harm that would be done by letting the FBI decide not to enforce it. A Federal investigative and law enforcement body that could take this kind of liberty with Acts of Congress would soon become a police-state instrument.

Public Law 88-200 was, as we have noted, approved on December 13, 1962. The fraudulent use of the Peace Corps name, seal, or emblem was no more reprehensible on December 14th, and thereafter, than it had been on December 12th. But on the 12th, the FBI could not have investigated an alleged case of their misuse; and on the 14th, it could not have refused to do so. On the intervening day, the *reprehensible* had become also the *illegal*.

This would appear to be self-evident. Yet not long ago, in a discussion group, we heard a man say that he would never forgive the FBI for not taking Oswald into custody. Not only did he brush aside the fact that the Bureau had no jurisdictional right to do so, but he put forth an argument which he obviously felt to be a clincher.

An assault upon the life of the President, he pointed out, is *now* a federal crime. This, he said, showed that the American people, and Congress, would have wanted it to be treated as such in Dallas: they just had not realized until after the assassination that the requisite law was missing.

The killing of a President, he insisted, is no more reprehensible now than it was on November 22, 1963; and in view of the importance of the crime, the FBI should have taken charge then as it would today. The first half of this statement is true, but irrelevant; the second half, both false and dangerous. Just as the Communist press has, in effect, denounced the FBI for not anticipating a Supreme Court ruling in McCarran Act cases, so this man denounced it for not anticipating an Act of Congress.

It seems hard, sometimes, for our lay minds to grasp and hold on to the fact that the importance of a crime has nothing to do with its being or not being *federal*. Murder, not only of a President but of any human being, is indubitably a far more important crime than is the misuse of the Peace Corps emblem. But with a few exceptions, murder is a local crime—the chief exceptions being where it takes place on Government property or on the high seas; or where the victim is a federal officer, a visiting foreign head of state, or a member of certain designated categories of representatives of a foreign power.

Since the Peace Corps is a federal agency, its emblem is Government property; and the right of the Federal Government to protect what is its own has long been established. Public Law 88-200 broke no new ground with regard to federal jurisdiction: it merely added certain new items to the list of those protected.

To make murder in general a federal crime would, on the other hand, be not only unconstitutional but destructive of the very basis of our system; for most murders have neither national nor interstate implications. Even if such a transfer of authority were to be achieved by amending the Constitution, it would make imperative the creation of a vast national police force; and in terms of the practicalities of law enforcement, it would be patently absurd.

By and large, murder remains a highly personal crime of impulse: a fact which Hoover stressed at the hearing on the FBI's 1968 budget. Stressing the relationship between impulsive killings and the availability of guns, he said that 31% of the cases of murder and aggravated assault in 1965 had occurred within family units; and that 48% had re-sulted from "altercations," usually between acquaintances.[1]

The FBI's jurisdiction embraces laws that are remarkable for their number and diversity. But it holds no area in which the Bureau can adopt a Hamlet-like stance and ponder, "To enforce, or not to enforce . . . ." If it should ever start gearing its investigations to its own rating of what is important; or to its forecasts of what the Supreme Court or Congress will do, we as a free people should have to say, "Chaos is come again."

This would be equally true if the FBI should ever start responding to outside demands instead of simply and liter-ally to instructions given it by an appropriate authority com-mitted to enforcing federal law. In terms of what such re-sponsiveness would contribute to eventual chaos, it would not matter whether a demand would require the FBI to "pick up and jail all Communists"; to provide "continuing vigilance" in behalf of a civil rights worker whose children were threatened by an anonymous phone call; or to step in and assume command where an urban race riot has broken out.

The FBI is not an agency set up to do whatever needs to be done; but those who want action in behalf of one or another "good cause" sometimes talk as though it were just that. A prize example dates from the late summer of 1964—after the Bureau had reported to President Johnson that certain race riots had been neither Communist-inspired nor Communist-controlled, although they had to some ex-tent been Communist-exploited.

On September 13th, Si Cassady, Editor of *The Valley News*, El Cajon, California, welcomed the FBI report and called for action on a grand scale:

[1] *FBI 1968 Appropriation*, p. 37.

The FBI is a national agency. Let's put it to work, Mr. President, in every state to root out the seeds of racial bigotry and injustice wherever they are sprouting, and whoever may be planting them.

This would be quite an assignment for a federal investigative and law enforcement body. These "seeds" are being planted in the minds of children in countless homes. They are disseminated by a host of organizations, publications, and individuals. They are transmitted from mind to mind, often, by the tone of voice in which a person declares himself to be unprejudiced. They are fertilized by small talk across multiple lunch tables and on the golf courses of country clubs. The prime methods by which they are planted and cultivated violate no federal law—and are protected by the Bill of Rights. Just as the FBI cannot take over the work of the policeman on the beat, so it cannot take over the work of John Q. Citizen.

When the Bureau was formed in 1908, the matters placed under its jurisdiction were treason; crime on the high seas; violations of the neutrality laws; crimes, including murder, on Indian reservations and other Government properties; violations of the National Bank Act; opium smuggling; impersonation of a federal officer with intent to defraud; fraudulent uses of public lands; fraudulent bankruptcies; violations of the antitrust laws; and violations of the antipeonage law. It was against these crimes that Attorney General Bonaparte's small force—which did not, during his term, exceed sixty men—pitted its efforts.

To turn directly from the Attorney General's *Annual Report* for fiscal 1909 to the hearing on the FBI's appropriation for fiscal 1969 is to gain an unusual vantage point from which to survey the changes that six decades have wrought in our land. Until we take such a look backward across the years, we are not likely to realize how much of the history of our time is reported in the growth of the body of federal law—and in the consequent activities of the Bureau.

To be sure, continuities are also reported. Most of the laws originally put into the Bureau's keeping are still there—usually in amended and expanded form—and continue to author multiple investigations. We have spoken earlier, for example, of the amendment and re-amendment of the National Bank Act. In fiscal 1967, which ended on June 30, 1968, there were 2,259 violations of what is now called the Federal Bank Robbery Law.[2]

Crimes on Government reservations, theft or embezzlement of Government property, impersonation of a federal officer with intent to defraud, fraudulent bankruptcies, antitrust violations, and violations of the neutrality laws: these are hardy perennials. They have gone on year after year, decade after decade.

One law that made heavy demands upon the original Bureau is, however, rarely invoked. This is the anti-peonage statute. When Bonaparte created his detective force, more than eighty alleged cases of peonage were stacked up in the Justice Department, awaiting investigation. During the Bureau's early years, peonage was a matter that was given "especial attention." But the crime as technically defined in law is almost nonexistent now; and new statutes have made possible a broader coverage of related offenses.

Considerable space in the text of the hearing on the 1969 budget is given over to a discussion of espionage: Soviet, Cuban, and Chinese. On the law enforcement front, the Bureau's license to act against espionage agents—and also against saboteurs—dates back to the spring of 1917, when we entered World War I. On the intelligence front, it dates back to a Presidential order issued in September 1939, after the outbreak in Europe of World War II.

One by-product of World War I was America's swift entrance into the motor age—and the age of car thefts. To a car thief a state line, far from being a barrier, was the line

---

[2] *FBI 1969 Appropriation*, p. 73.

beyond which he was outside the jurisdiction of those who had authority where the theft was committed. Thus, in 1919, the Motor Vehicle Theft Act—now expanded to cover stolen aircraft, also—was put on the books: the Act which made it a federal crime to transport a stolen motor vehicle across a state boundary. In fiscal 1967, 21,861 automobiles were recovered in FBI cases.

The Bureau is often accused of jumping eagerly into car theft cases that properly belong to the local police—because the area is one, allegedly, in which it can easily run up an impressive record of accomplishments. It seems worthwhile to note, therefore, that in calendar 1966, which covered half of fiscal 1967, the police of the country reported a total of 557,000 stolen cars.[3] This would mean that approximately one in every twenty-five was recovered by federal action. Surely, this is not a high percentage to be represented by federal cases—particularly in the view of the fact that multiple car-theft rings operate nationwide.

Such rings, Hoover indicated at the budget hearing, are often uncovered "as a result of investigating what initially appears to be the theft and interstate transportation of a single automobile." Convictions were secured in fiscal 1967 against 115 persons involved in such rings; and federal prosecutions were pending against 226 others.

The 1920's produced few laws that were designed to cope with the wrenching social-economic changes wrought by World War I. Congress appears to have been as disinclined as was the country at large to come to grips with the problems which these changes introduced.

For the Bureau, however, the 1924–1934 decade was one of swift growth toward professional standards and nationwide services to law enforcement bodies. Some innovations were purely administrative; others were underwritten by law.

[3] *op. cit.*, p. 72.

Thus, in 1924, "pursuant to an act of Congress," the Division of Identification became a repository for criminal identification records previously located in several different places. In 1927, the Fugitive Division was created.

In June 1930, Congress enacted Public Law 337, which authorized the Bureau "to collect, preserve and exchange criminal identification and other crime records with duly authorized officials of local, State and Federal law enforcement agencies." Under this law, more and more extensive services have been rendered—notably, with respect to fingerprints. And under it now a National Crime Information Center, which operates around the clock, has been established on a computerized basis.

In 1932, the Bureau's technical Laboratory was founded. In fiscal 1967, it conducted a total of 330,516 examinations of evidential items—for its own purposes, for local and state law enforcement bodies, and for other federal agencies.

In 1932, also, a division was created for the international exchange of criminal-identification data. By the end of its first year, 55 bureaus around the world had entered into a cooperative exchange with it.

One monstrous product of the 1920's was the bootlegging gang. By the early 1930's, the almost unchallenged growth of the gangs had made them unreachable by the only laws and law enforcement agencies with which they had to contend: namely, state and local.

In many cases, local officials had become their servants. Even when gangsters were indicted, moreover, they had little to fear. Intimidated juries hesitated to convict. Witnesses could be bought off, or made to vanish. Prison guards could be bribed or threatened into tolerating, or even helping to arrange, the escape of a convicted gangster.

Finally, Congress took the initiative. On a single day in 1934—May 18th—it passed six laws designed to send Bureau agents out to make war on the gangs. As a group, these six statutes have become known as the Federal Crime Act. In June, three further laws were added to the list.

Public Law 73-230 provided punishment for the killing or assaulting of Federal officers.

Public Law 73-231 made it a Federal crime to extort money or other thing of value by means involving interstate commerce. It covered extortion by telephone, radio, or other process subject to interstate regulation.

Public Law 73-232 amended the Federal Kidnapping Act to make it cover cases where no ransom was demanded; and to take the FBI into any case not solved within a 7-day period.

Public Law 73-233—the Fugitive Felon Act—made it a Federal crime to flee interstate to avoid prosecution or the giving of testimony in certain types of cases.

Public Law 73-234 made it a federal crime for an officer or employee of any federal penal institution to aid, or to conspire to aid, the escape of a prisoner.

Public Law 73-235 broadened the National Bank Act to make it cover robbery of any bank organized or operating under the laws of the United States.

Public Law 73-246 made it a federal crime to transport in interstate commerce stolen property valued at $5,000 or more.

Public Law 73-276—the Federal Anti-racketeering Act—protected interstate commerce and trade against interference by violence, threats, coercion, or intimidation.

Public Law 73-474 was the National Firearms Act. Here, primary jurisdiction was given to the Alcohol and Tobacco Tax Division of Treasury; secondary, to the FBI.

Seldom has the difference between the Bureau's not having and having a license to act been more promptly demonstrated. By the time these statutes had been in effect for two years, the dramatic maraudings of the gangs born of bootlegging were, in a practical sense, things of the past.

Testifying before the Senate Subcommittee on Permanent

Investigations, on September 25, 1963, Attorney General Robert Kennedy spoke about a package of laws—all of them passed in September–October 1961—which had given the FBI jurisdiction "for the first time" to act against large-scale interstate gambling.[4] The seven statutes which comprise this package have the same type of precise relevance to the outlaw activities of today's crime syndicates that the above laws had to those of the earlier groups.

Four of the seven statutes were new: those that prohibited interstate transportation of wagering paraphernalia, interstate transmission of wagering information, destruction of property moving in interstate or foreign commerce, and interstate travel or transportation in aid of racketeering. Three had been amended, to broaden their coverage—the Federal Firearms Act, the Fugitive Felon Act, and the law dealing with the interstate transportation of stolen goods.

Most laws, of course, do not come in any such packages as those of May–June 1934 and September–October 1961. They come separately, and deal with vastly diverse problems. Thus, they extend the FBI's license—and responsibility—to act by a steady, gradual process, each of them adding its bit to the work that must be done.

We can illustrate this fact by taking as our starting point the passage, on December 13, 1963, of *Public Law 88-200*— the one forbidding the fraudulent use of the Peace Corps "name, seal or emblem"—and then noting the character of five other laws put on the books between that date and August 27, 1964.

Public Law 88-201, approved on the same day as *88-200*, makes unlawful the interstate sale or delivery of any seat belt which does not meet certain standards set by the Secretary of Commerce.

Public Law 88-251, approved on December 30, 1963,

[4] *Hearings of the Senate Permanent Subcommittee on Investigations on Organized Crime and Illicit Traffic in Narcotics*, Vol. I p. 8, (1963).

extends the escape and rescue statutes to cover individuals confined under the Juvenile Delinquency Act.

Public Law 88-316, approved on June 6, 1964, prohibits schemes in interstate or foreign commerce to influence the outcome of sporting events by bribery.

Public Law 88-252, approved on July 2, 1964, is the Civil Rights Act of 1964.

Public Law 88-493, approved on August 27, 1964, broadens the FBI's jurisdiction over assaults on or killing of federal officers to make it cover additional designated foreign personnel and security officers of the Department of State of the Foreign Service.

A more recent seven-week period—that between July 7th and August 30, 1965—brought into being a still further range of statutes that illustrate what it means to speak of the FBI as having a broad and general assignment.

Public Law 88-69, approved on July 7, 1965, amends the act which prohibits interstate transportation in aid of racketeering to make it include travel in aid of arson.

Public Law 89-92, approved on July 27th, is the Federal Cigarette Labeling and Advertising Act—which makes it unlawful to manufacture, import, or package for sale or distribution within the United States any cigarette the package of which fails to bear a health caution statement.

Public Law 89-110, approved on August 6th—the Voting Rights Act of 1965—further implements the 15th Amendment with regard to the prohibition of discriminatory practices in voting.

Public Law 89-117, approved on August 10th, is the Housing and Urban Development Act of 1965. It extends the insurance program of the Federal Housing Administration as it relates to the insuring of home mortgage loans, and prohibits the making of false statements in connection with obtaining such loans.

Public Law 89-141, approved on August 28th, is the statute that did not exist when President Kennedy was assassinated. It provides penalties for killing, assaulting, or kidnapping the President, Vice-President, and certain officials; and it makes the FBI specifically responsible for investigating such cases.

In 1963, we would recall, there was no law under which the Bureau could even investigate the crime. It could act only after President Johnson had ordered it to do so.

Public Law 89-152, approved on August 30th, amends the Universal Military Training and Service Act of 1951 to make it an offense knowingly to "destroy or mutilate a Selective Service registration card."[5]

When Hoover presented his budget for 1969, on February 23, 1968, he included in it a chart which showed the number of investigative matters the FBI had received during fiscal 1967. Investigative matters are not, of course, cases that are being prepared for presentation in court. They are *alleged* violations of federal statutes—from whatever source the allegations may come. While many can doubtless be set aside, because they deal with matters with which the Bureau is already familiar, because they are patently "wild," or for some other reason, by and large they require some type of preliminary investigation.

Thus, the categories of crime listed on the chart are, in general, those with which the Bureau had concerned itself during that fiscal year. Also, in historical terms, they constitute a record of the activities which our nation has found it necessary to outlaw at the federal level.

The oldest of all federal crimes is on the list: namely, treason—which is the only crime defined in the Constitution itself (Article III, Section III). In fiscal 1967, the FBI received 91 "investigative matters" relating to treason and misprision of treason.

Most of the crimes over which the newly formed Bureau assumed jurisdiction in 1908 are there; and so are the matters that have been made criminal within the past decade.

[5] *FBI 1968 Appropriation*, p. 151.

There were 173 matters, for example, related to sports bribery; and there were 11,870 related to interstate transportation in aid of racketeering. On another front, the FBI handled in that fiscal year 5,366 civil rights cases.[6]

And the story goes on. During the five months that followed that appropriation hearing, Congress put on the books—together with many other statutes—the Civil Rights Act of 1968, with provisions covering matters as diverse as open housing and interstate travel with intent to cause or encourage a riot; the Truth in Lending Act, which outlaws the practices on which loan-sharking has long thrived; and the Omnibus Crime Control and Safe Streets Act of 1968, which was passed on July 19th.

In this over-compressed report on the expansion of the FBI's law enforcement function, we have altogether ignored its intelligence and security functions, and have said less than enough about its service activities. These matters will be handled in later contexts. Our limited purpose here has been to indicate that if we want to think with any degree of precision about the Bureau's license to act, and its responsibility to act—and also if we want to immunize our minds to various standard types of propaganda—we must get the feel of what is signified by the concept of *jurisdiction*.

[6] *FBI 1969 Appropriation*, pp. 71, 78.

SIX

THE INTELLIGENCE ASSIGNMENT

THE GENERAL INTELLIGENCE DIVISION (GID) which Attorney General Palmer created in 1919 was abolished by Attorney General Stone in 1924. Between its unmourned demise and the outbreak of World War II, the Bureau had no intelligence assignment in relation to national security—although it had jurisdiction over the national security laws.

In September 1937, however, President Franklin D. Roosevelt ordered it back into the intelligence field. The world's condition of non-peace has kept it there: each successive President has reaffirmed and updated its assignment. To give President Roosevelt's Executive Order its historical context, we must recall certain events that punctuated Europe's movement toward war.

On March 11, 1938, Hitler invaded Austria. On the 13th, he proclaimed its political and geographical union with Germany. In Italy, Mussolini's Grand Council voted its approval.

On September 30th, at Munich, Britain and France, crediting Hitler's word that he would make no further territorial demands, recognized his claim to the Sudeten area of Czechoslovakia, in which the population was largely of German origin.

By March 1939—the months in which the Spanish Civil War ended—it was obvious that the Munich Pact had not insured "peace in our time." Between March 14th and 22nd, the Republic of Czechoslovakia was dismembered. Hungary seized the Carpatho-Ukraine. The Nazis annexed Memel and set up a protectorate over Bohemia and Moravia.

In an effort to draw a line beyond which Hitler would know that he could not carry his expansionist drive without bringing on general war, Britain and France pledged themselves to defend the territorial integrity of Poland. Hitler responded by announcing a German-Italian alliance, military and political.

Throughout all this, most Americans continued to regard Europe as away off there—beyond the protective ocean. With increasing determination, however, both Nazi and Soviet agents were treating the United States as near and penetrable.

On April 27, 1939, Hoover reported to the House Subcommittee on Appropriations a sharp upswing in alleged violations of the espionage laws. Since one of the most overworked stereotypes in the stockpile of anti-FBI propaganda items is to the effect that the Director habitually exaggerates and overdramatizes the threat of espionage, in order to get more money out of Congress, we shall report the precise manner in which he took up the subject.

His testimony runs to 42 pages; the part on espionage, to 17 lines. It is preceded by a much longer part on antitrust and criminal matters. Having disposed of these, the Director said:

In regard to espionage, I would like to point out to the committee that in the five years preceding 1938 there was an average of 35 espionage cases per year. In 1938 there were 634 such cases. That is an increase of 599 cases over the previous year. With our present personnel it is not possible to give prompt attention to these cases.

We estimate that for 1939, going at the rate we are going now, we will have 772 such cases, as against 634 last year.

As you probably know, all the investigations of foreign agents engaged in espionage work within the United States and its Territories is carried on by the F.B.I.; the Military Intelligence Division, and the Navy Intelligence Division have requested us to handle all of that civilian work.

We have been requested by the War Department and the Navy Department to establish offices in Puerto Rico, Hawaii and Alaska, in addition to stations in the Panama Canal Zone and in the Philippines. We have not acceded to these requests. Even if this appropriation is granted it is doubtful that we can accede to them.[1]

That was all. With what he had to say compressed into 17 lines, he went on, "Passing from espionage cases, I want to refer to Court of Claims work."

This compound of flat statements would seem hard to misinterpret. Yet by the time it appears on p. 243 of Fred J. Cook's *The FBI Nobody Knows,* it has suffered a sea-change. Mr. Hoover said, "We estimate that for 1939, *going at the rate we are going now,* we will have 772 [espionage] cases . . . ." Cook's account contains not a whisper of the phrase we have italicized; and 772 has become, in effect, a figure pulled out of a hat: "The preciseness of this anticipation might seem suspicious to the skeptic . . . ." But Congress "appropriated another $300,000 to finance a counter-espionage program by the G-men."[2]

---

[1] Justice Department Appropriation Bill, 1940, p. 126.

[2] Fred J. Cook, *The FBI Nobody Knows* (New York, Macmillan, 1964), p. 243.

We have read this hearing. If Cook has, we do not know how he could have missed facts given on the first page which seem to show the above appropriation to have been a grant of funds which Congress knew in advance would be needed.

The FBI had entered fiscal 1939 with less money for the year ahead than had been needed for fiscal 1938; and Congress had cut $300,000 from an interim request. Further, the Bureau of the Budget had rejected an appeal by Attorney General Robert H. Jackson—whom Cook, in a different context, describes as a liberal—that it include in the FBI's 1940 budget an emergency fund of $150,000.

Congress was not being obdurate. The developing world crisis had confronted the legislative body with enlarged appropriation requests from many different agencies. It had, as a practical expedient, adopted the policy of giving them all less than they wanted, and of instructing them to come back for more when necessary.

We find nothing in the text to support Cook's statement that the $300,000 was for "a counter-espionage program by the G-men"; and certainly nothing to suggest Mr. Hoover's having over-emphasized the problem of espionage. It is hard to see how the Director could have reported facts in any form less dramatic than the one he employed.

By the summer of 1939, the question of how the Government should work to control foreign agents and their collaborators had become crucial. Hoover felt that responsibility should be concentrated and a pattern of close cooperation established. War and Navy agreed: their intelligence units had already asked the FBI to handle "within the United States and its territories" the civilian aspects of such espionage investigations as they were conducting from the military angle.[3] The State Department, however, felt that its Office of Security must keep unshared control over "sensi-

[3] *Justice Department Appropriation Bill for 1940*, p. 126.

tive" information—because of its extreme delicacy and its relationship to foreign-policy decisions.

One fact which appears to have weighted the scales in favor of a coordinated plan was that nobody wanted a repetition of the bungling which had, during World War I, resulted from snarled lines of responsibility. Another was that, without coordination, various federal bodies might all be keeping tabs on the same individual, each from the angle of its own work, without the pieces ever being put together to form a pattern.

Espionage is rarely a simple crime. To commit it, an agent has commonly to commit other crimes, also. If these lie, as they often do, in several jurisdictions, confusion and cross-purposes can all too easily become the order of the day.

An enemy agent who unlawfully obtained "information affecting national defense" would violate Section 3, Title 50, U.S. Code: an espionage law over which the FBI has jurisdiction. But if he had entered the country illegally, the Immigration and Naturalization Service would also have a case against him—as would Internal Revenue if he had received from any domestic or foreign source moneys not reported as income. The Federal Communications Commission would have a case if he had kept in touch with other members of his espionage ring by means of an unlicensed radio transmitter.

If each of these federal agencies investigated him without pooling their findings, no one of them would know the full extent of his activities—or all their ramifying connections. No one of them would have authority to weigh the merits of the several cases against him and decide under which law he should be prosecuted.

President Roosevelt concluded that information must be pooled and that decision-making must be cooperative. On June 26, 1939, therefore, he issued the following directive to members of his Cabinet:

It is my desire that the investigation of all espionage, counter-espionage, and sabotage matters be controlled and handled by the Federal Bureau of Investigation of the Department of Justice, the Military Intelligence Division of the War Department, and the Office of Naval Intelligence.... The directors of these three agencies are to function as a committee to coordinate their activities.[4]

The President asked Cabinet members to instruct all agency heads within their departments to transmit to the FBI any information relevant to the subjects named.

Again, we must note how Cook reports these events in *The FBI Nobody Knows*, p. 243:

As war neared in Europe, the first of many bureaucratic head-buttings developed in Washington over what agency was to have the glamorous job of catching spies. Hoover was determined to preempt the stellar role for the FBI, but every department with a detective force at its disposal wanted to get into the act. Roosevelt threw his support to Hoover....

The "glamorous job of catching spies"—which involves far more of tedium than of glamour—was not up for grabs. It took no determination on Hoover's part to "preempt" what had been under the Bureau's jurisdiction ever since the first espionage and sabotage laws were enacted in 1917. The question was how best to handle national-security problems the ramifications of which could reach into a number of jurisdictions, and how to provide for a pooling of national-security data.

The President's directive did not transfer to the FBI any jurisdictional territory that belonged to another agency. Only Congress can make such a transfer. What the directive did was to establish machinery through which joint deci-

[4] J. Edgar Hoover, "The Role of the FBI in Federal Employee Security Program," *Northwestern University Law Review*, July–August 1954, footnote 2, p. 1.

sions could be reached as to which agency should handle a given case when the suspect was taken to be guilty of several federal crimes.

A decision of this type might reflect the solidity of the evidence available with regard to each offense, or any of various other factors. If, for example, an agent could be indicted for illegal entry into the country or for failure to report income, the Government might well choose not to seek an indictment for espionage—since its doing so would require the exposure in open court of highly classified materials.

In Europe, events moved swiftly in the late summer of 1939. On August 23rd, the Nazi-Soviet Mutual Non-aggression Pact was signed. This Pact made war inevitable—because it provided for the partition of Poland. On September 1st, Hitler invaded that country. On September 3rd, Britain and France, honoring their commitment to Poland, declared war on Germany.

On September 17th, Soviet forces moved into the portion of Poland which the Pact had assigned to the USSR. On the 29th, the partitioning of that country was confirmed by a Soviet-German Treaty of Friendship.

It was in the midst of these events that President Roosevelt, on September 6th, acted to enlarge the FBI's national-security function to make it cover the gathering and correlating of intelligence. He did so by means of a message to all law enforcement bodies throughout the country:

The Attorney General has been requested by me to instruct the Federal Bureau of Investigation of the Department of Justice to take charge of investigative work in matters relating to espionage, sabotage, and violations of the neutrality regulations.

This task must be conducted in a comprehensive and effective manner on a national scale, and all information must be carefully sifted and correlated in order to avoid confusion and irresponsibility.

To this end I request all police officers, sheriffs, and other law enforcement officers in the United States promptly to turn over to the nearest representative of the Federal Bureau of Investigation any information obtained by them relative to espionage, counterespionage, subversive activities, and violations of the neutrality laws.[5]

Four months later, on January 5, 1940, Hoover told the Subcommittee on Appropriations about the steps he had taken to ready the Bureau for its intelligence function, and also about the consequences of this new assignment and the outbreak of war in Europe as measured in terms of workload.

The field offices which had been requested earlier by Army and Navy Intelligence had been opened in the Canal Zone, Puerto Rico, and the Philippines. Field offices had been opened, also, near six large shipping centers or military bases: in Albany, Baltimore, Savannah, Grand Rapids, Phoenix, and San Diego.

With an eye to preventing espionage and sabotage, the Army and Navy had asked the FBI to assume jurisdiction for them over "plant-production activities" in places that manufactured articles for their use. A procedure which involved no policing, but which was educational and consultative, was currently being applied in 540 plants; and it was capable of expanding to reach as many as 12,000 in "a time of greater emergency." Most plant owners had welcomed it and were giving "excellent cooperation."

At Washington headquarters, a General Intelligence Division—forerunner of today's Domestic Intelligence Division—had been created to coordinate and supervise all work related to "espionage, sabotage, and other subversive activities and violations of the neutrality regulations." Its Translation Section made available for use the substance of subversive foreign-language "communications, documents, and

[5] *Hearings of the House Subcommittee on Appropriations on Justice Department's Appropriation for 1941*, p. 121.

papers." Its Code Section broke down codes and decoded intercepted messages.

Also, special investigations were being made of persons reported to be active in "any subversive activity or in movements detrimental to the internal security." With reference to those who might have to be more fully investigated in the event of an acute national emergency, the results of the special investigations were being kept on file.

While these activities had absorbed many man-hours, that which had most strikingly added to the work load had been the deluge of complaints alleging violations of the national defense statutes. For fiscal 1938, the number of such complaints received from private individuals and local law enforcement bodies had been 250; for fiscal 1939, 1,651. But: "For the current year we will probably have a total, at the rate we are now going, of 78,000 complaints." They were currently being received at the rate of "214 new matters a day."[6]

These figures give some clue to the amount of chaos and injustice that might have resulted had *local* investigations been attempted of all the items sent in to the FBI. Because of the President's directive and Hoover's subsequent refusal to accept proffered help from volunteer "investigators," vigilantism was kept at a remarkably low level during World War II.

The darkest injustice of the war period in this country was indubitably that practiced against the West Coast Japanese. That was an Army operation; and, significantly, Hoover opposed it. No security purpose was, to his mind, served by the wholesale uprooting of our Japanese population.

Knowing as much as he did about where danger lay, he knew enough about where it did not lie to recognize the injustice of a dragnet categorizing of any minority group as dangerous. Skilled and responsible intelligence work is important not only because it leads to the identification of those who pose a threat to our country but also because it

[6] *op. cit.*, p. 152.

removes the need to view the innocent with alarm. At its best, it is an arch-enemy of hysteria; and so far as we can determine, the FBI variety has, on the whole, been very good.

Those who have a vested interest in declaring the Bureau's intelligence work to be a trespass out of bounds—an harassment of people, not for their actions, but for their beliefs—have made much of the fact that its intelligence assignment was not given it by an Act of Congress, but "only" by a Presidential order. We must recall, therefore, the terms of a Supreme Court decision handed down on April 2, 1956—in *Commonwealth of Pennsylvania v. Steve Nelson.*[7]

Steve Nelson, described as "an acknowledged member of the Communist Party," had been convicted under the Pennsylvania Sedition Act, and sentenced to a 20-year prison term and a fine of $10,000 plus costs. The Superior Court of Pennsylvania had upheld the conviction. The State Supreme Court had reversed it.

In so doing, it had concentrated on "the narrow issue" of whether or not the federal Smith Act had superseded the Pennsylvania Sedition Act—and, by implication, similar statutes in other states—by fully occupying the same territory. Its finding was to the effect that such supersession had, indeed, taken place: sedition directed against the Federal Government had become exclusively a federal, not a state, crime.

Since this decision eliminated altogether the State's action against Nelson, the Commonwealth of Pennsylvania, supported by various other states that had sedition laws on their books, appealed to the United States Supreme Court. "Because of the important question of federal-state relationship involved," the United States Supreme Court agreed to rehear the case.

[7] (350 US 497, 100 L ed 640, 76 S Ct 477); *U.S. Supreme Court Record,* October Term, 1955, pp. 41 ff.

In the end, it upheld the action of the State Supreme Court in setting aside Nelson's conviction. The field of sedition, it concluded, was wholly "occupied" by the Federal Government. It reached this conclusion by applying to the Nelson case three "tests" of federal "occupancy"—these being derived from many past decisions.

(1) The "scheme of federal regulation" as embodied in relevant statutes was "so pervasive as to make reasonable the inference that Congress left no room for the States to supplement it."

(2) The federal statutes "touch a field in which the federal interest is so dominant that the federal system (must) be assumed to preclude the enforcement of state laws on the same subject." Here, the United States Supreme Court quoted from the ruling of the Pennsylvania Supreme Court:

"Sedition against the United States is not a *local* offense. It is a crime against the Nation. As such, it should be prosecuted and punished in the Federal courts . . . It is not only important but vital that such prosecutions be exclusively within the control of the Federal Government . . . ."

(3) For the States to enforce diverse sedition laws would create a danger of conflict between the terms of state and federal statutes with respect to the same crime:

Since 1939, in order to avoid a hampering of uniform enforcement of its program by sporadic local prosecutions, the Federal Government has urged local authorities not to intervene in such matters, but to turn over to the federal authorities immediately and unevaluated all information concerning subversive activities. The President made such a request on September 6, 1939, when he placed the Federal Bureau of Investigation in charge of investigation in this field.

At this point in its ruling, the United States Supreme Court inserted the full text of President Roosevelt's message to local law enforcement bodies.

Further, it quoted from an address which Hoover had made during a two-day Federal-State Conference on Law Enforcement Problems of National Defense, August 5–6, 1940. The FBI Director, the court indicated, had stressed two dangers resident in non-federal efforts to deal with espionage, sabotage, and subversion. First, he had pointed out that local authorities are not in a position to judge the importance of an " 'isolated incident,' " because its significance may not appear until it has been " 'fitted into a national pattern of similar incidents,' " Secondly, he had emphasized the fact that few local or State authorities have had extensive enough experience in the handling of espionage, sabotage, and subversion to have developed the requisite skills.

After weighing these indicated points, the United States Supreme Court declared itself to be "convinced that the decision of the Supreme Court of Pennsylvania is unassailable." By the logic of its approach to this ruling, and by the weight that it gave to both President Roosevelt's message of September 6, 1939, and Hoover's 1940 address, the Court made "unassailable," also, the right and duty of the FBI to carry out both its law enforcement and its intelligence functions in the national-security field.

On April 4, 1956, the *Daily Worker* declared editorially that the Supreme Court's scrapping of "the conviction of Steve Nelson on state sedition charges" was "a tremendous victory for civil liberties and for the struggle to keep the Bill of Rights alive." The editorial did not by any means, however, accept the full implications of the Court's ruling. Rather, it proclaimed this ruling to be a first step in the right direction. The next step, it suggested, should be to eliminate *federal* statutes that dealt with similar matters. This step, however, would actually be in the opposite direction from the one taken by the Court.

In the years since 1956, the Supreme Court has handed down various rulings that have greatly limited the applicability of the Smith Act. Also, as we have noted earlier, it has declared unconstitutional most of the key provisions of the McCarran Act. But these decisions have related to specific parts of specific laws passed by Congress.

At no time has the Court questioned the right of Congress to legislate in the national-security field. At no time has it questioned the right and responsibility of the FBI to enforce national-security laws in such form and for as long a time as they are on the books; or the right of the Justice Department to prosecute violations of these laws. And at no time has it brought into question the right and duty of the Bureau to conduct such intelligence operations as were called for by President Roosevelt in 1939—and, in turn, by every President since that year.

SEVEN

THE PROBLEM OF SIZE

WE BELIEVE that Hoover is speaking the truth when he says that he would have preferred to keep the FBI smaller than it now is. Yet he is interminably charged with trying to maneuver himself into a position where he can ask for more moneys with which to enlarge his already "swollen bureaucracy."

Thus, William Turner, in an October 1962 interview over KPFA, made much of an alleged pursuit of car-theft convictions to be used in "justifying the Bureau's appropriation." One interviewer, Elsa Knight Thompson, asked, "Do they label the different sections? Do they say sixty second-hand cars received, or is it just a total as a result of FBI work and the prosecution of cases—we have convicted so many people?" Turner had to answer, "Well, sometimes—well, in the matter of cars they do specifically state how many cars they recover."

Qualifying this, he continued, "They don't state that they recovered. They state 'that were recovered in FBI-investigated cases.'" This wording, he said, lets the Bureau claim credit for many cases actually solved by the local police—cases that agents "investigate" only after the police have informed them of the cars' whereabouts and of their being from out of state.[1]

At the time of this radio interview, the most recent budget hearing was that of January 24, 1962. The published text carries two summarizing charts related to car-theft cases: one on p. 7, and the other on p. 59. In both, the phrasing is precisely that which Turner said the Bureau does not use: *automobiles recovered*. In a paragraph that leads up to the second chart, however, we come upon the phrase *recovered in FBI-investigated cases*. Since both phrasings apply to the same set of figures, Turner would appear to be emphasizing a non-existent distinction.

As anyone familiar with the format of the Director's budget presentations would know, car-theft convictions are *not* used to swell a grand ambiguous total of FBI accomplishments. The Subcommittee on Appropriations knows them to be exactly what they are and can evaluate them accordingly. Yet three years after the KPFA program, Turner was still saying, "Stolen cars are the FBI's statistical bread and butter."[2]

Long before Turner, there was the New York *Daily News* of March 1, 1940, which declared, "If Congress doesn't want an American OGPU, Congress had better ask itself whether it hasn't been giving Mr. Hoover too much money." But how much desire to create an "American OGPU" was Hoover manifesting in 1940?

In October of that year, President Roosevelt approached Attorney General Robert H. Jackson with a plan to have Mr. Hoover assume direction of all federal investigative and

---

[1] *Report of Former Agent Turner*, KPFA (Pacifica Radio, Berkeley, California), October 1962. Transcript, pp. 6–7.

[2] William W. Turner, "Crime Is Too Big for the FBI," *The Nation*, November 8, 1965, p. 326.

intelligence bodies. When the Attorney General laid the plan before the FBI Director, the latter turned it down.[3]

More telling than any single action, however, is the fact that the appropriation hearings show him to have been, *consistently*, more anxious to keep down the size of the FBI than to build it up. One of his characteristic statements— which we quote, in this instance, from the *FBI 1962 Appropriation*, p. 15—is, "We have absorbed the work with our present personnel."

The "work" was that which had resulted from the passage of the 1959 Labor-Management Reporting and Disclosure Act and the 1960 Civil Rights Act. The text of the hearing leaves no room for doubt that he could have had additional funds for the asking. But he said that what he had would do.

This hearing was on March 6, 1961. He next appeared before the Subcommittee on January 24, 1962. At that time, he made known his need for 218 new employees "for assignment in the field service." During the ten-and-a-half-month interval between these hearings, Congress had enacted thirteen laws that had added, or would add, to the Bureau's work load.

With respect to three of them—the Area Redevelopment Act, the Peace Corps Act, and the Arms Control and Disarmament Act—the FBI's work consisted only of investigating Executive appointees and making full field investigations of applicants when asked to do so by the employing agency. On the other hand, it was given primary jurisdiction over the Lead and Zinc Stabilization Act; over an amendment that broadened the statute relating to interference with the Government's communications system; and over an amendment to the Federal Aviation Act of 1958.

This amendment covered highjacking of aircraft, interference with flight crews, carrying of concealed weapons aboard aircraft, commission of various crimes aboard air-

[3] Don Whitehead, *The FBI Story* (New York, Random House, 1956), pp. 169–170.

craft, and the giving of false information about any of the above acts. During the first 90 days after this amendment's passage, the FBI investigated 25 cases that would not have come under the original Act.

The remaining seven laws, however, were what really made the difference. They were the ones of which we spoke in the preceding chapter in connection with organized crime: those that let the FBI "for the first time" take effective action against large-scale interstate gambling.

When Hoover testified on January 24, 1962, he indicated that no case had yet arisen under the Lead and Zinc Stabilization Act. Under the other twelve new laws, however, the FBI had, between March 6, 1961 and January 1, 1962, opened 3,289 cases—the vast majority of them related to organized crime. *Therefore*, he could not say, "We have absorbed the work with our present personnel." He had to ask for funds to cover 218 new employees.[4]

The growth of the Bureau cannot reasonably be talked about as an isolated phenomenon; nor can any size be designated as *right* in abstract terms. Critics who by-pass this fact in order to portray the FBI as "enormous" or "gigantic" clarify nothing.

In his article "Crime Is Too Big for the FBI," in *The Nation* for November 8, 1965, Turner sets up a contrast between the efficiency of the Federal Bureau of Narcotics and what he alleges to be the inefficiency of the FBI in relation to organized crime. In doing so, he speaks of the former as "a modest Treasury Department force of 450 (compared to the FBI's nearly 16,000)." Such a comparison is meaningless—and Turner must think that his readers are inordinately stupid if he expects them to be impressed by it. The work assignments of the two agencies are simply not commensurable.

If we want to go in for meaningless comparisons, we can quite as easily make the FBI "small" as make it "mammoth."

[4] *FBI 1963 Appropriation*, pp. 15–17.

In 1967, with its nationwide field of operations, its jurisdiction over a veritable host of federal laws, its intelligence and security assignments, and its various service divisions—Identification, Laboratory, and the rest—it had on its payroll "only" 15,780 persons, while the New York City Police Department had 27,749. Of the FBI's total personnel, "only" 6,138 were Special Agents, while New York City had 25,849 policemen and detectives.[5] Such a comparison is numerically accurate—and makes no sense at all. Back of the figures, again, are non-commensurable elements.

In a passage dealing with the 1930's, Max Lowenthal, in *The Federal Bureau of Investigation*, p. 333, quotes as though it were important a statement by Senator McKellar of Tennessee:

I have been astounded at the tremendous growth and use of large sums of money for the "secret service," as it is called, of the Department of Justice.[6]

But why should the Senator have been "astounded"? He was a member of the Congress that passed the Federal Kidnapping Act of 1932; the Federal Extortion Act of 1933; and, in 1934, the whole packet of laws known as the Federal Crime Act. Lowenthal implies—as McKellar apparently did—that Hoover had arbitrarily willed the Bureau's growth. But Hoover did not author these laws.

Neither did he author the transfer, in 1933, of war-risk insurance cases from the Veterans' Administration to the Bureau. The Attorney General's *Annual Report* for 1934, p. 129, declares that "there were over 10,000 pending suits which had been filed against the United States"; and that they all had to be investigated "to determine the complete industrial, medical, and social history of each of the individ-

---

[5] 1967 *Municipal Yearbook*, p. 453; *FBI 1968 Appropriation*, p. 16.

[6] Max Lowenthal, *The Federal Bureau of Investigation* (New York, William Sloane Associates, 1950), p. 333.

uals in whose behalf the suits had been brought." In 1934 alone, the Bureau had handled 1700 such investigations: a fact available, certainly, to Senator McKellar, and to Lowenthal when he wrote his book.

Available, also, were figures about the rising crime rate. Quite probably by reason of the depression, certain types of violations went up sharply in the 1929–1934 period. We take our data from the Attorney General's *Annual Report* for each of the indicated years.

In 1929, there were 14 convictions for theft of Government property; in 1934, 137. Between 1924 and 1929, there had been a steady rise in convictions under the National Bankruptcy Act: from 20 in the former year to 95 in the latter. But in 1934, there were 193. In 1924, there were 32 convictions under the National Bank Act. In 1934, partly because Congress had broadened the Act's coverage, there were 240.

Far from being extravagant, Hoover had shown himself to be a penny-pincher of the first order. The regular appropriation for fiscal 1934 was $3,022,348; but after passing the anti-gangster laws, Congress added the amount which it felt to be necessary for their enforcement: namely, $1,500,000. At the end of the fiscal year, Hoover reported "an unexpended balance of $220,325.22."

Without trying to define a *right size* for the FBI, we can say that the safety point lies between its being too small and too large. The record has endowed these vaguely phrased limits with at least a modicum of meaning.

It reports, for example, that just prior to the Bureau's creation, the Justice Department's investigative resources were so inadequate that only a token number of prosecutions could be attempted. As Attorney General Moody said, evil had to be "allowed to flourish." No size could be right for the FBI which drastically reduced the Department's ability to prosecute crimes.

What took place under Attorney General Gregory during World War I also helps to define the phrase *too small*. It can never be safe for a law enforcement body—federal or local—to be so short of manpower that it is tempted either into relying on volunteer help or into taking legal shortcuts that constitute a trespass upon individual rights.

On January 5, 1940, Hoover told the Appropriations Sub-committee about a different danger that stemmed from a manpower shortage. Having been ordered into the national-security field by President Roosevelt four months earlier, the FBI was being deluged with complaints about violations of the national security and defense statutes. As of December 1, 1939, 1,847 such complaints had not even been assigned for investigation; and the Director had no way of knowing whether or not this backlog contained critically important cases.

That situation was unique. But since crises are endemic within the FBI's jurisdictional domain—now in one sector of it, and now in another—unassigned cases are almost certain to stack up from time to time. If the backlog were consistently to be so large that there was no way of knowing how many vital cases were concealed in it, this fact would surely serve as a warning that more agents were needed.

Similarly, a warning would be signalled by the agents' being habitually so overburdened that either inefficiency or acute injustice—or both—would result. The FBI is always on the edge of this danger in this period when crisis overlaps with crisis—interminably.

Speaking of the "substantial amount of cost-free overtime service" performed by Special Agents, Hoover told the Sub-committee on Appropriations, on February 16, 1967, "We make steady efforts to hold the overtime service to a minimum, but it continues to rise." In fiscal 1966, it had totaled "3,610,656 hours as compared with 3,468,941 hours during the previous year." The 1966 overtime average was 2 hours, 34 minutes a day.

As of February 1, 1967, the average work load of each agent was 26 investigative matters—as compared with 19 in 1961. "I think that anything in excess of 20 matters is excessive . . . ."[7]

Even the above figures are now dated. For fiscal 1967, the overtime totaled 3,817,030 hours; and as of February 1, 1968, the average load of investigative matters being carried by each agent was 28.[8]

The "enormous" FBI is now, in brief, very close to the line beyond which it would be intolerably too small. The stark fact is that such things as bank robberies, infringements of civil rights, espionage activities, and a host of other matters come up at unpredictable times in unpredictable numbers—and their investigation cannot be postponed until some more convenient day.

The term *too large* could mean either too large for the work load or too large for checks and controls to be effective. We see neither danger as impending. Yet we must emphasize a peculiar fact: namely, that a federal investigative body is safer to have around if it is overworked in times of crisis than if its manpower is geared to its maximum crisis need.

When Attorney General Bonaparte was testifying before the Appropriations Committee in 1909, he was asked how his detectives could be kept from prying into private affairs wholly unrelated to federal law. In reply, he spoke not only of discipline and supervision but also of *busyness*.

Laying before the Committee a list of "all the different matters on which the present force . . . has been employed since its organization," he matched manpower against work load. The agents, he then observed, had no time left over "to roam about looking into the idiosyncrasies of private conduct on the part of either private citizens or public officials."[9]

[7] *FBI 1968 Appropriation*, pp. 22, 42.
[8] *FBI 1969 Appropriation*, pp. 24, 45.
[9] *Hearings of the House Appropriations Committee on Sundry Civil* Appropriations Bill for 1910, p. 1039.

The same is emphatically true of today's FBI agents. The demands of the job cannot be foretold even from hour to hour—a fact which creates a singular manpower problem. Agents have to be overworked a good part of the time, it seems, if they are not to be underworked the rest of the time. The *right size* for the Bureau, we would suppose, is somewhere below, but not critically below, the level of peak necessity.

One delicate task which the Director must repeatedly perform is that of locating the point at which a work load that would be tolerable only during a period of crisis *has become the normal one.* Beyond this point, there would be no safe way of dealing with the predictable succession of unpredictable crises.

Beyond this point, therefore, it would not be prudent for him to say, "We have absorbed the work with our present personnel." Wisdom dictates his spelling out his need for added manpower—as Hoover did in presenting his budget for 1968. He asked for funds to cover 100 more agents.

Considering the laws enacted by Congress during 1966, and the rise in both various categories of crime and requests for FBI services, the number seems small rather than large. But we do not feel equipped to judge its adequacy. We do not believe that any outsider is equipped to measure the FBI's work load against its manpower and decide how well—or badly—the two are matched.

In fiscal 1964, for example, the FBI Laboratory handled 257,060 scientific examinations of evidential items—in connection with its own cases and at the request of other agencies, federal, state, and local. By fiscal 1967, the number had gone up to 330,516. During this period, however, no increase was made in the Laboratory's work force.

We are not in a position to interpret this fact. Improved testing methods may have taken care of part of the added load. Or more overtime may have been put in. We found it wholly unshocking, however, to have Hoover ask, when he presented his budget for 1969, for funds to cover six additional agents and eighteen additional clerks for the Laboratory.[10]

In addition to alleging that Mr. Hoover has trumped up reasons to enlarge the FBI, some of his more persistent critics propose that the Bureau be made smaller by what amounts to piecemeal dismemberment. Thus, they propose that other agencies be set up to handle organized crime and civil rights cases; and they recommend the return of car-theft cases to the jurisdiction of the states.

Since intelligence work in Latin America was transferred from the FBI to the CIA when the latter was created, and since most applicant-type investigations were transferred to the Civil Service Commission in 1952, there is nothing unreasonable about suggesting that future "lump" transfers may become advisable. But there are common-sense standards by which each such proposal must be measured.

To be transferrable, a "lump" of work must be unitary: its removal must not leave stringy jurisdictional loose ends. The transfer must not put asunder what the logic of daily work puts together. This, we would recall, was one reason why Mr. Hoover said No to the proposal that the FBI be given the task of enforcing the narcotics laws. Their enforcement, he said, should not be separated from "the broad function of legal narcotics control."

The transfer must not make for needless duplication of effort, for a colossal waste of skill and experience, or for the scrapping of patiently built informant-systems. Finally, it must not put upon any law enforcement body tasks beyond its power to handle. By these standards, current proposals for cutting down the size of the Bureau do not seem to make sense. Their spirit, indeed, seems to be that of demolition; not of construction.

FBI work provides an interesting counterpart to the craftsman's dictum that form follows function. The only fields in which its Special Agents can develop expertness and

---

[10] *FBI 1969 Appropriation*, pp. 30–31.

fruitful relationships are those in which the Justice Department instructs them to investigate alleged violations of law. The civil rights field offers a case in point. Except for a concerted drive against the Ku Klux Klan in the 1920's, Justice was, prior to 1939, almost passive in the civil rights field. As soon as Attorney General Frank Murphy created, in that year, the Department's Civil Liberties Unit—soon renamed the Civil Rights Section—the FBI set up a matching unit.

By February 1956, Hoover was able to report to the Appropriations Subcommittee that all agents were being instructed in the handling of civil rights cases and that 172 of them had "received specialized training in the field."[11] During 1955, the Bureau had handled "1,275 civil-rights matters"—and this was before the passage of any of the modern civil rights bills.

Today, the FBI both trains its own agents in the enforcement of the new laws and tries, on a broad front, to improve the civil rights performance of local police forces—forces which, after all, must handle many cases over which no federal agency could have any jurisdiction. In the summer of 1964 alone, the Bureau held 228 conferences that dealt with the 1964 Civil Rights Act "and its relationship to law enforcement on all levels."[12] More than 20,000 persons from 6,406 agencies attended these conferences.

Proposals that organized crime be made the specialty of some investigative body other than the FBI, while "ordinary" crime be left to the Bureau, are simply unrealistic. Turner, for example, would quite apparently rate bank robbery as "ordinary." In his *Nation* article, he says that it has become a "greenhorn's sport." But some five months after his article appeared, nine members of La Cosa Nostra—the Mafia—were arrested on a charge of operating a "big-time bank robbery gang."[13]

[11] *FBI 1957 Appropriation*, p. 66.

[12] *FBI 1966 Appropriation*, p. 40.

[13] *Washington Post*, April 13, 1966.

If the proposed division of effort were put into effect, how many criminals would escape while two groups of federal agents waited for each other to act or picked themselves up after a head-on collision? It is their total failure to deal with such complexities that make unpersuasive the critics' proposals for dismembering the FBI.

Finally, how could interstate car-theft cases be returned to the states without imposing an intolerable burden upon their authorities and resources? It is true that most stolen cars are not now taken across a state line. But if FBI agents were withdrawn from the field, it would at once become to the advantage of a thief to operate interstate.

If, for example, a man stole a car in Ohio, disposed of it in Illinois, and fled to Iowa, he would have committed no crime in the state where he would have to be taken into custody. If the FBI could not act, it would take extradition proceedings to call him to account.

Besides, how could the states cope with interstate car-theft rings? On February 1967, the FBI had around 60 such rings under investigation.[14] As Hoover observed at a budget hearing on January 24, 1964, "It is only logical that responsibility fall on an investigative agency having jurisdiction wherever investigation is needed."

The CPUSA learned long ago that the bigger the "big guy" Bureau could be made to seem, the less prone many Americans would be to examine the credentials of the "little guy" Party before leaping to its defense. In Communese, therefore, Hoover is "the nation's chief cop"; the FBI is a "swollen bureaucracy," a "mammoth stoolpigeon machine." Such terms have an obvious utility within the Communist frame of reference. But if we are going to talk sense within our own frame of reference, we cannot simply borrow the Party's stereotypes.

[14] *FBI 1968 Appropriation*, p. 81.

Hoover's concept of what the FBI should be has provided a measure of temporary insurance against the FBI's taking on needless size. It will continue to grow as its legally assigned responsibilities multiply. But it will not, under his influence, take on any flabby fat. Neither, to judge by the record, will it grow for the sake of stretching out its tentacles of power.

The future is long, however. This fact bids us recognize that the only long-range way to keep the Bureau from becoming "mammoth" is to reduce the need for its growth; and this means both reducing the crime rate and raising the level of local and state responsibility and competence.

In 1962, when some 356,000 cars were stolen, it "was determined that 62 percent of the persons arrested for auto thefts were under the age of 18 . . . and 42 percent of the stolen vehicles had the key in the car or the ignition was unlocked."[15]

Just as FBI agents cannot enter "every state to root out the seeds of bigotry and injustice," so they cannot enter our homes to bring up our children to respect the law. They cannot enter our communities to foster campaigns to eliminate the conditions that breed crime by breeding boredom, cynicism, joblessness, and frustration. They cannot trail us around to remind us to lock our cars when we park them.

The FBI can do little to move state legislatures to enact laws that would reduce the need of federal laws. Hoover has, for example, long been urging the passage and strengthening of state gun-control laws—just as he has urged the passage of a federal law that could be dovetailed into these; but the response of most state legislators has been invisible. Congress, under Titles IV and VII of the Omnibus Crime Control and Safe Streets Act of 1968, has finally passed various measures related to the interstate shipment of certain categories of firearms; but it has stopped short of requiring

[15] *FBI 1965 Appropriation*, p. 31.

the type of registration that we take for granted with respect to our cars—and dogs.

The point we want to make here, however, is simply that the FBI cannot slow down its own growth rate. If we want this to be slowed, we must seek—at local and state levels, and throughout the private sector—workable alternatives to federal law.

We stress the phrase *workable alternatives*. Those who denounce as Communist-inspired or as unconstitutional every new law by means of which Congress seeks to cope with pressing social and economic problems do not help the situation one iota.

The democratic homework assigned us by conscience and complexity is very far from finished. On many fronts, it has assumed an urgently critical character. Thus, more federal statutes are sure to be passed before workable alternatives can be found; and there are sure to be a great many cases in which *only* Federal action can be a match for problems national in scope.

But this makes it all the more important that we reserve federal law for situations where nothing else can be made to serve as well. The closer we can come to enacting *all necessary* and *no other* federal laws, and most particularly none that are born of either local inertia or public hysteria, the sounder our society will be; and the better our long-range chances will be of having an FBI that is neither small nor large in arbitrary terms, but of an appropriate size.

EIGHT

CHECKS AND CONTROLS

THE CHIEF danger posed by the FBI's growth is that of its becoming unwieldy and decentralized. As an organization takes on size, the centripetal forces that unify it face ever-sharper competition from centrifugal forces; and where the latter outpull the former, they create vacuums to be filled by factionalism, grievances, self-seeking, inertia, buck-passing, and errors born of faulty communication.

Yet size is not the prime determinant of an organization's being, or not being, *responsible*. The basic question to be asked is whether it has or does not have a solid structure of *accountability*.

When Alan Belmont testified before the Warren Commission, he was Assistant to the Director in charge of investigations. Hence, he was asked to explain the setup of the Bureau—"to provide a framework for describing the investigation of the case of Lee Harvey Oswald." In reponse, he drew, as it were, a verbal chart of the FBI's chain of command and of the provisions that keep an investigation on the line.

The Director is at the top, with an Associate Director under him. Within the total setup, there are ten working divisions, each under an Assistant Director. Four deal with investigative matters, five with administrative. Each of these larger groupings is headed up by an Assistant to the Director. "The 10th division is the inspection division and reports directly to Mr. Hoover."

The field offices, now 58 in number, "are geographically located in accordance with the amount of work in a particular area." Each is headed by a Special Agent in Charge, who has under him an Assistant Special Agent in Charge. These men "are responsible for the proper conduct of the work within their divisions." They are "answerable to Mr. Hoover"; and in relation to each type of work which they perform, they are supervised by the appropriate division at headquarters.

Since crimes are committed on earth, not in limbo, each case has a geographical point of focus—and is assigned to the field office "where the major part of the work is to be done." This office becomes, for that particular case, the *office of origin*. But leads may develop elsewhere. An *auxiliary office* is one which, having received a report on a case and a request couched in specific terms, follows up leads and reports its findings.

Thus, every field office is at once an *office of origin* for some cases and an *auxiliary office* for others. All requests and reports are cast in standard duplicate form, so that what is on file at headquarters with respect to each case as it develops is matched by what is on file out in the field. Urgent matters are transmitted by means more rapid than the duplicate forms—such as teletype. All offices are connected to both Washington and all the other offices by teletype. Also, the FBI has its own radio transmission system: "... our offices can communicate with headquarters and with each other."

"If," Belmont continued, "anywhere in the field, there is a matter which has some urgency, or there is a question of policy, it would and does come to my attention, and indeed to the attention of Mr. Hoover.

"I am kept daily advised, as is Mr. Hoover, of all matters of policy or urgency or where there is a question of procedure. This is inherent in our system of close supervision."[1]

How good are these provisions for accountability? We can best give an oblique answer. When the wife of the old philosopher in James Stephens' *The Crock of Gold* described as *perfect* the bowl of porridge that she set before him, he replied, "Perfection is finality. Finality is death. Nothing is perfect. There are lumps in it."

Inevitably, there are "lumps" in the FBI's system of checks and control. One is the simple fact that human judgment is fallible. Another is that urgent matters do not always declare themselves to be so. Oswald's conduct did not spell urgency to any of the several agents who interviewed him.

A further "lump" is the fact that not even the best program of applicant selection and training can weed out every potential misfit. The seeming rarity of gross misfits argues well, however, for the FBI's program of selection—and all the more so because the Bureau had not been able to hold to a steady, gradual rate of growth.

Skyrocketing national-security demands forced Hoover, for example, in February 1941, to ask for supplementary funds to "provide for 700 additional field service agents, 500 of whom would be used on national-defense investigations, and 200 on the investigation of the Selective Service Act."[2]

Quite apart from the problem of finding 700 good men at that time, when there was an across-the-board demand for them, the Director cannot have been happy about making such a request, for in January 1940, he had warned about

---

[1] *Hearings Before the President's Commission on the Assassination of President Kennedy*, Vol. V, pp. 2–4.

[2] *Hearings of the House Subcommittee on Appropriations on First Deficiency Appropriation Bill*, 1941, p. 179.

the hazards that could attend an abrupt wartime buildup of the force, emphasizing that neither applicant standards nor policy standards must be lowered. He had warned, also, that in any such "national emergency as we are faced with now there is great danger that an investigative force may degenerate into 'witch-hunting.' "[3]

We have spoken earlier of how the Bureau's work load was jacked up to a new plane by the passage of the anti-gangster laws in 1934 and by those relating to interstate gambling, in 1961. On a very different front, Congress, after not having enacted a single civil rights bill for almost seventy-five years, has put five such laws on the federal books since 1957.

On the whole, the FBI's program of applicant selection and training has stood up well under the impact of expanded work and successive crises. If "lumps" have persisted, so have efforts to get them out: to trace to its source every administrative or investigative delinquency and try to insure against its repetition.

To the internal controls must be added the external: the letter of the law, the person of the Attorney General, departmental policies, Congress' fund-watching committees, and courts. "The FBI," Hoover wrote in the Foreword to Whitehead's *The FBI Story*, "should never be permitted to become an independent agency, operating without the checks and controls under which it now operates." We see no present danger of its achieving such independence—or of its wanting to do so.

Its critics charge, however, that its subordination to the Justice Department is observed only in pantomime—that the Attorney General rubber-stamps whatever Mr. Hoover wants. Max Lowenthal, for example, writes on p. 331 of *The*

---

[3] *Hearings of the House Subcommittee on Appropriations on Sundry Civil Appropriations Bill for 1941*, p. 155.

Federal Bureau of Investigation that the most necessary of all controls over the Bureau has long since been scrapped.

Attorney General Bonaparte, he states, "told Congress in 1908 and 1909 that the only safeguard against abuses by this Bureau that would be effective, and the one safeguard that was indispensable, was the daily knowledge by the Attorney General of what his detectives were doing." Attorneys General Bonaparte and Wickersham both "reported to Congress that this was their actual practice, faithfully adhered to, and effective in preventing illegality and political police espionage."

Yet, Lowenthal continues, Attorney General Palmer, in 1921, dismissed this safeguard as "impractical"; and its reimposition has become ever less possible: "By 1950, the Bureau had 100 times as many detectives as in the period when Mr. Bonaparte said that if it was to be prevented from indulging in the practices of a political police, the Attorney General would have to know, every day, everything its detectives were doing, in detail."

He treats this argument as tantamount to proof that the FBI now lacks proper safeguards against "illegalities" and police-state practices. To our minds, his proof not only fails to hold water but leaks like a sieve.

For one thing, we find no record of Bonaparte's having said what Lowenthal implies. The closest parallel is the following statement, made on February 8, 1909:

Now, from the record I have shown the committee, I have endeavored, so far as the comparatively small force that we have organized is concerned, to arrange a system that would enable me to tell this committee, or anyone else who has a legitimate right to inquire about it, what any member of that force should be doing at a particular time.[4]

[4] *Hearings of the House Subcommittee on Appropriations on Sundry Civil Appropriations Bill for 1910*, p. 1032.

Bonaparte also said, as we have noted in an earlier context, that the system of supervision should be such that the Attorney General could be held accountable if anything went wrong.

His "system," however, was one that put the primary responsibility upon Bureau Chief Stanley W. Finch. Finch summarized the reports which the agents handed in each day; and the Attorney General kept posted by reading these summaries. While it was doubtless the best system that Bonaparte could contrive with his limited resources, it was rudimentary compared with today's checks and controls. It does not seem to have contained any provision that insured the accuracy of an agent's report on his own work; and this report is what Finch summarized.

Lowenthal appears to contend that a Department head creates a threat to our liberties if he makes the Director of an investigative body responsible for its daily work. Freedom, in short, flies out of the window if *delegated* authority comes in at the door. By his logic, the Secretary of the Treasury would have to know, every day, in detail, what was done by every agent of the Secret Service, the investigative unit of Internal Revenue, and the Intelligence Division of the Coast Guard.

What Lowenthal says about the position taken by Attorney General Palmer is, in general, accurate—although the latter, even in the contexts from which Lowenthal quotes, seems to have been referring to the size of the whole Justice Department rather than to that of the Bureau of Investigation. We spoke in Chapter III of the hearings held in 1921 on *Charges of Illegal Practices in the Department of Justice*. During these hearings, Palmer took recurrent refuge in statements that he could not be expected to know everything that was going on.

Thus, Senator Walsh asked at one point about the wording of a directive that had gone out to Bureau agents over the signature of "Frank Burke, assistant director and chief."

Palmer expressed doubt that such wording had been used. Then:

Senator Walsh: I will read it to you. I really was curious to know, Mr. Attorney General, how much of this you knew about.

Mr. Palmer: Well, Senator, there cannot be any secret about the fact that the Attorney General does not know everything about all the details of the work in the whole Department of Justice. There can be no question about that. If I were to confine myself to that, I would do nothing else.

This passage, on p. 541 of the *Hearings*, is given in Lowenthal's notes as a source.

On several occasions, Palmer used the size of the Department—not specifically that of the Bureau—as an explanation of why he did not know what was going on. But size was not actually the problem. The problem was that there was neither an adequate structure of *accountability* nor any clear awareness that one was needed. From the Attorney General down, the policy appears to have been that of giving general orders and telling subordinates to use their own discretion about methods.

In a set of instructions about how the mass deportation arrests were to be handled, for example, agents were told that when people were taken into custody their meeting places and residences "should be thoroughly searched":

I leave it entirely to your discretion as to the method by which you should gain access to such places. If, due to the local conditions in your territory, you find it absolutely necessary for you to obtain a search warrant for the premises, you should communicate with the local authorities a few hours before the time for the arrest is set and request a warrant to search the premises.[5]

Palmer did not disclaim knowledge of the wording of these instructions. It was his own; and he defended it as proper. Even though the Fourth Amendment states that it

[5] *Hearings*, pp. 30–31.

protects the persons and property of "people"—not just citizens—against unwarranted search, the Attorney General would not agree that it protected aliens, and he showed no concern whatever about the fact that the premises of a host of citizens not covered by the deportation act, and also of innocent aliens, were searched after their "mistaken" arrests. No investigative body, not even if it consisted of one agent, would be safe to have around if it operated under such instructions.

The Bureau's Division Superintendent for the Boston area, George R. Kelleher, certainly did not have under him an agent force too large to be properly supervised. Yet his testimony, like that of Palmer, exposed a glaring ignorance of how the mass arrests and searches were made. He, too, had left the choice of methods entirely to the agents' "discretion."[6]

By treating *size* as the core problem, Lowenthal tacitly asks us to believe that Palmer would not have tolerated the excesses of the "Red raids" if he had known about them. This is nonsense. In simple fact, Lowenthal's indispensable safeguard provides no protection whatever against abuses that are authored by, or countenanced by, the Attorney General. Are we to believe that only ignorance of what was going on kept Attorney General Daugherty from stopping the illegalities and corruption which, during his term, *seeped down from the top* to saturate the whole Justice Department, including the Bureau?

The FBI must remain—and, we believe, does remain—subordinate to the Attorney General in all respects prescribed by law and policy. But events of the dark years bid us ask an old question: *Quis Custodiet?* If a new Daugherty should occupy the post of Attorney General, what could prevent his infecting the Bureau with the spirit of illegality?

The FBI Director could not declare a reversal of roles and set himself up as the Attorney General's superior. But Mr.

[6] *Hearings*, pp. 483 ff.

Hoover and his associates have built into the Bureau certain safeguards which continue to operate while Attorneys General come and go. These pose no threat to the legitimate authority of any Attorney General. But they would, we believe, make it hard for a latter-day Daugherty to exploit the agent force for his own ends.

One safeguard is the standard of professional conduct in which all agents are schooled, and which indubitably "takes" with the vast majority. Another is the chain-of-command structure, which makes the organization a unit within which each person is accountable for what he does. A third is the stabilizing presence of agents—today, two-thirds of the total force—who have served for ten years or more.

Quite apart from any hypothetical problem of corruption, these safeguards enable the FBI to be responsive to the orders and policies of successive Attorneys General and yet maintain stability. A weather vane FBI would be dangerous; and Attorneys General, we must not forget, come and go. They are political appointees: members of the President's executive "family."

Since 1924, fifteen have held office under seven Presidents. The one to remain longest was Homer S. Cummings, 1933–1939. Three who stand out for their contributions— Harlan Fiske Stone, Frank Murphy, and Robert H. Jackson —each served for less than a year before being elevated to the Supreme Court. With the person to whom it is subordinate changing so often and at such unpredictable intervals, the FBI must, in large measure, be self-disciplined and self-stabilized.

Its being so does not exempt it from any law or regulation by which it is bound. Normally, for example, an agent who makes an arrest does so on a warrant which has been issued by the appropriate official—most often, by the United States Attorney of the region. Agents are authorized to make arrests without a warrant when a misdemeanor or a felony is committed in their presence or when they have actual grounds for believing that a felony has been committed.

But an agent who makes such an arrest must *immediately* submit a report in writing to the United States Attorney, to enable him to have command of the facts at the time the suspect is to be arraigned.

Moreover, the legal process initiated by an arrest is not one to tempt an agent to fake evidence. The Department must seek an indictment from a federal grand jury. If it is secured, the case goes to trial in a United States District Court. If a conviction is handed down, the defendant can appeal. At every point along the line—which can extend all the way to the Supreme Court—the evidence gathered by FBI agents must stand up under determined efforts to demolish it.

In *The FBI Nobody Knows*, pp. 25–26, Cook quotes Jack Levine—who, like Turner, is an ex-FBI agent turned critic—as having said that when he was working in the Detroit field office, he " 'found out from talking to agents who monitored [wiretaps] that many of these cases are not known to Bureau officials or by anyone in the Justice Department.' "

According to Levine, as reported by Cook, the agents knew they were breaking the law but did so to secure the high conviction statistics demanded by Hoover. In brief, having made unauthorized taps, they included the data thus secured in the body of evidence on which federal prosecutions were to be based.

To believe this, we should have to believe that experienced agents, well aware of the price of exposure, would tell all to a talkative rookie like Levine. How little reason they would have had to trust him with their dangerous secret is shown by his readiness to tell the world what he says they told him—thus putting their reputations and livelihoods in jeopardy, if what he said was accurate.

Further, to believe it, we should have to be given a convincing explanation of how the agents got around the policy-barriers and practical difficulties that would obstruct their entrance upon such a course of action. If Levine gave any such explanation, Cook does not transmit it to his readers.

Finally, and most important, we should have to believe that agents *could*, without detection, and often enough to make a significant difference in the number of convictions secured, smuggle illicit wiretap data into the Government's body of evidence. That they could do so is grossly implausible.

Among criminals, only the rank amateur is careless about how he transmits potentially incriminating data. In its chapter on organized crime, *The Challenge of Crime in a Free Society*, the President's Commission on Law Enforcement and Administration of Justice emphasizes that the telephone has been a favored instrument for such transmission—chiefly because wiretap evidence has not been admissible in federal courts.

Thus, even if the agents who were in the Detroit field office when Levine was there had contrived to smuggle tainted evidence into the Government's body of prosecutive materials, they would have had to reckon, in each case, with the defendant's knowledge of what he had communicated by telephone and *by no other means whatever*.

The defense lawyer, given this knowledge, would have been quick to challenge such illicit data. If the Government had had to dismiss a case because its evidence was shown to be tainted, the fat would have been in the fire so far as the outlaw agents were concerned. The FBI's precise record of whose work is in back of each item of evidence would have insured their being quickly identified.

We do not claim to be proving that no agent has ever abused his right of access to wiretap equipment. We are in no position to prove any such absolute. But we do not see how he could convert the fruits of unsanctioned taps into a statistical increase in convictions; and Levine—at least, through what Cook reports—offers no proof, not even approximate proof, of what he declares to have been a common practice.

A person who tries to decide between Hoover's warnings of what could make the FBI into a police-state instrument and his critics' charges that it *is* such an instrument ends up dealing with relative degrees of convincingness, not with absolute proofs. But on two counts at least the FBI's insistent detractors lend support to what the Director says.

They do so by the jerry-built character of their denunciations. And they do so by being inconsistent in ways that make Hoover's dogged consistency very reassuring by contrast.

Hoover never deviates from his contention that the FBI must operate within the letter of the law. The fervor with which his critics pounce upon any agent conduct that can, by any means, be portrayed as illegal would seem to argue their attaching even more importance than he does to such restraints. Yet every so often, they go into reverse and denounce him for being excessively law-bound—"legalistic."

Thus, in an article in the May 1965 issue of *Ramparts*—"The FBI and Organized Crime"—Cook contends that the strict controls under which agents work and Hoover's meticulous concern about the letter of the law "leave little room for that kind of free-wheeling detective work so essential if underground mobs are to be effectively infiltrated." He quotes a "source" as agreeing that the constant surveillance maintained over agents' activities reduces flexibility, but as saying that, because of the Bureau's size, such "ironclad control is almost essential to protect the rights of the average citizen."

Surprisingly, then, Cook writes that "this tight rule, this stickling for ultra-fine points of law militate against the release of investigative energies aimed at cracking the gigantic conspiracy of the underworld." We do not know how he reconciles this assertion with his acceptance of Levine's charge that agents are able, without detection, to make a common practice of illicit wiretapping and of smuggling the data thus secured into the body of prosecutive materials.

But in any event, he goes on to deplore Hoover's refusal to let the FBI enter a case without a clear jurisdictional right to do so. Such "insistence that the FBI must not go on 'fishing expeditions' is," he says, "a definite asset to criminals."

Coming from a person who has talked as much as Cook has about FBI "illegalities," this is curious doctrine. Also, it is impractical doctrine: the surest way for the FBI to help criminals get their cases thrown out of court, or their convictions reversed on appeal, would be for it to lay itself open to valid charges of having transgressed the law. But most of all, it is dangerous doctrine, the kind that sends a chill wind from the Palmer and Daugherty eras blowing across our minds.

In 1961, as we have already reported, Congress gave the FBI more room than it had previously possessed to move against organized crime—by enacting a package of appropriate laws. The results, as given by Attorney General Kennedy, were prompt and gratifying.

Other relevant laws have been put on the books since then. One of the most recent is the *Truth in Lending Act— Public Law 90-321*—which was passed by both houses of Congress on May 22, 1968. It converts into federal crimes the key practices on which loan-sharking has thrived.

Further laws can be enacted as the need for them becomes clear. But if "free-wheeling" agents were permitted to go on "fishing expeditions" and to make such forays *outside the law* as they might think necessary *to enforce the law*, where would the process end? How could the agents be kept from trespassing upon civil and constitutional rights?

Hoover's consistent answer is that they could not be halted on the safe side of such trespass: that a trend toward police-state practices would be under way. It is upon this premise that the FBI's structure of checks and controls has been meticulously built.

NINE

THE EAVESDROPPING PROBLEM

TITLE III of the Omnibus Crime Control and Safe Streets Act of 1968 is entitled *Wiretapping and Electronic Surveillance.* It aims both to curb private eavesdropping and to legalize, within the limits of specified safeguards, official eavesdropping in relation to a wide range of designated crimes.

Under its terms, each use of a tap or electronic "bug" by the FBI would require the approval of the Attorney General and, beyond this, the securing of a court order. The application for such an order would have to state clearly the nature of the evidence sought and the reason for believing that it could be obtained by means of the projected eavesdropping enterprise. No order granted would be general in character: it would not validate the securing of any data unrelated to those set forth in the application; and it would be for a specified time span.

The Act provides that neither this statute nor the Communications Act of 1934 shall limit the President's constitutional power to order such wire and oral interceptions as he deems necessary to protect the nation against hostile acts of a foreign power; to obtain essential foreign intelligence information; and in cases involving espionage, overthrow of the Government, or where there is clear and present danger to the structure or existence of the Government. Data thus secured may be used in evidence where such interception was reasonable but shall not be otherwise used or disclosed except as necessary to implement the President's constitu- tional power to protect the nation.

To date—that is, during the first four months of the Act's existence—the Attorney General has authorized surveillance only in national-security cases. Thus, no practical estimate can yet be made either of the law's utility as a weapon against crime or of the loopholes for abuse which it may contain in spite of the seeming care with which its provi- sions are formulated.

The FBI has, however, made at least one arrest related to private eavesdropping. On August 11, 1968, at the Minneap- olis–St. Paul airport, agents arrested a suspect on a warrant charging that he had carried on a flight from Kennedy Inter- national Airport an "'electronic device designed for surrepti- tious interception of wire or oral communication and wire- tapping.'"[1]

This warrant was legalized by Section 2512 of Title III of the Crime Bill. This prohibits—except "as otherwise specifi- cally provided"—anyone's sending through the mail, or send- ing or carrying in interstate or foreign commerce,

any electronic, mechanical, or other device, knowing or having reason to know that the design for such device renders it prima- rily useful for the purpose of the surreptitious interception of wire or oral communication . . . .

It further prohibits the manufacture, assemblage, posses- sion, or sale of such devices or their component parts for

[1] *Washington Post*, August 12, 1968.

purposes of interstate or foreign commerce; and their being advertised for sale "in any newspaper, magazine, handbill, or other publication" that the advertiser knows or has reason to know will be mailed or otherwise transported in interstate or foreign commerce.

This Section, in brief, is a newcomer in the long line of federal laws which Congress has enacted under the "commerce clause" of the Constitution. In his study of such enactments, Edward H. Levi, in *An Introduction to Legal Reasoning*, observes that one chief reason why our Constitution has been so durable in a world of change has been the fact that its framers left its wording "simple and ambiguous"—and thus made it a match for "unforeseen contingencies." It would be hard to think of a contingency that was less foreseeable in 1789 than today's development of the eavesdropping capability, mechanical and electronic.

The fact that Title III is on the books does not mean that the thorny problems that result from this capability have been solved. If and when an Attorney General begins invoking all its provisions, the resultant cases will be certain to lead to appeal after appeal. Predictably, then, it will be a matter of years before Supreme Court rulings have been handed down with reference to the Title's many delicate definitions and distinctions.

Meanwhile, the issues and controversies which the problem has been authoring for decades will continue to be with us. In this chapter, then, we shall act on the assumption that the new law has not made obsolete either the citizen's need for perspective on relevant issues or his need to keep his head in the midst of controversy.

The current eavesdropping capability is an affront to what we have called decent. A man's home is his castle now only if no one arranges to have it bugged or his phone line tapped. His private office is private only in the sense that no one can come through the door without permission. What is privately said in it may be recorded on a tape to which his chief competitor will listen in an equally vulnerable "private" office.

On September 14, 1968, the *Saturday Review* carried a cartoon by S. Harns which showed a coach and two baseball players conferring on the diamond. A third player, approaching on the run, warned: "Keep your voices down. I think second base is bugged." If this caption exaggerates a current danger, it does so only in mild degree.

There is no reason to think that devices of intrusion will pass from the scene: the knowledge of how to rig them up is too widespread. Thus, the problems which they foster are those of control. Who should be allowed to use them, and under what conditions? How can their illicit use be prohibited and, in practical terms, prevented?

The Fourth Amendment reads:

The right of the people to be secure in their persons, houses, papers, and effects against unreasonable searches and seizures, shall not be violated, and no warrant shall be issued but upon larly describing the place to be searched and the persons or probable cause, supported by oath or affirmation, and particu- things to be seized.

This is the great privacy Amendment; and it is indispensable to the safeguarding of our liberties.

Yet because the public interest exists side by side with the private, there have been ever since the Constitution was adopted different interpretations of the word *unreasonable* as it relates to arrests, searches, and seizures. This fact opens up a highly complex question: if a variance in interpretation is to be permitted in favor of the public interest, what are the limits upon official invasions of privacy?

Not only do circumstances alter cases, but circumstances alter. If the individual's privacy is threatened as never before by eavesdropping contrivances, it is also true that society is threatened as never before by forces of subversion, organized crime, and incitement to violence. What, then, would be just "reasonable" enough, and not "unreasonable," in the Government's use of eavesdropping equipment to invade the privacy of those whom it has "probable cause" to rate as criminal or subversive conspirators?

This question leads to another: if a limited trespass upon privacy is legalized, how can it be kept limited? The person and effects of an arrested individual are at least partially safeguarded by two provisions. One is that an officer who holds an innocent person as a suspect without probable cause to believe him guilty of the offense for which he is held is liable to penalties for false arrest. The other is that no arresting officer can seize at random what he finds in the possession of a suspect. But how can comparable safeguards be built into a law that authorizes eavesdropping?

If a telephone line is tapped, or a room bugged, even in the public interest and with legal sanction, the data gathered are unselective. The person, moreover, whose words are "seized" is not aware of the intrusion—and cannot, therefore, protest the seizure of the irrelevant.

Responsible discussion of legalized eavesdropping by Federal investigators has tended to move, then, in an ellipse around two focal problems: that of locating the point of balance between private rights and public interest; and that of establishing limits and safeguards to prevent a licensed but surreptitious invasion of privacy from getting out of hand.

Among persons who have coped with these problems, there is strong agreement that no authorization to wiretap or otherwise monitor a private conversation should be vaguely defined or cast in general terms. Hoover bluntly emphasized this point in 1939, when he asked the Attorney General not to endorse a law that would have given the FBI an almost unrestricted wiretap privilege: "I do not wish to be the head of an organization of potential blackmailers."

He re-emphasized it after President Roosevelt had, on May 21, 1940, authorized and directed Attorney General Robert Jackson to approve wiretaps in national-security cases.[3] Each tap, Hoover insisted, must be separately

[3] Press release by Attorney General J. Howard McGrath, Jan. 8, 1950.

authorized in writing, not by him, but by the Attorney General.

Further, he established within the FBI certain safeguards to minimize the threat to constitutional rights implicit in these newly authorized taps. One provided that *as few persons as possible* would engage in wiretapping or have access to the equipment; another, that *more than one person* would always know the nature of the information gained by a tap—and would know that it had been thus secured.

The problem of telephonic surveillance (wiretapping) antedates, of course, that of electronic surveillance (bugging). A quick backward look may illumine its present status.

In *Olmstead v. United States,* 1928, the Supreme Court ruled that admission in federal courts of evidence secured by means of wiretaps did not infringe the rights guaranteed by the Fourth Amendment. For several years thereafter, the extent to which federal investigative bodies sought such evidence depended upon who headed them up. Even within the Justice Department, practices varied: the Prohibition Bureau used taps; the Bureau of Investigation did not. But in 1931, Attorney General William D. Mitchell ruled that departmental policies must be standardized.

He did not stop the Prohibition Bureau from using wiretaps. He ordered the Bureau of Investigation to revise its regulations. These would, he said, provide a sufficient safeguard if they stated that "telephone and telegraph wires shall not be tapped without prior authorization by the Director of the Bureau . . . ." Hoover, however, authorized none until after the passage of the Federal Kidnapping Act in 1932, and then only in cases where he felt a life to be at stake.

The creation of the Federal Communications Commission in 1934 was a watershed event. Section 605 of the enabling Act said that "no person not being authorized by the sender shall intercept and divulge or publish the existence, con-

tents, substance, purport, effect, or meaning of such intercepted communication to any person . . . ."

In 1937, in *First Nordone,* the Supreme Court held that,
by reason of Section 605, wiretap evidence could no longer
be admitted in federal courts, since its admission would constitute divulgence. In 1939, in *Second Nordone,* it ruled out
the admission of evidence gathered by following up a wiretap lead.

Section 605, however, says intercept *and* divulge. We
have added the emphasis. The word *and* left the way open
for President Roosevelt to authorize the use of taps in
national-security cases—providing the Attorney General
authorized each of them, and no data thus gained was incor-
porated in the body of evidence on which the Government
based a prosecution.

Attorney General Jackson advised the FBI accordingly;
and all Presidents and Attorneys General since then have
reaffirmed this policy. President Johnson did so in his January 1967 State of the Union message, even though he called,
otherwise, for the outlawing of "all wiretapping public and
private . . . ."[4]

This long treatment of the national-security field as an
exception points both to its importance and to its being one
in which data not admissable in federal courts can still have
a preventive utility. Many Soviet-bloc agents conduct
espionage activities under cover of diplomatic immunity.
Evidence that cannot lead to their prosecution—since they
cannot be prosecuted in any case—can lead to their being
expelled from the country. Furthermore, an espionage agent
is not a lone wolf. If his purposes can be identified, information developed from wiretaps against him can guide authorities to others who make up the ring of which he is a part;
and the store of preventive intelligence materials can thus
be enlarged.

The Justice Department, as Hoover has indicated, would

---

[4] *The New York Times,* January 20, 1967, p. 1.

not always prosecute espionage agents even if it could: "Often, disclosure of their activities through public trial would compromise highly classified information and thus defeat the very purpose for which the espionage and other security statutes were enacted."[5]

Attorney General Ramsey Clark, like his predecessors, has authorized national-securing surveillance, both before and since the passage of the Omnibus Crime Bill. The wording of Title III would seem to signify that the prohibition upon divulgence that was built into Section 605 of the Federal Communications Act has been modified; but no case has arisen as yet to show whether or not the Attorney General intends, in relation to national security, to let wiretap evidence be used as a basis for prosecutive action.

Our own first approach to the wiretap problem was by an improbable route. In Lowenthal's book, pp. 320–321, we came upon a cryptic passage:

FBI practices were summed up in March 1940 by a Senate Committee. While the report did not specifically state that its charges were directed against the Bureau, Chairman Burton K. Wheeler of Montana, in a press interview, acknowledged that the report was in fact aimed at the police unit....

The illegalities committed by the police were catalogued by the Senate Committee. The catalogue reads very much like a list of charges made against Bureau agents in the years 1919 to 1924.

How could a Senate committee *sum up* "FBI practices" without saying that it was talking about the FBI? Curiosity sent us to Lowenthal's notes and, beyond these, to *Senate Report 1304*, March 12, 1940, and to the Hearings of the Subcommittee on Interstate Commerce pursuant to *Senate Resolution 224*.

This *Resolution*, introduced by Senator Theodore F. Green of Rhode Island, was directed against the use of wire-

[5] *FBI 1959 Appropriation*, p. 32.

taps and other eavesdropping devices for monitoring conversations of federal, state, and local officials. It had been prompted by charges that phone lines of several political figures in Rhode Island had been tapped—not by the FBI—during an investigation of alleged election frauds in 1933. When Senator Green learned of a rumor among newsmen that it was aimed at the FBI, he issued a statement to the press, on March 13, 1940, in which he categorically denied this.

His *Resolution* was referred to the Interstate Commerce Committee, of which Senator Burton K. Wheeler was Chairman. This Committee, in *Senate Report 1304*, recommended the passage of Senator Green's *Resolution* but suggested its being broadened to cover monitoring by or against any person for any reason.

Nothing in the *Report* suggests its being aimed, in any particular sense, at the FBI; and Senator Wheeler never "acknowledged" that it was. He merely said at a press conference, in response to a question, that if the *Resolution* was made as broad as the Committee would like it to be, it would cover all federal agencies, including the FBI.

Senate Resolution 224, adopted on March 30, 1940, led to a series of hearings by a Subcommittee of the Interstate Commerce Committee. In May and June, the hearings were focused on the Rhode Island election frauds; in November and December, on wiretapping by both private individuals and the police in New York City. FBI activities were not even called into question.

These hearings introduced us to the anarchy which has characterized the wiretapping field. It came to light, for example, that the Governor of Rhode Island, William H. Vanderbilt, and a state Assistant Attorney General had secretly hired the services of the Seaboard Bureau, a private New York detective agency headed by Frank Bielaski—a brother of A. Bruce Bielaski, Bureau Chief under Attorney General Gregory. Frank Bielaski had arranged to have tapped the phone lines of both the Attorney General of Rhode Island and Mayor McCoy of Pawtucket.

On May 23rd, he testified that the tap on McCoy's line had been a failure: no communication had been intercepted. Asked whether he meant that "there was not a single occasion when any conversation was overheard to which the mayor was a party," he answered, "This is right."

On June 6th, however, Severllon Brown, Editor of the Providence *Journal and Evening Bulletin,* testified that Bielaski had told him in the fall of 1939 that "they were receiving information from the telephone of Mayor McCoy."[6]

There was no way to determine who was telling the truth. Bielaski testified that he had only the unsupported word of one hired operative, Lee Edward Barton, as to what was or was not intercepted. No one else monitored the tap. No record was kept.

Barton, he insisted, was "a very fine gentleman." But while he was saying this, the "fine gentleman" in question was out of sight, seemingly occupied with *not* responding to a subpoena. The hearings showed this type of thing to be a commonplace in the wild domain of private wiretapping. And the manner in which the New York City police tapped wires was equally irresponsible.

Two subcommittees of the Senate Judiciary Committee have, more recently, held significant hearings: the Subcommittee on Constitutional Rights, in 1961, on *Wiretapping and Eavesdropping Legislation;* and that on Administrative Practice and Procedure, in 1965, on *Invasions of Privacy* (*Governmental Agencies*).

At a hearing of the former subcommittee on May 11, 1961, Attorney General Robert Kennedy was represented by Assistant Attorney General Herbert J. Miller, Jr., then head of Justice's Criminal Division. On July 13, 1965, Attorney

[6] *Hearings of the Subcommittee of the Senate Committee on Interstate Commerce, Pursuant to Senate Resolution 224,* Part I, pp. 153 (Bielaski) and 341 (Brown), 1940.

General Nicholas Katzenbach testified before the latter sub-committee. Both men called for drastic revision of federal statutes relating to wiretaps—to insure what Katzenbach called "a clear-cut national policy."

Miller defined certain "ills" that demanded remedy—the first of these being that the unqualified ban on disclosures confronted federal authorities with "the choice of either violating the law or else taking no action to prosecute known criminals."

For example, both *Public Law 73-231* and the Federal Communications Act were passed in 1934. The former made it a federal crime to extort "money or other thing of value by means involving interstate commerce"—which would cover extortion by telephone. But *Section 605* of the Communications Act made it well-nigh impossible to prosecute under *Public Law 73-231* a criminal who made an extortionary demand by telephone only.

To compound confusion, the Supreme Court, in *Rathbun v. United States*, had established an exception to the non-disclosure rule in a case where FBI agents had listened in with *the permission of the victim*. Section 605 allowed an exception only if they listened in *with the permission of the sender*. The court, in brief—not Congress—had altered one law in order to make another enforceable.

A second "ill," Miller indicated, was sanctioned lawbreaking at the state level. "It is common knowledge that wiretapping is practiced by state law enforcement officials. When the communications are interstate, it is a patent violation of Section 605 . . . to disclose the conversation as evidence in a state prosecution." Yet many state courts admitted such evidence.

Moreover, Miller said, the Supreme Court had held in *Schwartz v. Texas* that it did not violate the Fourth Amendment for a state to base a conviction on such evidence. Further, in *Pugwash v. Dollinger*, it had "refused to enjoin state officers from divulging intercepted communications in a state court."

Thus, the Assistant Attorney General said, we had men "charged with enforcing the law, openly engaged in deliberate violations in order to prosecute alleged criminals"; and the "common sense of the community" was on their side. Yet sanctioned illegalities can "all too easily spread until they defeat the very liberty which the too strict law is supposed to safeguard."[7]

Not least, the ban on disclosures has let interstate criminals use the telephone almost with impunity to commit crimes that can be kept verbal. It is, for example, a federal crime to offer a bribe in any area covered by federal law. Yet a criminal who has offered a bribe *by telephone*, even with FBI agents listening in, has been protected by Section 605.

Finally, while the Government has been denied the right to make effective use of authorized taps, it has been almost helpless to control unauthorized ones. Robert Kennedy, recalling a case that came up while he was Attorney General, stressed this fact in *The Pursuit of Justice*, p. 49. A fire chief in a western city discovered that the recording system of a fire-alarm station had been rigged to record calls on his private line. Even though Justice had learned the identity of the wiretapper, it had been obliged to close the case: he could not be prosecuted under any federal statute then on the books.

Attorneys General Kennedy and Katzenbach both asked for wiretap legislation based on the pattern of the Fourth Amendment. They wanted, that is to say, legislation that would first outlaw all taps, private and public; and that would then spell out, in the public interest, and by means of a warrant system, a few exceptions to the general rule.

Each tap, they held, should be separately authorized: by the Attorney General in national-security cases, to protect classified data, and in kidnapping and extortion cases, to permit swift action; and by court order in all other cases.

[7] *Hearings of the Subcommittee on Constitutional Rights of the Senate Judiciary Committee, on Wiretapping and Eavesdropping Legislation*, pp. 254–255, 1961.

The types of investigation for which eavesdropping permits could even be sought would be listed in the law itself and would be few—just enough to let the Government deal effectively with espionage, kidnapping, sabotage, subversion, extortion, and organized crime.

Both men believed that, with such a pattern of limited permission and careful safeguards worked out, Section 605 could safely be revised to allow disclosure in federal courts of data gained by means of authorized taps. Such data would no longer be half inside and half outside the law.

When we compare their proposals with Title III of the 1968 Omnibus Crime Control and Safe Streets Act, three differences are apparent. The crimes in relation to which Title III would allow eavesdropping permits to be sought are far more numerous than those listed by either Kennedy or Katzenbach. Again, the limitations imposed by Section 605 upon the eavesdropping activities of local and state law enforcement officers are reduced in the same measure, and within the same frame of safeguards, as are those imposed upon federal investigative bodies. And, finally, the new law deals with both telephonic and electronic surveillance, while the earlier proposals related solely to wiretapping; not to bugging.

Our layman tendency is to bracket wiretapping and bugging as twin problems. Yet in legal terms, the bugging capability differs *in kind* from the wiretap capability—a fact made explicit by the President's Commission on Law Enforcement and Administration of Justice in *The Challenge of Crime in a Free Society* (1967), p. 202.

The Federal Government has long had a recognized power to regulate "the national telephone communications network." A wiretap intercepts a conversation carried by this network. This fact has provided a basis for federal control of wiretapping.

A bug, however, is a self-contained eavesdropping unit; and there is nothing *interstate* about its use. Thus, it falls outside the province of the Federal Communications Act, which derives from the "commerce clause" of the Constitution.

Not even the use of a leased wire to carry a bugged conversation to the eavesdropper would bring the operation under this Act; for the wire, in such a case, is not the means of interception. It is simply a conveyor of what has been intercepted by means of a non-interstate device.

"At the present time," the Commission noted in 1967, "there is no federal legislation explicitly dealing with bugging." Laws to regulate it would have to break "new and uncharted ground." It will take, we must assume, a goodly number of prosecutions, convictions, and appeals to define the degree of success with which the 1968 law has done so.

Considerable confusion in the area of public opinion has resulted from a widespread failure to distinguish between wiretapping and bugging. The much-headlined 1966 case of FBI eavesdropping in Las Vegas—in connection with its gathering of evidence about a tax-dodging scheme allegedly used by an interstate gambling syndicate—brought forth, for example, a remarkable amount of both inaccurate and loaded reporting.

The agents' activity had not involved the use of a *wiretap*, but of *a bug and a leased wire*. Since some newspapers— among them *The New York Times*—reported this fact and explained its legal significance, it must have been available to the press. Yet a striking number of papers called it a *wiretapping* case.

Even the *Washington Post*, which would seem well located to get facts straight, did just this. Beginning on June 19, 1966, it ran three articles by one of its staff writers, Richard Harwood, which did more to confuse than to clarify the issue.

The first article carried a headline which described the FBI activity as a "Wiretapping Operation." In the text, Harwood quoted from the anti-disclosure clause of Section 605—which does not apply to the use of a bug or leased wire—and made the agents appear guilty of a flagrant violation of this Section.

In the second article—which still used the word *wiretap*—he made a token bow to the legal difference between a tap and a bug. But his manner of doing so made it seem almost a matter of opinion whether or not such a difference exists. He said that former Attorney General William Rogers "made a distinction" between the two; and that this "distinction (had) likewise been made by FBI men." He did not indicate that this distinction exists in law—because of the difference between what is and what is not part of an interstate communications system.

To think constructively about the complex problems posed by eavesdropping would be hard enough even if the situation were not further complicated by anti-FBI propaganda. But such propaganda, charging the illicit use of wiretaps, has been going the rounds for decades. It reached one high point in the 1939–1941 period, while the Nazi-Soviet Pact was in effect and after President Roosevelt had authorized the use of taps in national-security cases.

It was during this period that Morris Ernst, Counsel for the American Civil Liberties Union, undertook to check rumors against such facts as his skill and resources might enable him to bring to light. A decade later, he published his findings in an article called "Why I No Longer Fear the FBI."[8]

In the late 1930's, he reports, he had been hearing multiple charges that "the FBI was made up of 'witch-hunters'" who "tapped telephone lines indiscriminately, learning everybody's private business." As a liberal "with a long record of aggressive fighting for the preservation of personal liberties," he was "inclined to view all law-enforcement officers with a wary eye"—knowing how many of them break the law in order to get their jobs done.

[8] *Reader's Digest*, December 1950.

His curiosity, however, was aroused by Hoover's request that the Attorney General *not* support the proposed law that would have let the Bureau engage in almost unlimited wiretapping. So he decided to make his own checkup on various key rumors related to illegal wiretapping and other infringements of civil liberties by FBI agents.

He followed through on more than 100 charges of alleged agent misconduct—and concluded that "a real smear campaign has been carried on against Hoover's work. The FBI is unique . . . . It has a magnificent record of respect for individual freedom . . . ." Adding that he was, among liberals, "by no means alone in this opinion," he quoted from a letter which Roger Baldwin, former Director of the ACLU, had sent to Hoover:

"It seems to me that your bureau has accomplished an exceedingly difficult task with rare judicial sense."

Ernst ended by saying, "For me, that sums up the record."

His article and Lowenthal's book both appeared in 1950. Lowenthal, in a chapter called "Spies and Saboteurs," charges the FBI with uninhibited indulgence in illegal wiretapping. But he offers no evidence of having made any such careful investigation as was made by Morris Ernst; and we cannot see either Ernst or Roger Baldwin letting the wool be pulled over his eyes where an infringement of civil liberties was at issue.

More than a decade after Lowenthal there was Jack Levine, with his story about the illicit wiretapping in which agents indulged in the Detroit field office. And in his second article in the *Washington Post*, Harwood quotes from William Turner a similar charge with respect to agents in the Los Angeles field office—this time, in connection with their efforts against organized crime.

Harwood reports Turner's having said that, while he was an "inspector's aide" in the Los Angeles office, during the term of Attorney General William P. Rogers, " 'I found that agents had installed wiretaps and electronic "bugs" on hood-lums' " without Mr. Rogers' being aware of the fact.

We cannot disprove this statement, made by Turner in 1965. But it jibes very badly with what he said in 1962 over KPFA. He was asked during that radio interview about his work with FBI sound-equipment; and, specifically, whether or not he regarded as accurate Hoover's annual report, at the budget hearings, "on the number of taps that exist at any given time." He replied,

I would say it's fairly accurate, speaking from my own—I haven't been in every field office in every part of the country under all conditions, but from my own experience it's accurate.[9]

In an exchange about the FBI's wiretaps that fills more than a page of transcript, Turner had every chance to say, in 1962—when he was much closer to his FBI experience than he was in 1965—what he has later said about the agents in the Los Angeles office. Thus, so far as we are concerned, his one type of statement simply cancels out the other.

As we said with respect to Levine's charges, we would not claim to know that agents have never gone outside the law in their use of taps—with or without authorization. But as Morris Ernst appears to have discovered, such charges have a way, when they are critically examined, of turning from a solid state to a gaseous one.

In a memorandum on Presidential security which he issued shortly after President Kennedy's assassination, and which the Warren Commission quotes in its *Report*, p. 428, Hoover said that a practical approach to the problem "necessitates compromise." He was not, obviously, sponsoring the type of compromise that is the trademark of the self-serving opportunist; but rather, the mind-testing, soul-testing type that is, and must be, the trademark of an open

[9] KPFA transcript, p. 5.

society. It is a type which requires that enough attention be given, simultaneously and continuously, to each of various competing values so that our society will not be skewed out of shape by the loss of any one of them.

At point after point, while working on this book, we have found ourselves dealing with a problem, now of one sort and now of another, that "necessitates compromise." And this is emphatically true of the eavesdropping problem. The task of reconciling the private interest and the public interest is, in this area, far too complex to admit of any perfect and absolute outcome.

In *The Challenge of Crime in a Free Society*, p. 203, the President's Commission said in 1967, "The present status of law with respect to wiretapping and bugging is intolerable. It serves the interests neither of privacy nor of law enforcement." To what extent Title III of the 1968 Act has rendered tolerable the "status of law" in this field remains to be seen.

We think it can be said, however, that the broad eavesdropping problem will be with us for a long time to come; and that even when it has been "solved" it will remain unsolved. Individual cases will present unanticipated complexities. Science and technology will introduce further refinements of equipment—and will thereby create "unforeseen contingencies."

In short, the problem is one with respect to which we need to keep our heads and to develop a taste for facts. It is one in which we must remain vigilant to protest any official trespass upon constitutional rights that goes even one short step beyond what the public interest requires. It is, also, however, one in which we must recognize that the public interest exists: it does not make sense for criminals to be able, with impunity, to use communicative media to commit crimes. Not least, it is one in which we must refrain from making oversimplified demands, and in which we must develop a high level of immunity to stereotyped propaganda.

THE INFORMANT

BECAUSE THEY must operate in secret, those for whom the law of our land is *the enemy* have no choice but to hate and fear the informant. Thus, every conspiratorial body, criminal or subversive—La Cosa Nostra, Ku Klux Klan, CPUSA, or whatever—has machinery for screening new members and for binding to itself those who already belong.

In part, this is a machinery of ritual and indoctrination: to insure every member's feeling that to peach on his fellows would be the ultimate act of treason. In other part, it is the machinery of terror: to insure every member's knowing what will happen to him if he talks out of turn.

Yet there is always the risk that someone will talk: for gain, or to save his own skin; for revenge, or by reason of a troubled conscience. Even a long-trusted associate may become—in the language of hate and fear—a turncoat, squealer, fink, stool pigeon. Or he may, all the while, have been of and for the enemy: an undercover agent.

Most of us, of course, know about only such cases of informing as have become news. Like the visible part of an iceberg, however, these form an illustrative fraction of the larger whole—and also report its presence. There have been more than enough publicized cases to suggest how sizeable the submerged bulk must be.

On September 30, 1967, for example, it was reported in the press that seven members of the extremist Negro group called RAM—Revolutionary Action Movement—were either under arrest or being sought on warrant in connection with two alleged plots. One such plot was directed against President Johnson, J. Edgar Hoover, Mayor James Tate of Philadelphia, and Police Commissioner Frank Rizzo of that city; the other against the Philadelphia police force. According to the *Washington Post*, "Both plots were disclosed by informants who were members of RAM."

A week or so later, the press began reporting the trial of the 18 men accused of conspiracy in the 1964 Ku Klux Klan murder of the three civil rights workers in Mississippi. The Government's case—which led to the conviction of seven defendants—was built, in part, on the testimony of two ex-Klansmen who had become informants for the FBI.

Even a modest sampling of types that are a matter of public record indicates that informants are as diverse in motive and makeup as are noninformants. To specify one type, there is the teen-ager who goes to the police when a petty-theft gang with which he has become involved starts planning theft-with-murder. Theft, yes; murder, no. Such a boy represents a diverse company of persons who have broken with conspiratorial bodies when these have, by the informant's personal definition, gone too far.

One Klansman who testified before the House Committee on Un-American Activities in 1966 had, apparently, been able to countenance acts of intimidation but not the bombing of churches. For many members of the CPUSA Stalin went too far when, in 1939, he signed the pact with Hitler. For many others, Khrushchev went too far when, in 1956, he crushed the Hungarian revolution.

Many individuals have, in contrast, moved away from conspiratorial groups by a gradual, and even reluctant, process of mental and emotional defection; and have finally reached a point of no return. Their piecemeal disillusionment has lodged them closer to the social order which they have previously called the enemy than to their former co-conspirators.

One not-uncommon reason for a member of a crime syndicate to become an informant is stark fear: not of the law, but of his own associates. Joseph Valachi provides an example. After belonging to La Cosa Nostra for thirty years, Valachi was convicted on a narcotics charge and sent to Atlanta penitentiary—as was a co-defendant, Vito Aguici. Among the members of La Cosa Nostra who were already there was Vito Genovese, head of Valachi's underworld "family." Aguici told him that Valachi had talked too much at the trial, and thus made him a marked man; and Valachi recognized the ritual signs of his being slated for liquidation.

After weeks of frenzied fear, he killed a fellow prisoner whom he mistakenly took to be his own appointed killer. Under life sentence for this crime—and reportedly with a $100,000 bounty on his head, offered by his former associates—he became for the Government a valuable source of information.

Not only did he talk at length to the FBI and the Organized Crime Section of Justice, but he testified before the Senate's Permanent Subcommittee on Investigations during its 1963 hearings on *Organized Crime and Illicit Traffic in Narcotics*. His testimony fills most of Part I of the *Hearings* and a section Part III. Thus, as Attorney General Robert Kennedy said, testifying before the same Subcommittee on September 25, 1963, he broke "the underworld's code of silence."

The Attorney General went on to say:

Valachi's disclosures are more important, however, for another reason. In working a jigsaw puzzle, each piece in place tells us something about the whole picture and enables us to see additional relationships.

It is the same in the fight against organized crime. Valachi's information is a significant addition to the broad picture. It adds essential detail and brings the picture into sharper focus. It gives meaning to much that we have already known.[1]

Valachi's type of fear would not, of course, account for an individual's transferring his loyalty to the FBI and staying on as an informant within an underworld group to which he has previously belonged in body and mind. Here, the determinative factor has not infrequently been the jolting impact of high-level human conduct upon an individual who has lived all his life in the underworld, guided by its jungle standards. Such an impact can be all the more potent because the individual first encounters consideration and *restrained* authority in the person of an agent who represents the vast power of the Federal Government—and who makes no more use of the power at his command than the situation absolutely requires.

We are reminded here of a passage in a letter which Harlan Fiske Stone wrote to Felix Frankfurter on February 9, 1925: a letter in which he discussed the standards which he felt to be appropriate for the Bureau of Investigation:

I am firmly of the opinion that officials of the Department of Justice can more effectively perform their duties by acting the part of gentlemen than by resorting to tactics of a different character. The work of gathering evidence and conducting litigation should be done in a gentlemanly way.

Agents of the Bureau, he continued, must be "impressed" with the fact that "the respect to which they are entitled as

[1] *Hearings*, Part I, p. 6.

law-enforcement officers can only be obtained by their strictly observing the rights of citizens and the law of the land."[2]

This standard, translated into FBI policy, is no more binding upon an agent when he is dealing with a respectable citizen than when he is dealing with a person who has long been immersed in what Maxwell Bodenheim called "that brisk midnight known as crime." Its uniform application has, many times, paid strange dividends.

Thus, Hoover has indicated that those who volunteer to take on the incredibly dangerous role of informant within a crime syndicate "are frequently men and women with extensive records of past offenses who have come to respect the FBI because of fair and courteous treatment accorded them and members of their families by Special Agents."[3]

In yet another category is the informant who has become convinced that a body which he joined in good faith is the implacable enemy of the values which he took it to be serving. In terms of the number of conscientious defectors whom it has produced, the CPUSA had indubitably been the number one "wrong cause" in the United States in this century. But any organization that draws people to it by professing humanitarian aims and that then requires its members to serve these aims by means of deceit and violence is sure to turn out its quota of defector-informants.

In many cases, the defector from the intelligence or espionage apparatus of a foreign power has similarly changed sides by reason of conscience: what he has served has become in his mind the opposite of what he took it to be. Igor Gouzenko, for example, was a Soviet secret agent by training—and at the outset, we would assume, by conviction.

[2] Quoted by Alpheus T. Mason, in *Harlan Fiske Stone: Pillar of the Law*, pp. 149–150.
[3] J. Edgar Hoover, "The Confidential Nature of FBI Reports," *Syracuse Law Review*, Fall 1956, p. 6.

Having graduated from the Military Intelligence Academy in Moscow, with the rank of lieutenant, he was, at the age of twenty-four, sent to Canada in 1943 as code clerk in the Soviet Embassy. Two years later, he defected—taking with him 109 secret documents that led to the breaking up of a massive spy ring that operated in Canada, Great Britain, and the United States.

In a very different category from any of the above is the person who penetrates a criminal or subversive organization as a working member of an intelligence or law enforcement body. One instance of such undercover work became headline news on February 17, 1965, with the exposure of an alleged plot to blow up the Statue of Liberty, the Washington Monument, and the Liberty Bell.

Here, the undercover agent was 31-year-old Raymond Wood, who had been on the New York City police force for only ten months. To those who called it *lucky* that the plot had been uncovered in time, Police Commissioner Michael J. Murphy gave a curt reply: "There was nothing lucky about this. This man risked his life for months."

In the summer of 1964, a group of students, defying a State Department ban on travel to Cuba, went there under the auspices of the Student Committee on Travel to Cuba. After their return, eleven of them, under the leadership of Robert Steele Collier, a Negro, formed the Black Liberation Front, with headquarters in New York City. The group's intense racism and its bias in favor of Cuba and Red China convinced the Police Department that it should be watched. Wood, a Negro, was instructed to penetrate the Front and keep the department informed.

"He walked himself flatfooted in picket lines, until he was recognized as one of 'them.' He dressed, acted, and talked like 'them.'" Finally, he contrived to make a "No. 1 contact" that led to his being admitted to meetings. There, under intense scrutiny, he was told of the dynamite plots—plots designed to symbolize a violent repudiation of the American concept of freedom. Thereafter he kept the department alert to developments.

His worst time came when he had to go to Quebec with Collier to secure the dynamite. He had no chance to tell the department that he was leaving the country; and as one official said later, " 'If he had been killed, we would not have known it. He was completely on his own.' "[4]

Back from Quebec, Wood helped to bury the dynamite in a vacant lot in the Bronx—and alerted the department. The data he gave "led to the arrest, on February 16, 1965, by the police and FBI, of three Negro men, Robert Steele Collier, Walter Augustus Bowie, and Khaleel Sultaryn Sayyed; and Michelle Duclos, a white woman from Canada." All were charged with conspiring to destroy Government property.[5] In what has been called the fastest promotion in the department's history, Commissioner Murphy bestowed upon Wood the rank of detective.

On November 30, 1964, *The Nation* carried an editorial called "Hoover the Vulgarian." In this, we read, "It is, of course, characteristic of Mr. Hoover that he should—against the great weight of historical evidence—find informers to be 'truly patriotic individuals.' " And this statement is characteristic of a considerable body of anti-informant propaganda.

It is characteristic in its use of the derogatory term *informer* rather than the neutral term *informant*. It is characteristic in its assumption of a high moral tone: one that rejects *on principle* the practice of giving information about crime or subversion to a law enforcement body. And it is characteristic in that it makes Hoover's attitude toward informants seem peculiar to him, and to be one that puts

[4] *Washington Post*, February 17, 1965, p. A3. New York Daily News Service.

[5] *FBI 1966 Appropriation*, p. 60.

him outside the honorable fellowship and tradition of law enforcement.

The phrase "the great weight of historical evidence" has no weight. Since the vast majority of informants have been known as such only by those to whom they have reported, no reliable study of the traits—if any—that distinguish them from the general run of human beings has ever been made.

The high moral tone needs to be evaluated. A *principled* objection to the use of informants would have to be an across-the-board objection. It would have to condemn alike those who have informed on the Nazis, the Communists, the Klans, La Cosa Nostra, and a wide range of other criminal and conspiratorial groups. By this standard, the robe of high morality in which the anti-informants have moved among us shares with the Emperor's new suit of clothes the singular characteristic of being nonexistent; and it is time for the child within our own minds to break the spell by saying so.

The CPUSA has been a prime author of charges that informants are an evil breed and that Hoover, by using them, betrays a taste for "perjured evidence." But the Party's stakes in developing this line are, we must realize, very high. Since it has not been able to prevent defections, it must, in self-defense, work to make the act of informing so repulsive—and so costly in terms of defamation and harassment—that defectors will stop short of going to the FBI.

Furthermore, undercover agents cannot be kept from talking—or testifying. Thus, it becomes of the utmost importance to prevent their being credited, particularly by those sectors of our society that are vital targets of Communist propaganda: young people, intellectuals, minority groups, peace groups, and others. The anti-informant line serves as a covering *argumentum ad hominem*: since there is no way to know who will turn out to be an undercover agent, whoever it is must be discredited in advance—as a nefarious informer.

Finally, it is imperative that any Party member or any collaborator with the Soviet espionage apparatus who is arrested for breaking the law must be cast at once as a martyr: a political prisoner. Whoever testifies against him must, then, be cast as a "kept witness" and "perjurer."

All this might seem to suggest that the Communists are opposed *on principle* to the act of informing and to the FBI's use of informants. But not at all: after Hitler's invasion of the USSR, in June 1941, members of the CPUSA did not hesitate to inform on the Nazis with whom they had collaborated during the period of the Nazi-Soviet pact.

It is more shocking, somehow, to find the double standard fuzzily applied by critics of the FBI who claim to be liberals in the Western sense. The defectors and undercover agents, for example, whom we meet in Cook's *The FBI Nobody Knows* as witnesses against Communist defendants are presented as a sorry, unstable lot: the sort of people who *would* become informants and whom J. Edgar Hoover *would* be inclined to credit. Yet in his article "The FBI and Organized Crime," Cook not only recommends more infiltration of underworld "mobs" but suggests that the infiltrating must be done by persons of a very different breed from FBI agents: tougher, and less scrupulously law-bound. He never does explain why such persons would be more trustworthy than those who have testified against Communist defendants. Neither does he explain why he both disapproves and approves of the use of informants—blaming the FBI both for relying upon them and for not having more of them.

Of all the cases that have stimulated outraged cries against the use of informants, the best known is the trial of the Communist Party leaders, in 1949, for violation of the Smith Act. Yet the testimony of the Government's witnesses stood up under the most exacting cross-examination. The convictions handed down in the lower court presided over by Judge Medina were upheld by the Court of Appeals and, subsequently, by the Supreme Court.

In appealing their case, the convicted Party leaders specifically challenged the propriety of the Government's reliance on the testimony of former Communists and undercover agents. But Judge Learned Hand, in delivering the opinion of the Court of Appeals, observed that courts have countenanced the use of informants "since time immemorial" and that their use does not go counter to American traditions of law. It is usually necessary, he said, to rely upon informants or accomplices "in cases of conspiracy, or in cases where the crime consists of preparing for another crime"—because of the clandestine nature of the activities involved.

Nonetheless, the ex-Communists and undercover agents who testified at this trial—and whose testimony was validated by every test that "due process" provides—were, and have been ever since, rated as perjurers, and not by the Communists alone. Many non-Communists have taken out on these Government witnesses their dislike of the Smith Act, and in some cases, it would appear, their reluctance to believe that anything worse than legitimate dissent is ever fostered on the Left.

As Judge Hand's *Opinion* would suggest, Hoover's attitude could better be called standard than peculiar to him. It was not he, for example, but Senator Robert Kennedy who, on March 3, 1965, engaged in a sharp exchange with Bernard Fensterwald, Counsel for the Senate Subcommittee on Administrative Practice and Procedure—because the latter described as a "fink" an informant named Baron who had provided data on "corruption and dishonesty within the Teamsters' Union":

Senator Kennedy: I never heard that.
Mr. Fensterwald: A "stool pigeon." Does that word strike a chord?
Senator Kennedy: I thought it was a citizen who was reporting information and evidence in connection with illegal activities.

Mr. Fensterwald: That is correct. That would be a very good definition.

Senator Kennedy: That is your definition of "fink."

Mr. Fensterwald: Wait.

Senator Kennedy: Let me say, I am shocked to hear that. There have been a lot of people, if I may say so, Mr. Counsel, who have provided information to the U.S. Government in connection with Communist activities, underworld activities, and narcotics activities at great risk to their very lives, and I think that it has been very, very helpful to the United States.[6]

Again, it was not Hoover but Attorney General Katzenbach who said at Emory University, on April 24, 1965, that he found it "profoundly disturbing that someone who, at personal risk, is willing to come forward and report illegal activities should be dubbed a 'fink' or 'stool pigeon' . . . . We know from repeated experience how central such courage and conduct can be to the effective enforcement of law."[7]

It was Assistant Attorney General Warren Olney III who, on September 3, 1954, addressing the Peace Officers Association of California, in Los Angeles, devoted a good part of his speech to the 1949 Smith Act trial: the evidence; the upholding of the convictions; the criticisms to which the Department had been subjected because of its use of ex-Communists and undercover agents as witnesses; and the extent to which these witnesses had been mercilessly slandered.

The Justice Department, he said, "makes no apology" for using former Communists as witnesses. "In advance, in every case, their testimony has been carefully checked and evaluated. In all instances they have been open to complete, severe, and extensive cross-examination by able counsel."[8]

It was Assistant Attorney General William F. Tomkins who told the International Association of Chiefs of Police,

---

[6] *Hearings before the Senate Subcommittee on Administrative Practice and Procedure, on Invasions of Privacy (Governmental Agencies)*, Part I, p. 274, 1965.

[7] Transcript of speech (1965); Department of Justice, Washington, D.C.

[8] Transcript of speech (1954); Department of Justice, Washington, D.C.

meeting in Philadelphia in 1956, that the Government "invites all former Communists who have sincerely repudiated the principles of the Party" to join the ranks of those citizens "who are doing what they can to protect our country from Communist subversion."[9]

It was the President's Commission on Law Enforcement and Administration of Justice which, in 1967, in *The Challenge of Crime in a Free Society*, p. 198, summed up various reasons why it is so difficult to initiate a strong offensive against organized crime. It said, in part:

The millions of people who gamble illegally are willing customers who do not wish to see their supplier destroyed. Even the true victims of organized crime, such as those succumbing to extortion, are too afraid to inform law enforcement officials. Some misguided citizens think there is social stigma in the role of "informer," and this tends to prevent reporting and cooperating with police.

The credentials of those who comprised this Commission—professors of law, law enforcement officials, and experts in a wide range of relevant fields—were above reproach.

If Hoover is proved vulgar by his appreciation of the services rendered by informants and undercover agents, he moves in a distinguished company of "vulgarians." But he as an individual is not actually the subject at issue; and those who make him appear to be so are just selling us a bill of goods.

Regardless of who the FBI Director might be, Justice would continue its legal war against criminals and subversives. It would continue to maintain surveillance over their organizations and to prosecute such of their members as have demonstrably transgressed federal law. To this end, it would continue to receive data from confidential informants,

[9] *The Police Yearbook*, 1956 (Washington, D.C., International Association of Chiefs of Police), p. 29.

to subject these to exacting checkup, and to use those that stood the test. And the highest courts in our land would continue to treat such evidence as admissible.

And why, in the name of common sense, should it not be admitted? Why should this *one type* of firsthand, eyewitness testimony be excluded. The burden of proof rests with those who say that it should be—particularly if they also demand that the FBI accumulate evidence of the same type for use against defendants whom they happen to want to have convicted.

No process of checking up on the reliability of prospective witnesses—be they informants or not—is one hundred percent proof against error and skillful perjury. But in the rare cases where doubt has been cast upon the trustworthiness of an informant-witness, the Government has almost invariably had enough surplus evidence so that it could expunge the questionable testimony and continue to press the prosecution of the case. There is nothing to suggest that the use of informants leads to the conviction of innocent persons.

When we analyze the arguments of the anti-informants, we find that most of them, deprived of their trappings, are simply assertions that informant-witnesses should not be *allowed* to appear against defendants who belong to some "elect" category: who are Communists, or Klansmen, or whatever. The fact that such defendants have engaged in activities that make them need special protection against exposure does not obligate our society to provide it for them. They have every established right to "due process." They have no right to demand special privilege before the law.

PART THREE

THIS CONTROVERSIAL
BUREAU

ELEVEN

THE FBI IN THE AMERICAN SCENE

MOST AMERICANS are against crime, conspiracy, and subversion. But they are not all equally disturbed about the same crimes. They do not make identical estimates of the extent to which conspiracy and subversion are real and present dangers. They do not all become simultaneously convinced that a certain phase of our national life should be brought under federal law. They do not attach the same relative importance to states' rights and individual rights. With disagreement about all these matters rampant, it is not to be expected that all Americans will see the FBI in the same light.

The Bureau does not, of course, map out its own areas of jurisdiction. It acts under federal law and under directives from the Attorney General or the President. But it operates out in the field—out where Acts of Congress are brought to bear upon personal lives, established customs, and the aims of various organized groups.

If the feelings of any vocal sector of the public run high

with regard to the passage of any law, they tend to run even higher with regard to its enforcement. In extraordinary measure, then, the dedicated commitments, angry cross-purposes, and passionate partisanships of our age are mirrored in what people have said about the FBI. Thus, we can profitably explore certain reasons why it has been, is, and can be expected to remain a controversial bureau.

One reason is obvious: namely, that there are among us groups that have a vested interest in keeping it controversial. When a conspiratorial body, criminal or subversive, is put on the spot by an FBI investigation, it needs to be able to cry, "Foul!" Such a cry is an expedient means of diverting public attention from the group's activities to the question of whether or not the Bureau has employed illegal methods.

For the tactic to work, however, the cry must be heard by a sizeable number of persons whose minds have already been made uneasy about FBI practices. Thus, propagandists for subversive and criminal interests can be expected to stay on the job of extracting from what the Bureau does and what its Director says any elements that can be converted into matters of strident issue.

There is nothing new about this. In the March 1910 *Century Magazine* Attorney General Bonaparte recorded some of the maneuvers and pressures that had punctuated his term of office: most of them the brain-children of financial and industrial interests that were seeking a way to halt, or to avoid, antitrust actions.

No sooner did he assume his post than he began to be visited by "prominent lawyers representing different corporations or clusters of corporations with which the Government was, or expected soon to be, in litigation . . . ." All too patently—as they suggested "delay," or "indulgence" to their clients—they were feeling him out to see whether or not he could be reached by any form of influence which they could command. When they became convinced that he could not be either bribed or intimidated, the visits stopped—and the attacks began.

They were spearheaded by two newspapers "somewhat notoriously identified with 'interests' allied to the persecuted Trusts . . . ." A man in a position to know had warned Mr. Bonaparte that these papers had instructed their Washington representatives to "write (him) out of the Department of Justice." He had been skeptical. But very soon the indicated papers began to "favor" him with "commentaries unblemished by any taint of truth."

Soon the campaign was in full swing. He was said to neglect his office; to be impossible to work with; to be a power-seeker and headline-seeker; to be "feuding" with President Roosevelt. Again and again it was rumored that the latter was about to fire him. As their back-and-forth letters and memoranda show, Bonaparte and the President exchanged, and enjoyed together, multiple items about their being at swords' points.

On only one front did the attackers achieve a measure of success. By a sustained policy of misquoting, they made it hard for the Attorney General to reach the public with an ungarbled account of what he was doing and why.

Today, groups with a vested interest in making the public uneasy about FBI practices form a far more diverse company than did the anti-Bonaparte propagandists. We can learn from the most recent FBI *Annual Report* and from the budget hearings for fiscal 1968 and 1969 how many-purposed are the organizations on which the Bureau now has reason to keep tabs.

Among them are the Communist Party of the United States of America (CPUSA); the W.E.B. DuBois Clubs; the Maoist Progressive Labor Party; the Trotskyite Socialist Workers Party and its youth affiliate, the Young Socialist Alliance; the Nation of Islam—"an all-Negro, violently antigovernment and antiwhite organization"[1]; the Revolution-

[1] *FBI 1968 Appropriation*, p. 62.

ary Action Movement (RAM); 14 Klan and Klan-type organizations; the National Socialist White People's Party (formerly the American Nazi Party); the National States Rights Party; the Minutemen; La Cosa Nostra (the Mafia); and other crime syndicates. No one of these is likely to be reticent about circulating charges that the FBI employs brutal and illegal "police-state" methods.

But even if no propagandists were on the job, the FBI would, for reasons deeply rooted in our system, be a recurrent center of controversy. One such reason is that it operates in the two "charged" areas of federal law and domestic intelligence.

In the former, its work in behalf of "one nation indivisible" is bound many times to impinge upon jealously guarded states' rights. In the latter, its work in behalf of national security is similarly bound to impinge upon jealously guarded civil and constitutional rights. Thus, in the course of doing its law-defined work, it comes up, again and again, to delicately defined boundaries that it must not cross—not even for the sake of getting its work done.

Whether or not it *has* crossed them is certain to be a recurrent matter of angry argument; for whole stretches of these boundaries are so vaguely defined as to blur the point at which trespass begins. The specialist in constitutional law is often far more hesitant about locating this point than are the standpatter, the crusader, and the ideologue.

While some persons are sure to resent the FBI's doing what it must do under the law, others are equally sure to resent its *not* doing more than the law allows of what they want done. In brief, it is predictable that a wide range of determined spokesmen for different and often competing causes will take turns denouncing the Bureau.

Almost independently of what it does, moreover, and simply by reason of what it is—or could all too easily become if it got out of bounds—the FBI bears the burden of man's ancient, well-justified fear of a secret police. It can never expect wholly to slough this off. The burden goes with the job.

It is made heavier by the fact that the Bureau cannot shout from the housetops a full account of what it does. Much of its work must remain unpublicized, many of its findings classified. Thus, it is hard for the lay citizen to know whether or not the FBI bows with good grace to laws that inhibit its own activities. By the same token, it is easy for those with a vested interest in portraying the Bureau as a Gestapo to initiate rumors that elude checkup—and that tend, by repetition, to become part of what "everybody knows."

While it is contrary to the public interest for the FBI to be falsely accused of using police-state methods, it would be far more so for us to stop caring whether or not they were used. The answer to the bland assurance "It can't happen here" is that it did happen here—between 1918 and 1924.

A further burden goes with the FBI's job. It is that of being part of a legal system which Martin Mayer has called "the most complicated ever devised by the wit of man." Anthony Lewis presents one aspect of this complexity in *Gideon's Trumpet*:

An Englishman or a Frenchman lives under one national law; not so the American. Our Constitution created a system of dual government, state and federal .... On the criminal side, take the case of a car thief. He breaks the law of New York when he drives away in a Chrysler parked on East Eighty-seventh Street, Manhattan, with the key conveniently left in the ignition; if he drives across the George Washington bridge to New Jersey, he also violates a federal law against interstate transportation of stolen vehicles.[2]

[2] Anthony Lewis, *Gideon's Trumpet* (New York, Random House, 1964), pp. 12–13.

The FBI is obligated to enter the case at this point. But jurisdictional complexity would set in if the car thief—perhaps because he saw someone looking at the car with what he took to be suspicious eyes—committed a murder. With a few specified exceptions, murder is a local not a federal, crime; and it is of a higher order of seriousness than is the theft of a car.

Thus, if the FBI arrested the suspect on a warrant that charged him with the federal crime of interstate transport of a stolen car, he would be turned over to the New Jersey authorities by the United States Attorney of the region, to be prosecuted for murder—after he had been indicted on the federal charge. Evidence gathered by the FBI would also be turned over. But if the suspect was acquitted of the murder charge, the federal Government could reactivate its charge.

All this points to a further reason for the FBI's often being a center of controversy. Cases in which both federal and state authorities have jurisdictional rights are legion. If such a case arouses public interest, the Bureau can become equally fair game for those who are quick to see the Federal Goverment as imposing its will upon the states and those who see it as weakly yielding to the states' rightists.

To complicate matters further, Congress, in framing a law, cannot always define the area of federal jurisdiction except in presumptive terms. Often the determinative factor is the crossing of a state line; but with certain types of crime only investigation can reveal whether or not such a line has been crossed. Congress, therefore, may write into a statute a *presumptive clause*: a clause which specifies the conditions under which a crime is to be regarded as federal until, or unless, evidence proves it to be local in character.

We can illustrate with the Federal Kidnapping Act. As originally framed, in 1932, this Act did not contain a presumptive clause; but one was added in 1934—to send the

FBI into any case not solved within a 7-day period. A kidnapper, in brief, who was not apprehended within a week was legally *presumed* to have fled to another state. The law stood thus for twenty-one years. Then came the tragic Weinberger case.

On a July afternoon in 1956, in the Long Island community of Westbury, Peter, the month-old son of Mr. and Mrs. Morris Weinberger, was asleep in his carriage in the yard of his home. For an interval of not more than fifteen minutes his mother left him alone, while she went into the house for a fresh diaper and other necessities. When she returned, he was gone. The kidnapper had left a note demanding $2,000 for his return, and specifying how he was to receive it.

To quote from *Time* of July 16, 1956, "Inevitably someone called the New York newspapers." They, in turn, scrambled to call the Nassau County police headquarters to check their tips—and were asked "to hold up the story until after the ransom deadline next day, in hope the kidnaper would collect the ransom and return the baby."

All except the *Daily News* agreed. It demurred; and by 8:20 that night its early edition was on the street with a brief bulletin on the case. Half an hour later, its big second edition was out with banner headlines about the kidnapping and, on an inside page, a full account of it.

Other papers were at once released from their pledge; and the police forthwith lost all control of the situation:

Next day, the Long Island countryside swarmed with reporters, photographers and TV cameramen. Newsmen interviewed the Weinbergers' neighbors and the neighbors' children. At 10 A.M., when Weinberger placed the ransom at the nearby spot specified in the note, three newsmen were allowed to watch for the car. To no one's surprise, the kidnaper did not keep his date.

Chief of Detectives Stuyvesant Pinnell later said, " 'We would have got a hell of a lot further if there had been no interference from the press.' " But this was an instance of self-defense. He had failed to notify the papers and pledge them to secrecy before unofficial tips could reach them. Once the scramble for news was under way, moreover, he had irresponsibly poured out information that should have been kept secret and had, apparently, yielded to the importunities of newsmen at every point. His whole performance had, in fact, been a masterpiece of bungling.

The September 3rd issue of *Time* reports the outcome. After the requisite seven days had passed, the FBI initiated its investigation. With few clues to go on, agents gave concentrated attention to the ransom note. It was handwritten in green ink; and the m's and r's were peculiarly formed.

In addition to checking 75,000 fingerprint cards of people in the area who had police records, the agents scrutinized every public document that might yield a matching sample of handwriting. Court records, auto-license applications, voter registrations: these and other documents were, during a six-week period, examined to the number of more than 2,000,000.

Finally, on a probation paper in a set of such papers that had been removed from the files for disposal, as outdated, they found a signature in green ink with the tell-tale m's and r's. With the suspect thus tentatively identified, other supportive pieces of evidence could be fitted into place. Angelo John La Marca, "sometime mechanic and cab driver," was arrested and "stolidly confessed": he had decided upon kidnapping as the only means by which he could secure $2,000 to pay accumulated bills. Driving through Westbury, on the lookout for a possible victim, he had chanced to pass the Weinberger house and had seen the unattended carriage during the few minutes that Mrs. Weinberger was absent.

On the morning after the kidnapping, he had taken the infant back to Westbury, hoping to return him and collect the ransom. But he had found the area "swarming" with policemen, reporters, photographers, and a miscellany of other people—so that he could not approach the designated spot. Thereupon, he had taken the baby into a thicket not far from his own home in Plainview and had abandoned him there.

The gross mishandling of the Weinberger case moved Congress to again amend the Federal Kidnapping Act. On August 6, 1956, it cut the presumptive period down to twenty-four hours.

On January 30, 1957, Hoover told the House Subcommittee on Appropriations that the FBI had already entered "17 cases which, under the previous 7-day presumptive clause, we would not have entered, as all resolved themselves within a 7-day period." In only two instances had the solution of the crime shown it to be truly *federal*: in the other fifteen, no state line had been crossed.[3]

Does this mean that Congress, having judged the presumptive period to be too long, has made it too short? Hoover did not presume to say that he felt this to be true; but he stressed the fact that the 7-day period had usually served to prevent the Bureau's entrance into non-federal cases.

Paradoxically, the Weinberger case, even though it moved Congress to amend the law, provided no clue whatever to how long or how short the presumptive period should be. Even if the FBI had begun its investigation at the end of twenty-four hours, it would still have done so after the infant had been abandoned. And when the kidnapper was eventually apprehended, it became clear that he had not crossed a state line. Thus, while the case was solved by the FBI, the solution showed it to be non-federal in character—and a shorter presumptive period would not have made it federal.

Our system of dual government—federal and state—makes necessary, in the framing of certain statutes, a resort to the expedient called a *presumptive clause*. But in practice, a statute which contains such a clause can foster enough

[3] *FBI 1958 Appropriation*, p. 34.

ambiguities to make some persons impatient with the FBI's delay in entering a crucial case and provide other persons with a basis for saying that its entrance constitutes a "trespass."

At a hearing on January 29, 1964, Hoover discussed a law that is far more controversial than is the Kidnapping Act:

Among the prohibitions of the Civil Rights Act of 1960 is the interstate transportation of explosives with the knowledge or intent that such will be used to damage or destroy property for the sake of interfering with its use for educational, religious, residential, business, charitable, or civic purposes.

But how can anyone know, prior to an investigation, whether or not the explosives were transported interstate? Hoover explained:

There is a presumptive clause in the legislation that interstate transportation has taken place where an explosive is used in the manner proscribed . . . .

Is every bombing of property to be treated, then, as a federal crime?

The Justice Department's Civil Rights Division, he went on to say, has ruled otherwise. It has not felt that the law was intended to "relieve local and State authorities of their primary responsibility . . . ."

The Department, therefore, has instructed the FBI to bring to its attention "all known bombings, and related outrages"; and to conduct "full investigations in every instance where the Department has so authorized." The results are referred to the Civil Rights Division; and it decides whether or not further action is warranted.[4]

Thus, under the 1960 Act, the FBI enters a bombing case on the "rebuttable presumption" that the explosives were

[4] *FBI 1965 Appropriation*, p. 57.

transported interstate. The establishment of a local source for these explosives would rebut the "rebuttable presumption." It would, in short, take the case out of the federal field; and from that point on, the FBI could do not more than offer its evidence to state authorities.

This is one reason why, where a bombing has occurred, the FBI agents try to secure the cooperation of state and local police from the very start—and thereby invite the charge that they are "pals" of the "segregationist cops." The percentage of bombing cases from which the Federal Government has to withdraw, at one stage or another, is very high. State and local authorities are better equipped to carry on if they have been continuously involved in the investigation.

In the vast majority of cases, they are thus continuously involved. When the FBI initiates an investigation under a presumptive clause, it does not take matters out of the hands of local officers. On the contrary, it seeks to make its work an effective part of a cooperative effort.

With regard to bombings in and around Birmingham, Alabama, in the summer of 1963, James A. Wechsler wrote in the *New York Post* of September 18th that Hoover had not even tried to bring home racial violence to those responsible for it. "He hasn't tried, I presume, because he is reluctant to risk his status as a sacred cow with the Southerners who control the FBI's budget . . . ."

But who are these "Southerners"? Only one member of the House Subcommittee on Appropriations that passed judgment on the Bureau's budget for fiscal 1963 was from below the Mason-Dixon line: namely, Robert L. Sikes of Florida. The Chairman was John J. Rooney of New York. The other five members were Don Magnuson, Washington; Fred Marshall, Minnesota; Frank T. Bow, Ohio; Glenard P. Lipscomb, California; and Elford A. Cederberg, Michigan.

The phrase "Southerners who control the FBI's budget" has become a stereotype. Yet at no time during the past dozen years at least has there been a Southern majority on the Subcommittee on Appropriations. At this writing, there are ten members instead of the seven that there were in 1963. Rooney is still Chairman. Representatives Sikes, Bow, Lipscomb, and Cederberg are still members. The five men now on the Subcommittee who were not there in 1963 are John M. Slack, Jr., West Virginia; Neal Smith, Iowa; John T. Flynn, Jr., Georgia; Charles S. Joelson, New Jersey; and Mark Andrews, North Dakota.

In sharp contrast to Wechsler's version, there were reports circulated in the fall of 1963 to the effect that the FBI had investigated as many as 50 bombings around Birmingham during the summer of that year. We do not know by whom these were authored; but they were wildly inaccurate.

Hoover's own report lies between the two extremes. The FBI informed the Civil Rights Division with respect to all the bombings known to have taken place in the Birmingham area. The Department authorized full investigations of just six of them. These six were promptly and thoroughly investigated.[5]

Wechsler's column illustrates a point of which we have become very much aware in the course of our work on this book: namely, that what we as citizens need to know about the FBI is often buried under statements that reflect strong convictions about current issues but that are only tenuously related to either plain facts or the precisions of federal law. This point can be more fully illustrated by juxtaposing contrasted responses to Bureau action in relation to the murder, on June 12, 1963, of Medgar Evers, field representative of the NAACP, in Jackson, Mississippi.

The crime seemed clearly to have been stimulated by Evers' work in registering Negro voters. Attorney General Robert Kennedy instructed the FBI to enter the case under Section 241, Title 18, United States Code: the 1870 law that is designated in the Code as *Conspiracy against the rights of citizens.*

[5] *FBI 1965 Appropriation*, p. 57.

On June 22nd, on the basis of evidence which the Justice Department found to be sufficient, FBI agents arrested Byron De La Beckwith. Their warrant charged him with having violated the above statute. They could not have arrested him for the local crime of murder; but he was turned over to the Jackson Police Department to be tried for murder.[6]

Two successive trials ended with hung juries. After the second, the judge, in April 1964, released De La Beckwith on bond. In November of that year, William L. Wallace announced for the state that no third trial would be held unless new evidence was brought to light.[7]

On the day after Evers' murder, Wechsler reported in the *New York Post* that in October 1962 the NAACP leader had had an anonymous phone call threatening the lives of his children. "It had not occurred to him to ask for FBI protection . . . ."

There was no law on the federal books under which the FBI could have established protective surveillance over Evers' children, or anyone similarly threatened. Moreover, there is nothing in Wechsler's account to suggest that the FBI was even informed of the phone call. Yet he asserts that, because of that call, Evers himself should have had the benefit of "continuing vigilance" even after the threat to his children had dissipated.

Such vigilance, he contends, should still have been in effect eight months later, in June 1963 to have reduced the likelihood of Evers' being murdered. "Instead he went to a lonely death, as he had feared he would, while the G-men slept."

This view of Wechsler's opens up crucial questions; for what he says, in effect, is that the FBI should have acted *on its own,* and *outside the law,* to perform a police function which the Justice Department could not have authorized. Furthermore, the number of persons who received anony-

---

[6] *FBI 1965 Appropriation,* pp. 57–58.
[7] *The New York Times,* November 21, 1964.

mous threats in 1963, as in each recent year, would come close to being legion. By what standard would he have had the Bureau draw the line between those who did and those who did not qualify for federal "vigilance"?

Should the FBI have made its own estimate of the relative merits of various persons? Should it have decided that Evers, because he represented the NAACP and was registering Negro voters, was more deserving of protection than was, say, a Negro sharecropper who represented no organization but who put his life in jeopardy by registering to vote?

On June 24, 1963, two days after De La Beckwith's arrest, *I. F. Stone's Bi-Weekly* declared, "The FBI lives in cordial fraternity with the cops that enforce white supremacy . . . . The FBI hasn't solved a single one of the shootings that have marked the Negro's struggle for freedom."

The next day, Wallace Dabbs wrote in the Columbus, Mississippi, *Commercial Dispatch* that the South is losing its respect for the FBI because of the high-handed way in which the "fed" boys trespass upon the domain of local police forces. The FBI agents, he said, had no right to arrest De La Beckwith. If they had any evidence against him, they should have turned it over to the Jackson Police Department, for it to evaluate—and to use at its own discretion. Instead, "they dug through those 1957 Civil Rights Bills" and charged De La Beckwith with "conspiring to deprive Evers of his civil rights."

The *Dan Smoot Report* of July 15th used the Evers case as the basis for a charge that "civil rights for negroes, in the eyes of politicians hungry for votes, means that harming a negro is a national disaster which requires federal action even when such action violates the Constitution; but that negro violence against whites is a routine matter beneath the notice of federal authorities."

Between the polemical extremes lay much solid reporting. The Washington *Afro-American* of June 25th, for example, recalled the circumstances of Evers's murder; explained the nature of the law under which De La Beckwith was arrested; described such evidence against him as had been made public; and noted that, according to Hoover, the Attorney General would turn De La Beckwith over to the Jackson Police Department, "following his arraignment on federal charges," if that Department would file a murder charge.

This one article told more about the case, and about federal law and its enforcement, than did the other four put together. The other four could scarcely be said to be about the Evers case at all. Rather, they used it as a means of reaching our emotions, not our minds, and persuading us to denounce what their respective authors wanted to have denounced.

To an extent that we did not anticipate at the beginning, the task of evaluating the FBI has turned out to be one of separating sense from nonsense, fact from fiction, and straight reporting from loaded polemics. The chapters, therefore, that comprise the rest of Part III might be catalogued under the heading *People Have Said. . . .*

T W E L V E

OUT OF COMMUNISM'S LEXICON

IN THEIR guerrilla war against the FBI, the Communists are untiring. For decades, they have been injecting into the troubled atmosphere of our time a rigid, repetitious brand of anti-FBI propaganda. We have come upon unmistakable excerpts from it in surprising places; and our having done so is not surprising. What is hammered home insistently enough for a long enough time has a way of becoming "true." The Communists learned this fact from Lenin. So did Hitler.

The fact that the Communists rate the FBI as evil does not, of course, prove that it is good. But it is a matter of simple prudence for us to know the character of the Party line, with respect to the Bureau as with respect to other subjects, so that we can recognize it for what it is—and has been down through the years.

The CPUSA's approach to the FBI has been dictated by what it cannot do. Obviously, for example, it cannot entice the FBI into a "united front"—and thus acquire leadership over it. There would be no point, then, in its making a tactical pretense that the gap between itself and the Bureau is less wide than it seems to be.

It cannot lull the FBI into an illusion that Communism has so changed its character that to regard it as conspiratorial is "old hat." The Bureau is familiar with all the Party's ins and outs; and it has remained on guard against the very types of action in which Party members are instructed to engage.

It cannot, where the FBI is concerned, obey Lenin's command to "penetrate without being penetrated, influence without being influenced." Instead, the FBI has penetrated the CPUSA on a massive scale—with the latter unable to return the compliment. The flow of defectors has likewise been one-directional: from the Party toward the Bureau.

Unable to employ to any good purpose, in relation to the FBI, its usual tactics and strategies, the CPUSA has held itself to one unvarying effort. It has tried to foster in the American people—and particularly in groups committed to a defense of civil and constitutional rights—enough distrust of the Bureau to move them to do for the Party what it has not been able to do for itself: namely, bring about some curtailment of the Bureau's power to do its job.

To this end, its propaganda has, without letup, portrayed the FBI as the arch-enemy of American principles and freedoms. In like vein, it has cast Hoover as the arch advocate and practitioner of all that is repressive and reactionary.

The nature and continuity of this anti-FBI campaign can be illustrated by two book reviews that appeared in the Party press fourteen years apart. One, by Harry Raymond, is a review of Max Lowenthal's *The Federal Bureau of Investigation,* in the January 1951 issue of the Party's theoretical journal, *Political Affairs.* The other, by Fred G. Eberhart, is a review of Fred J. Cook's *The FBI Nobody Knows,* in *The Worker* of January 19, 1965.

The two books have three things in common which are reflected in the reviews. First, their authors, Lowenthal and Cook, are "bourgeois"—a fact emphasized, and capitalized on, by both Raymond and Eberhart. Secondly, they are critical enough of the FBI and Hoover to make the Communist reviewers eager to have them read. Yet, as their third similarity, both are marked by what these reviewers are obligated to pinpoint as a grave defect: neither Lowenthal nor Cook puts a Marxist-Leninist interpretation upon the FBI's activities. Raymond and Eberhart, each in turn, deplore the absence of this interpretation—and proceed to provide it.

Thus, the two reviews yield both a compact summary of what the Communists say, and like to have said, about the FBI and its Director and a reminder of the rigid ideological compulsions under which the Party press labors.

Raymond heads his review "J. Edgar Hoover's American Gestapo"—and concentrates on portraying the FBI as a "police state" instrument. Lowenthal's book, he writes, has suffered "a storm of abuse" from "prostitute writers of the commercial press"; and its author will be "lucky if he is not slapped into jail and persecuted under the McCarran Act for his painstaking efforts in historical research."

The FBI "has for some time been assuming the role of Himmler's Gestapo . . . . It has penetrated shops, trade unions, churches, schools, homes, and community organizations. It directs a virtual reign of terror against public employees . . . ." It is "a sinister instrument of the monopolies in their drive to war and fascism." It views as subversive the Negroes' struggle "against Jim-Crow, against the lynchers, for equal rights . . . ." Lowenthal's book "should shock all Americans into a realization of the extent to which our country is being systematically subjected to a Gestapo rule of fear and terror."

Regrettably, however, in Raymond's view, Lowenthal "does not see [the FBI] in its true historical light as part of the developing pattern of the rule of U.S. capitalism in the era of imperialism and the drive to world war and fascism." He fails to relate its functions "to the plans and aims of the imperialist ruling class."

Eberhart's review—which bears the heading "The Master Deceiver's Power Laid Bare"—might seem like a direct imitation of Raymond's did not the Party press offer abundant evidence that the pattern and jargon are standard. For example, just as Raymond denounces "prostitute writers of the commercial press," so Eberhart charges that Cook's *The FBI Nobody Knows* is being denied a fair hearing because of "a conspiracy authored by Hoover, the press, the Congress, the Judiciary and others who control the organs of public opinion."

J. Edgar Hoover's career, he writes, has been marked by "a relentless drive for power, an affection for perjured evidence, and, above all, a phobia against radicals, civil rights advocates, peace promoters and the broad spectrum of those who are the most loyal defenders of democracy." For its exposure of this nefarious career and the machinations of the FBI, he warmly recommends *The FBI Nobody Knows*.

Regrettably, however, in Eberhart's view, Cook exhibits a sad lack of ideological awareness. He fails to relate the FBI "to the structure of America society" and to see Hoover as "the instrument of a government that is fearful of an idea whose time has come."

The similarity of outlook that binds these reviews together across a span of foutreen years becomes all the more striking when we think of the sheer eventfulness of those years. When Raymond reviewed *The Federal Bureau of Investigation*, Stalin was still alive—with the Communist orbit as his monolithic possession, terror as his instrument, and Parties around the world as bond servants of Soviet policy. When Eberhart reviewed *The FBI Nobody Knows*, Khrus'ichev had come and gone—and had left behind him the wrenching effects of destalinization, an upsurge of nationalism in East Europe, the Sino-Soviet conflict, the USSR's nuclear prowess, a failing agriculture, and a vast industrial complex faced with the problem of how to reverse a declining growth-rate without a hazardous resort to "capitalist" methods and incentives.

To read Eberhart with all this in mind is to be struck by the static character of the CPUSA's posture in a changing world. The fact that the Party talks of what is "fated" to happen at some unspecified future time creates an illusion of dynamism. Also, wherever it is free to execute strategic zigs and zags, it can create an illusion of change in its own character. But the future that is talked about is ideologically closed; and the zigs and zags merely signal an effort to accomplish by new means what old means have failed to accomplish.

What makes the Party's anti-FBI propaganda so revealing is that, in relation to the Bureau, the Communists lack maneuvering space. They have no option except to go on repeating themselves. Thus, we can learn from this special sector of their propaganda more than the obvious fact that they dislike Hoover and the FBI. We can learn to recognize, through and under all manipulated appearances of change, the static and dated character of "dynamic" Marxism-Leninism.

A sampling of items from the Party press for the past three decades will show how invariably, when they talk about the Bureau and its Director, the CPUSA's propagandists come out by the same door by which they went in. For a first example, we go back to an editorial—"A Warning to the People"—in the *Daily Worker* of May 11, 1940.

The Nazi-Soviet pact was then in operation; and the CPUSA was dedicated to opposing our aid to Britain and France and, above all, to keeping us out of the war. Thus, we find "Gestapoman Hoover" and President Franklin D. Roosevelt cast as collaborators in evil. Hoover's "plug-ugly activities" are designed to force the people, in the name of security, to surrender their liberties; and Roosevelt, intent to further his own "war plans," encourages Hoover's "brutalities."

Hitler's invasion of the USSR, in June 1941, threw this Party line into reverse; and not until his defeat was certain did the propaganda machine run smoothly again in its prewar groove. But by 1947, the "petty, power-mad J. Edgar Hoover" was being assailed as head of a "frame-up gang."

In that year, also, the Truman doctrine became a threat to Soviet ambitions. Therefore: "The Hoover-Truman bloc has raised the red scare and the menace of Soviet expansion in a deliberate attempt to throw sand in the eyes of the people . . . .

". . . . the Soviet Union does not have troops in the countries outside its borders except by international agreement. Nor is there any threat from the side of the Soviet Union with regard to the independence of other states."

This passage is from a "Speaker's Outline on the Present International Situation," issued by the Education Department of the Communist Party of New York on March 21, 1947. Five months later—with Rumania, Bulgaria, and Albania already reduced to the status of Soviet satellites—Stalin took over Hungary. Czechoslovakia came next, in May 1948; Poland, in January 1949.

The June 29, 1949, issue of the *Daily Worker* carried an article—"Life of the Party"—by Elizabeth Gurley Flynn: "Surely the American people must see the FBI with new eyes today. The time has come to investigate its methods, its scandal-mongering lists, its blackmailing data, its misuse of public funds, its usurpation of power, its tentacles gripping all parts of our country . . . . The old secret police of the Czar, the Okrana, built up just such a stranglehold on millions of people." She did not mention Stalin's secret police.

In the May 1950 issue of *Political Affairs*, Gilbert Green declared it to be "one of the big tasks of our Party . . . to make the labor movement and all democratic mass organizations realize that this tremendous F.B.I. stoolpigeon machine is concentrated not only against the Communist Party, but against every democratic organization and movement in this country."

In the December 1953 issue, Pettis Perry wrote, "We have to bring home to all strata of the population the truth of FBI harassment, their snooping and Gestapo-like attempts to intimidate men, women, and children . . . ."

Since such propaganda has been going round and round for decades—with no new direction to take—it is not surprising that Raymond's review in 1951 and Eberhart's in 1965 seem cut to the same pattern from the same bolt of cloth.

One propaganda theme which deserves special notice cropped up in 1939–1940—and has been a favorite ever since. The stimulus to its introduction was the Presidential Order which, in September 1939, took the FBI into the national-security field and moved Mr. Hoover to create a General Intelligence Division: forerunner of today's Domestic Intelligence Division.

This theme exploits the fact that Hoover was, at the office end, in charge of the General Intelligence Division created by Bureau Chief Flynn during the Palmer era. Flynn kept the GID's field activities under his own control. The Communist tactic consists of (1) making Hoover responsible for the abuses of that period; and then (2) portraying the modern Intelligence Division as nefariously "more of the same."

William Z. Foster—for many years the most powerful leader in the CPUSA—writes of the Palmer "Red raids," in his *History of the Communist Party of the United States*, p. 175. "These monstrous raids, authorized by the 'liberal' President Wilson, were carried out by Attorney General A. Mitchell Palmer and his hatchet man, J. Edgar Hoover."

This casting of Hoover as "hatchet man" of the raids is an expedient rewriting of history, persuasive only because the actual history of that period is a large blur in the public mind. Hoover neither set the pattern of the raids nor participated in them.

On June 8, 1940, when the campaign against the Director was in full swing, Congressman Emanuel Celler of New York defined Hoover's role in the Palmer era in an address over radio station WJZ. On June 11th, he read the text of his address into the *Congressional Record*.

Referring to charges that Hoover "was actively engaged" in the Palmer raids, Celler said:

This is utterly false. The late William J. Flynn was the man in charge. At that time Hoover was a special assistant attorney general, and he handled the prosecution of many cases. He had nothing to do with the arrest or so-called persecution of individuals. He simply handled the cases in court as they were presented to him.

He then made a point which needs to be emphasized:

Hoover was appointed to his present position by Harlan F. Stone, now Justice of the United States Supreme Court, and who was at that time the Attorney General. Justice Stone is an outstanding liberal. He appointed Hoover to his present position as head of the F.B.I. only after a most careful investigation. If Hoover had been involved in any of these so-called Palmer raids or persecutions, certainly Justice Stone would not have appointed him.[1]

We spoke in Chapter XI of the 1921 hearings, presided over by Senator Walsh, on *Charges of Illegal Practices in the Department of Justice*. Hoover attended these hearings, as a departmental attorney, and was asked on several occasions to confirm or provide some item of information.

[1] *86 Congressional Record*, Part 16, p. 3744, Appendix.

The Subcommittee's probe was determined and thorough. But its 788 pages of testimony and evidential materials yield no suggestion whatever—by a member of the Department, a member of the Subcommittee, or a witness—that Hoover was implicated in or responsible for the abuses and illegalities that were being explored.

Those who had issued the orders that led to the dragnet raids and to illegal searches and seizures were identified and questioned. Hoover was not among them. The persons who had charge of the raids in various areas were identified and, in some instances, questioned. Hoover was not among them. He was not among the individuals called to testify and explain their conduct—on any count.

It seems to us to be one hundred percent improbable that the Communists, in 1939–1940—just when they happened to need, for their own purposes, to make Hoover responsible for the abuses of the Palmer era—would unearth facts the existence of which neither Attorney General Harlan Fiske Stone nor the Walsh Subcommittee, for all their probing, found any reason to suspect. Yet this propaganda line has remained a Party favorite.

Also, various "bourgeois" critics of the FBI have pulled it out of the atmosphere and given it a wider circulation. Thus, Fred Cook, in *The FBI Nobody Knows*, p. 244, describes the intelligence division created by Hoover after the outbreak of World War II as a "revival of his once-discredited, much-hated General Intelligence Division . . . ."

The CPUSA's war against the FBI is not an isolated phenomenon. It is simply one aspect of its war against our system as a whole. We stress this fact because many non-Communists make charges against the Bureau and its Director that sound as though they were deliberate borrowings from the Party line. Even when such charges are ill-founded, however, or cynically "loaded," they lack the ideological trademark.

More often than not, they appear to reflect a belief, arrived at by one course or another, that the Bureau is a threat to our type of society and a misfit within our governmental structure. Such beliefs can be honestly held, whether or not they are justified; and no issue is made clear by calling everyone who holds them a Communist.

Yet even when they are honestly held, they can be dishonestly presented. One depressing figure on today's landscape is the non-Communist who, in his commitment to a cause, loads the evidence against whomever or whatever he has designated as villainous. This figure may crop up at any point on the opinion spectrum. He may have any of a well-nigh unlimited range of targets. The fact that he loads the evidence does not make him a Communist—even though the Communists do likewise. It just makes him intellectually dishonest.

The propaganda pattern that we have traced in the Communist press can also be traced in the writings of any one long-term Party spokesman. Those of Herbert Aptheker, former editor of *Political Affairs* and one of the CPUSA's leading theoreticians, offer a case in point.

In the January 1965 issue of *Political Affairs*, Aptheker wrote, "Ever since Hoover's career as a federal investigator began—forty-five years ago—his every utterance and action has demonstrated commitment to extremely anti-democratic and reactionary views." Declaring the Director to be a "racist," he urged his dismissal for "outrageous misconduct and for gross failure to perform his sworn duty . . . ."

What has Aptheker said on other subjects? His *American Foreign Policy and the Cold War* provides answers. While this book was published in 1962, the Preface states that the chapters appeared in substantially their present form, between 1949 and 1962, in *Masses and Mainstream, Mainstream, International Affairs* (Moscow), and *Political Affairs*. Within the frame of reference which we enter by opening the book, Soviet policy is always "peace-loving" and "anti-imperialistic." That of the United States is "war-mongering" and "imperialistic."

About the Korean war, he says, p. 131, that "for every tortured Korean patriot, for every violated Korean woman, for every famished Korean child the American ruling class, the American government is guilty." North Korea was not only guiltless but free from internal dissent, because there "the people ruled."

On p. 164, we read that the Truman Administration undertook "the deliberate rebuilding of Nazism in Germany." German anti-Semitism is denounced. Soviet anti-Semitism is not mentioned. Aptheker's line, in brief, is unvaryingly the Party line.

What all this comes to is the fact that the CPUSA's anti-FBI propaganda is irrelevant to the question of whether or not the Bureau is doing a good job; and of whether or not it is the kind of investigative body that fits our American system. It is irrelevant for the same reason that several articles by Aptheker which appeared in *The Worker* early in 1966 were irrelevant to an effort to understand the war in Vietnam.

Having made a trip to North Vietnam, Aptheker wrote with an "I was there" flavor. Being always the theoretician, he made his conclusions sound like the end results of meticulous analyses. But the *substance* of his eyewitness report differed not at all from that of other articles in the Party press—by persons who had not been to Vietnam, North or South.

A good preparation for reading what the Communists say on *any* subject is to savor the significance of a passage on p. 339 of *Fundamentals of Marxism-Leninism* (1963 Edition). Issued by the Foreign Languages Publishing House, Moscow, this book is called a Manual; and in multiple translations, it serves as such for all Parties that are oriented toward the Soviet Union.

Under the heading "Freedom of Discussion and Unity of Action," we read, "Party discipline does not expect anyone to relinquish his own convictions if they are not at variance with the principles of Marxism-Leninism. But the Party makes it incumbent upon every member to obey the adopted decisions and conscientiously to carry them into effect even if the member does not agree with them . . . ."

The next paragraph begins, "The Party has strict rules as regards those who do not obey the adopted decisions." As a unit, these statements tell us what we can and cannot learn from reading an article in the Party press.

We can learn what the Party line is with respect to the subject handled. We can learn that the author has not refused to obey "adopted decisions." But we cannot learn what he as an individual thinks about what is appearing under his name. We have no key to the doubts or convictions he may have relinquished in order to keep his article from being at "variance" with "the principles of Marxism-Leninism"—as currently defined. And we cannot gain any unbiased information about the subject.

Responsible, fact-respecting appraisals of any part of our Government and its policies are always in order—no matter how critical they may be. But if the FBI, or any other agency, is to be found wanting, it must be found so by the standards of our own society; not by those of a Party that is ideologically forbidden to do otherwise than denounce, in approved terms, any institution or policy that makes harder the fulfillment of Communism's "historic mission."

THIRTEEN

BABEL, U.S.A.

IN SHARP contrast to the CPUSA's ideological stockade, within which every word has its marching orders, our society is a place where we are equally free to talk off the tops of our minds or out of the depths of our convictions; out of our abysmal ignorance or out of our hard-earned knowledge.

It is a place where reporters, columnists, editors, radio and TV commentators, personal acquaintances, and outright propagandists make a daily stab at making up our minds for us. Also, it is one in which the members of multiple cliques and pressure movements develop their own in-group ways of talking—among themselves, and at and about everyone else.

In brief, it is an open society; and within it, the problem of deciding what to credit, out of all we read and hear, can be, at times, almost overwhelming. It becomes acute when we try to appraise an agency like the FBI—or, for that matter, any other federal body—around which statements of every degree of accuracy and inaccuracy have been accumulating for years.

So long as we do not focus our minds on these statements, they simply merge into the welter of what we have read or heard somewhere. But the situation changes drastically when we try to judge them as true or false; or, lacking a basis for such judgment, to appraise their plausibility. Then we have to make note of what contradicts what; to assign different weights to different types of evidence; and to ask on what authority this or that assertion is made.

Our first example need not be solemnly regarded. It is just a column in the *Las Vegas Review-Courier* of September 6, 1963, in which Bob Richards lets go at the FBI for handling a certain case in a way that he counts as unfair to Las Vegas. Most of the column can simply be rated as what one man has felt like saying. Thus, with regard to the FBI, Richards asks:

Has it been transformed from a tight-knit organization of dedicated lawmen into a posse of poseurs with law degrees whose chiefest duties are polishing up the handle of J. Edgar Hoover's big brass door . . . ?

But in one sentence, facts are at issue: "It is axiomatic among newsmen that whenever the FBI releases the name of a Most Wanted Criminal it means they've already got their quarry staked out and will charge in for the pinch just as soon as the public has got the word they want the guy."

It may be "axiomatic among newsmen"; but it is not true. And here the Bureau has not been secretive. From 1950, when the Most Wanted program was initiated, to 1964, the average lapse of time between the naming of a criminal as Most Wanted and his capture was 146 days. In fiscal 1966, it happened to be 137.[1] Some Wanted persons are arrested

[1] "Profiles in Crime," *FBI Law Enforcement Bulletin*, July 1966, p. 2.

almost at once. Some have never been found. As of January 4, 1965, 224 had been located out of 242 posted since 1950.

We doubt that the phrase "axiomatic among newsmen" has any literal meaning. But if we pretend that it has, we face the question of why newsmen, of all people, would reach a conclusion so wide of the mark. The press is informed when a name is added to the Most Wanted list and when a listed criminal is arrested. Items reporting such data are a commonplace. Would not a newsman, then, who intended to write on the subject and who wanted to get facts straight have access to enough "morgue" materials to prevent his sponsoring a wildly untrue "axiom"?

If we seem to be over-attending to a smallish matter, we do so for two reasons. One is the frequency with which criticisms of the FBI are supported by airy nothings impressively phrased. The other is that critics have carried to the point of tedium their ridiculing of the Most Wanted program.

Dick Gregory, for example, in his syndicated column of November 1, 1964, called the FBI "probably the biggest fraud in the world"—and advised those who wanted to confirm this to go to the post office and look at the top ten. "No. 1 is probably a purse snatcher. No. 2 maybe some guy who took an illegal flight to avoid arrest probably for some maternity rap . . . ."

The FBI does not list purse snatchers or men fleeing a "maternity rap." We can assume that Gregory knows this. But he was not really writing about the "top ten." He was ridiculing the list as part of an effort to prove that the FBI avoids tough problems—particularly those that have to do with racial discrimination—and concentrates on petty crimes that let it astonish a gullible public with its feats.

All Most Wanted persons have been singled out because their records mark them as potential threats to those among whom they move. The majority are sought for crimes over which the FBI has primary jurisdiction. But some, under the Fugitive Felon Act, are listed at the request of local police departments. Far from being "staked out," so that agents can, in a glare of publicity, "charge in for the pinch," they are being sought by all investigative means.

The program has succeeded far beyond what we ourselves thought probable when it was first announced. Of the 265 men located between 1950 and the end of fiscal 1968, 95 were arrested as a result of citizen cooperation. But why should anyone bother to cooperate if he has been persuaded—by Richards or Gregory or whomever—that the FBI is just engaged in a publicity stunt?

One type of repetitive charge is far more serious than the above. It is to the effect that Mr. Hoover, an insatiable power-seeker, is constantly maneuvering to expand the FBI's domain at the expense of some other agency.

Thus, Chalmers M. Roberts wrote in the *Washington Post* of October 5, 1964, "The FBI-Secret Service feud has long been well known. The Secret Service men have felt Hoover wanted to swallow their much smaller agency." Again: "The FBI, many believe, never forgave the CIA for taking over its Western Hemisphere jurisdiction after the war."

Rumors about FBI-Secret Service and FBI-CIA "feuds" have been circulating for years. Yet in no context have we found either type to be supported by explicit, responsible evidence. Thus, it makes sense to give less weight to such rumors than to statements put on record, *voluntarily*, by persons who hold or who have held key posts within the agencies to which the FBI is declared to pose a threat.

When Chief James J. Rowley of the Secret Service testified before the Warren Commission on June 18, 1964, he was questioned in detail about the relationship between his agency and the FBI—apparently because Drew Pearson had suggested in his "Washington Merry-Go-Round" of December 16, 1963, that a lack of cooperation between them "may have contributed to the tragedy in Dallas . . . ." But not even by reading between the lines can we find anything in Chief Rowley's testimony to support the "feud" thesis.

He stated his objection to a proposed bill that would have codified a division of authority with regard to the protection of the President, with part of the task assigned to men appointed by the Attorney General: "If anything happened like Dallas, we could get into an Alphonse and Gaston pantomime." But since Mr. Hoover shared his opinion of this bill, Chief Rowley's statement can scarcely be said either to reflect a "feud" or to have provided a basis for one.

More impressive, however, than such negative evidence is the fact that he *volunteered* one pro-FBI statement after another. It is hard to see why he would have done so had he viewed the Bureau as a dangerous predator.

He told of having borrowed FBI agents in Puerto Rico in the late 1940's, saying, "That was the beginning of the cooperation, when I was in the White House, with the FBI"; and he affirmed its continuance. He declared himself to have been wholly satisfied with the Bureau's pre-assassination policy of transmitting "risk" names. And he reported that his men on the White House detail like to attend the FBI National Academy.[2]

Spokesmen for the "feud" thesis have suggested that Chief Rowley was too "magnanimous" to show his true feelings. But while magnanimity could have called for the withholding of criticism, it would scarcely have called for the volunteering of warm approval on counts that went far beyond any questions asked. Besides, he was speaking under oath—and he is not a man who would commit perjury.

When Hoover testified, on May 14th, he was given every chance to downgrade the performance of the Secret Service. Had he been wanting to take over that agency, he could easily have implied that it was less efficient than it should

---

[2] *Hearings Before the President's Commission on the Assassination of President Kennedy*, Vol. V, pp. 447 ff.

be. Instead, he staunchly supported its record and policies—and urged that it be given manpower to match its work load.

He spoke also of the close cooperation that the FBI had enjoyed with the CIA. Here, Allen Dulles, former Head of the CIA, broke in with a remark that he was in nowise obligated to make: "I would like to testify to the fact that cooperation existed during the whole period I was Director . . . ."[3]

Dulles, we might note, "testifies" to the same effect in his *Craft of Intelligence*. On p. 122, for example, he describes both the division of labor between the FBI and the CIA and the pattern of cooperation. He illustrates the latter with an account of the "coordinated effort that resulted in the capture of Soviet spy-master Rudolf Abel."

Rumors that the FBI had grudgingly relinquished its work in Latin America to the CIA in 1946, and that it had not cooperated with the new agency, must have been put into circulation almost as soon as the CIA was formed. By the late 1940's, they were rampant enough so that Senator Leverett Saltonstall felt that the situation should be clarified.

At a hearing, therefore, of the Senate Appropriations Committee on February 7, 1950, the question of FBI-CIA relationships was taken up. Certain items of evidence that were there introduced seem worth recalling.

On November 18, 1947, Rear Admiral Roscoe Henry Hillenkoetter, Director of the CIA, wrote to Hoover: "The fine support which the Bureau has rendered the Central Intelligence Agency has been, I am convinced, a major contributing factor during the difficult formative period of our growth."[4]

[3] *op. cit.*, p. 109.
[4] *Hearings of the Senate Appropriations Committee on 1951 Appropriations for Departments of State, Justice, Commerce, and the Judiciary*, p. 156.

When the first Assistant Director of the CIA, Colonel Donald H. Galloway, resigned in November 1948, he sent a memorandum to his superior, Admiral Hillenkoetter, commending the FBI for its cooperation. This was "never more apparent," he wrote, "than during the time when the Bureau representatives in Latin America turned over their stations to the representatives of the newly organized Central Intelligence Agency. I feel that the success of the turn-over was due in large part to this attitude on the part of the FBI."[5]

No credible evidence to support the rumors about FBI resentment and non-cooperation was brought to light. It seems fair, then, to ask those who are still retailing the old rumors to bring their evidence into the open—where it can be matched for credibility against the statements volunteered by the CIA Director and Assistant Director, who were in a position both to know and to care. Until they do so, they can scarcely ask us to be persuaded by what "has long been well known" or what is believed by their nameless "many."

Walt Whitman spoke of the abysmal second-rateness of "poems distilled from poems." Rumors distilled from rumors are equally undistinguished—even when they are hoary with age.

Drew Pearson wrote in the column from which we have already quoted, "On J. Edgar Hoover's desk recently has been a study of overlapping jurisdiction between the FBI and the Criminal Investigative Division of the Army, with Hoover wanting to take over all the CID's work in the continental United States."

Overlapping jurisdictions are a commonplace throughout the executive branch. The established means of resolving such problems as they create is that of conference. Thus, the making of preparatory studies is also a commonplace; and

[5] *Ibid.*

Hoover's desk would be a logical place for such a study to be found.

Its presence there, however, would not indicate that the FBI Director wanted "to take over all the CID's work in the continental United States." Pearson affirmed that various unnamed members of the CID had told him this was the case; but unless we feel obligated to believe anything we read, we need not be impressed by such "pig-in-a-poke" evidence.

Jurisdictional areas, it is important to realize, are not as separate and capable of neat jurisdiction as are the pieces of a jigsaw puzzle. For example, primary jurisdiction over the Federal Firearms Act is lodged with the Alcohol and Tobacco Tax Division of Treasury, while the FBI has secondary jurisdiction. If a crime which violated this Act was committed with a gun that had been smuggled into the country, Customs would also be involved. Who would do what with respect to a crime that violated laws within several jurisdictions would be determined by conference.

Often, moreover, conferences are held, not to resolve, but to prevent, Alphonse-and-Gaston problems. The Labor-Management Reporting and Disclosure Act of 1959—to take one instance—threatened to create a jurisdictional fog-belt between the domains of the FBI and the Labor Department. This fact led not to a feud but to a conference. On February 8, 1960, Hoover reported to the Subcommittee on Appropriations that an agreement had been worked out "specifying those criminal divisions of the law to be relegated to each Department."[6]

Throughout the executive branch, there are more than enough jurisdictional overlappings to provide bases for hypothetical "feuds." In the nature of things, conferences are often marked by strong disagreements. Why should they not be? But far more dramatic than rumored "feuds" for the

[6] *FBI 1961 Appropriation*, p. 12.

existence of which we are offered only anonymous testimony is the workaday process by which our vast, complex governmental structure is kept in fair working order.

Back of the rumors that cast Hoover as a predator is the assumption that he wants the FBI to get bigger and bigger, and its territory to grow and grow. This assumption has so long been circulated as truth that the will to question it seems to have atrophied. Yet, so far as we can determine, the record is to the contrary: it reports the Director's having turned down some prize chances to enlarge his domain.

The most striking chance was that provided, in 1940, by President Roosevelt's suggestion that Hoover assume direction over all federal investigative and intelligence bodies. The position which this plan would have given him would have been roughly equivalent to that of Secretary of Defense on the military side: he would have had under him the heads of the various agencies.

To have so rich a plum handed to him would surely have been a power-seeker's dream. Yet when Attorney General Jackson laid the proposal before Hoover, the latter turned it down. According to Jackson, he said, "General, that plan would be very good for today, but over the years it would be a mistake."[7]

It is a matter of record, also, that Hoover, in 1951, asked to be relieved of a type of authority which he already possessed. At the end of World War II, the FBI was in charge of a wide range of applicant-type investigations. Thus, the Director had every chance to build up the kind of "blackmailing dossiers" that he is repeatedly accused of wanting. Yet he asked that most such investigations be removed from the Bureau's jurisdiction. The vast majority, he said, were irrelevant to either federal law enforcement or domestic intelligence—those for the D.C. Office of Civil Defense, the Voice of America, foreign aid programs, and various other

[7] Whitehead, pp. 169–170.

bodies. In August 1951, Attorney General J. Howard McGrath, acting on Hoover's request, asked Congress for enabling legislation. In October 1952, the bulk of such investigations was transferred to the Civil Service Commission—the appropriate agency.

More recently, at a hearing on January 29, 1964, Chairman John J. Rooney of the House Subcommittee on Appropriations put a question to Hoover: "There is a proposal, as you undoubtedly know, to turn over to the Department of Justice the enforcement of the narcotics laws. Would you care to comment on this?"

Hoover ticked off objections. The enforcement of such laws, he said, should not be separated from "The broad function of legal narcotics control." Besides, "the Narcotics Bureau has done a very good job under very great difficulties."

Technically, the FBI could handle the job. "But I am against, and have been for years, the growth of the FBI. I think we are entirely too big today, bigger than we should be. I would have liked to see the FBI remain small; but that has been impossible because Congress has yearly enacted legislation expanding the investigative jurisdiction of the Bureau."[8]

We accept this as an honest statement because, having studied his budget requests from 1940 to the present, we have found no instance of his asking for funds for added manpower except as an unavoidable response to added work. We have already spoken in Part II about the relation of new laws on the federal books to the growth of the FBI.

The increase in the agent force, we must note, cannot be plotted as a steady upward curve, although the growth in population, federal laws, and federal crimes can be thus plotted. In 1945, there were 4,000 Special agents; in 1946, 3,159. A high point was reached in 1952—before the applicant-type investigations were transferred: 7,029. After four-

[8] *FBI 1965 Appropriation*, p. 61.

teen years of expanding work, the figure for February 1, 1966, was lower than that for 1952: it was 6,415.[9]

No one could hope to trace to their source or to measure by the yardstick of evidence more than a tiny fraction of the multiple charges that have been made against the FBI and its Director. But even an occasional exploration of the shadow-land behind one or another rumor can serve to remind us that what is "axiomatic," "well known," or believed by "many" need not be automatically credited.

Al Smith's injunction, "Let's look at the record," is still serviceable. So is the question that was the intellectual trademark of Missouri's Thomas Hart Benton, who stood tall in the Senate from 1820 to 1850: "The facts—what are the facts?"[10]

[9] *FBI 1965 Appropriation*, p. 19.

[10] Albert Castel, "Thomas Hart Benton—Champion of the West," *American History Illustrated*, July 1967, p. 12.

FOURTEEN

EXPOSÉ AFTER EXPOSÉ

O N JUNE 10, 1965, the *Saturday Review* carried a boxed item by Helen Nelson called "State of the Nation": a tribute to *The Nation* on its 100th anniversary. The author recalled that the magazine's first editor, E. L. Godkin, had said, " 'our criticisms may be ill-judged, but are always honest' "; and she added, "A look at the record shows how well the promise has been kept."

Since 1918, she went on to say, *The Nation* has been "the magazine of crusading liberalism that it is today." Finally, she reported that one feature for which it is well known is its exposé series on the FBI.

The Nation's editors would surely accept this rating as fair and accurate. And since they have not only published but featured the exposé articles, these can be taken to illustrate their concept of honest criticism and crusading liberalism.

The Nation has long shouted from the rooftops its dislike of J. Edgar Hoover. Thus, in its editorial "Hoover the Vulgarian," we read, "Mr. Hoover, for all his fame and prestige is an oaf . . . . He has learned nothing in all his years of high office; his manners, his language and his ideas are as vulgar now as when he first joined the FBI. . . . Fortunately, he cannot hold on to the office forever, but must we wait till death taps him on the shoulder?"

We would not argue with this: the Editors have every right to express their opinion of the Director as strongly as they wish. The exposé articles, however, are not editorials. They are offered to some 30,000 subscribers, and many more readers, *as material to be credited*. It is relevant, then, to ask what level of reportage they represent.

Hoover is not indispensable to the continuance of our system. We are not; and neither is *The Nation*. But some things are. We would contend that one of them is a definition of *liberalism* that makes intrinsic to it an elementary fairness toward those who are criticized, respect for the rules of evidence, respect for the integrity of the word, and a sense of responsibility toward those whom we tacitly ask to believe what we say. Remove these, and the crusading factor in *crusading liberalism* is bound to erode the liberal factor.

Erosion can go so far that what is left is crusading extremism called *liberal* by its practitioners—because they define as liberal the ends they have in view. Even so does the John Birch Society define as *conservative* its different brand of crusading extremism.

The exposé series began on October 18, 1958, with Fred J. Cook's "The FBI." Jack Levine's "Hoover and the Red Scare" appeared on October 20, 1962; Harold Feldman's "Oswald and the FBI" on January 24, 1964; and William W. Turner's "Crime Is Too Big for the FBI" on November 8, 1965.

Because Cook's "The FBI" has been expanded and updated in his *The FBI Nobody Knows*, which we shall explore in a later chapter, we shall pass it over at this point. An evaluation of Turner's article also belongs in a later context. For the present, then, we shall limit ourselves to the

Levine and Feldman pieces. *The Nation* must have rated both as important, for each title, in turn, is prominently featured on the magazine's cover.

Levine's "Hoover and the Red Scare" is announced as *By a Former FBI Special Agent*. A note assures the reader that Levine "resigned voluntarily." He did: having entered the Bureau on September 12, 1960, he resigned on August 4, 1961—after a 14-week training period and a little more than seven months of service in the Detroit field office.

In view of all that he purports to reveal, the brevity of his term of work should be kept in mind, as should the fact that he was not in the Domestic Intelligence Division. His own statement, as given in an October 1962 interview over WBAI—the New York affiliate of Berkeley's Pacifica Radio, KPFA—would indicate that the nearest he came, in Detroit, to anything that could be called security work was to make "some background investigations of applicants for government jobs." Primarily, he worked on "criminal" matters—such as frauds against the Government and embezzlement of bank funds.[1]

It is important to hold in mind, also, the fact that in the FBI, as in any intelligence body, what an agent knows depends upon *his need to know.* If sensitive information is not related to work that he has to perform, he has no legitimate access to it.

This is equally worth remembering with regard to the statements and writings of persons who have set up shop as permanent experts on Communism by reason of their once having been in the FBI. The key question to ask such an "expert" is whether or not he worked on domestic intelligence investigations. If he did not and did not have extensive security experience in the field, it is prudent to rate his knowledge of Communism as a layman's knowledge—with the impressive tag of the FBI attached.

[1] *The Report of Former Agent Levine,* a Documentary Broadcast by WBAI for Pacifica Radio. October 1962. All our quotations from this interview will be taken directly from a copy of the 5-reel tape secured from WBAI.

Levine's article cannot be properly weighed as an isolate. It has to be put into the context of his relationship to the FBI: his reasons for becoming an agent; his resignation; his efforts to get reinstated; and his subsequent campaign to discredit the Bureau and Hoover.

Materials in the public domain yield two quite different answers to the question of why Levine went into the Bureau. On WBAI, he said that he had thought it would be a rather "fascinating" experience. He had just graduated from law school and was "very curious to see what the FBI was like." He found working in a New York law firm "a little dull at the moment" and "just wanted a change of pace, so to speak."

One of the interviewers, Mr. Elman, asked:

At the time, though, you had no idea that—or did you have any idea that any of this information which you later accumulated was the case?

Levine replied:

No, well, I—I had heard quite a lot of bad things about the FBI, and quite a lot of good things; and it was very difficult to really reach any conclusion on what the FBI was like or what kind of work they did unless you were—on the inside.

Fred J. Cook, who makes Levine the hero of Chapter I of *The FBI Nobody Knows*, lists this WBAI interview among his sources: note, p. 48. Yet in sharp contrast to the above, he states unequivocally that Levine was "lured" into the FBI "by the lofty ideal it projected of honest, dedicated law enforcement and unselfish public service."[2]

With respect to the young agent's reason for resigning, we can similarly pay our money and take our choice. When he was asked about it by Elman, on WBAI, he said:

[2] Fred J. Cook, *The FBI Nobody Knows*, p. 1. (New York, Macmillan), 1964.

Well, I was—I was rather shocked and horrified by a number of different experiences and observations and incidents which I encountered in the Bureau, which just completely disillusioned me, and—I was just very unhappy being—being in this type of organization, and being—a part of something which I couldn't justify in many ways.

But this statement, made when he had been out of the Bureau for 14 months, matches very badly with what he wrote to Hoover on August 28, 1961—just 24 days after his resignation. The text of his letter appears in the *Hearings* of the House Subcommittee on Sundry Civil Appropriation Bill for 1964, p. 500. It was read into the text on February 1, 1963—because Levine's virulent campaign against the Director had led Committee members to inquire about the case.

Levine told Hoover that he had resigned only because his parents, overburdened with business responsibilities, "had been urging him to return to New York to relieve them of some of these . . ." Further:

It was with the greatest regret and sorrow that I took leave of the Bureau. Being a part of this organization of dedicated men which you have moulded with such devotion . . . has been an inspiring experience . . . .

Saying that his parents' problems were under control, he applied for reappointment as a Special Agent.

His record, Hoover told the Subcommittee, was weighed but judged to be "substandard." When Levine was informed that his request was denied, he wrote again, asking for a reconsideration of his case; and on October 6th, he called at the Bureau in person to press his request. Only after it had again been denied, did he begin to spread abroad, to all who would listen, his "revelations" about the FBI and its Director.

What does "Hoover and the Red Scare" come to as an exposé? The thesis, which *The Nation* seems to have found sensational, can be briefly summarized. The CPUSA, says Levine, is so weak, and so largely composed of FBI informants, that it poses no threat. Soviet expionage constitutes a real danger; but the FBI's efforts to curb it have been so ineffectual that Hoover has not been able to use them to justify his huge budget requests and "autocratic powers."

Therefore, he works vigorously to keep alive the "myth of extensive Communist subversion." *Therefore*, he has loaded the CPUSA with FBI undercover agents, to make it appear much larger than it is. *Therefore*, he has enlisted the help of right-wing extremists, to keep the "myth" going—extremists who now threaten to get out of hand.

To underwrite this thesis, Levine purports to reveal the number of FBI informants within the CPUSA; how they are distributed; and the Bureau's "well-developed plan to neutralize the sabotage potential of the American Communists should a U.S.-Soviet war seem imminent." He even purports to reveal the substance of "a highly confidential memorandum to all bureau officials" which he says Hoover sent out in 1960.

Elman, on WBAI, was apparently curious about how a rookie agent would come by the range of intelligence data that Levine purported to reveal. He asked:

Would you say—would you say that the kind of information you were privy to, as a member of the FBI, was extraordinary; or would the information that you base your report on, and your article in *The Nation* on—would you say that this information is commonplace to all first-year investigators like yourself?

Incredibly, Levine replied:

Oh, yes, yes. You see, during the training program which all FBI agents receive, we get full and complete briefings on all aspects of the FBI's work and their investigations in the security field, as well as in the criminal field.

We are asked to believe, in brief, that materials which would inevitably be classified as "sensitive"—and some of which he himself called "very, very confidential"—were imparted to all trainees: men who had not yet even been tried out as agents. Yet on the same radio program, he stated that what he was able to tell was startling to various Division heads in the Justice Department and to people all the way up to the White House.

When we try to fit them together, his diverse statements about *who knows what* form so implausible a whole that we do not think that anyone is obligated to take his disclosures seriously enough to worry about them. But did the Editors of *The Nation* fully trust their accuracy? If not, why would they feature his article as important? But if so, they must be more credulous than the general run of newsmen and editors.

Levine told on WBAI how he had told various Congressmen about the shortcomings of the FBI and its Director and had found them too "intimidated" to speak out. He had then taken his materials to certain newsmen—among them, James Reston and Anthony Lewis of *The New York Times;* J. Russell Wiggins of the *Washington Post*; and Al Davis and Milt Viorst of the *New York Post*. They had asked for documentary evidence to support his charges.

To Levine, this signified that they feared the "tremendous furor" it would cause, and the effect it would have upon "advertisers" if they criticized Hoover—and this in spite of the fact that the papers which these men represent have all criticized him. He also suspected that they might fear "recriminations by Hoover in terms of investigations being conducted into their past life." But this seems a needlessly melodramatic explanation of a request for evidence.

Elman broke in on Levine, and the following exchange took place:

Elman: Were you told this by any of these newspapermen? Can you recall? I don't want to be testy, but can you recall any of the exact quotes that these people said to you when they—
Levine: Yes—uh—
Elman: —did reject your material?
Levine: Yes. I'll tell you a very interesting experience I had with Mr. Jack Anderson, who is a—an aide to Drew Pearson. He was—
Elman: Yeah?
Levine: He was relating this to me, just several months ago, in Washington . . . .

Elman's question about what had been said by the newsmen to whom Levine had offered his material went unanswered.

Harold Feldman's "Oswald and the FBI" begins thus:

The Warren Commission should, if possible, tell us how President Kennedy was killed, who killed him, and why. But beyond that, it *must* tell us if the FBI or any other government intelligence agency was in any way connected with the alleged assassin.

His thesis is that Oswald was probably an FBI informer; and that this is why his name was not given to the Secret Service. Also, he implies that the Bureau, after the assassination, conducted a determined cover-up campaign to keep the truth from the public; and that, to this end, it suppressed evidence, intimidated witnesses, and "leaked" what it wanted to have believed.

The Warren Commission has now, of course, rendered the verdict for which Feldman did not wait. In its *Report*, p. 22, it states that it found no evidence to support "the speculation that Oswald was an agent, employee, or informant of the FBI, CIA, or any other governmental agency."

While we shall refer to various findings of the Commission, Feldman's article, because it predates these, cannot be judged by them. It must be judged by how its author handles materials that were available to him by January 1964. Does he give all data then at hand an equal chance to reach the minds of his readers? Among the persons who had by then said their say, whom does he quote to support his thesis?

Having alleged the existence of a cover-up campaign, he tacitly rejects *as part of this campaign* whatever is said by the FBI. Yet he also criticizes the Bureau for not saying more. He calls it "secretive" because it did not disclose its findings or let itself be drawn into a public 'tis-'tain't argument over rumored information.

Still further, he implies that statements which support those made by the Bureau should be regarded as suspect—as having probably been "leaked" on FBI orders or slanted away from the truth by intimidated witnesses. In brief, he denies the Bureau its day in court—and proclaims its probable guilt.

To whom does he give a hearing? He quotes first from *Minority of One*, which is consistently hostile to the FBI. In the May 1963 issue, for example, Bertrand Russell accuses the Bureau of "fabricating evidence and even the existence of Communists to be hunted in order to drain public funds."

Feldman quotes from the January 1964 issue a passage which, in turn, quotes from the *New York Post* of November 25, 1963, to the effect that William M. Kline, United States Customs, Laredo, Texas, had said that "a federal agency in Washington" had asked that a watch be kept over Oswald's movements in Mexico.

On July 31, 1964, Kline executed and sent to the Warren Commission a 5-point affidavit. We quote points 3 and 5:

3. I do not recall being interviewed by Harold Feldman who I am informed represented the *New York Post*, nor do I recall

being interviewed by any person identifying himself as being employed by the "Nation Magazine."

5. I have no personal knowledge whatsoever that any agency of the United States Government maintained a surveillance of Oswald's movements, and I have never indicated to the contrary to any news reporter.[5]

Kline's point number 3 moved us to write to the *New York Post* to ask who had authored the article in question. We have had no reply—and are ready to grant that our inquiry may, for policy reasons, have been out of bounds. But we could not help being curious; for if what Feldman quotes from *Minority of One* was first quoted by that publication from an article in the *Post* which he had written, or for which he had provided the substance, he would seem to be his own first witness for the prosecution.

Next, he says that the extent of the contacts between the FBI and Oswald "is indicated in 'the revelation that the Federal Bureau of Investigation tried to recruit Oswald as an undercover informant in Castro groups two months before Mr. Kennedy's death.'" He credits this "revelation," for which the Warren Commission could find no basis in fact, to a dispatch from Dallas in the *Philadelphia Inquirer* of December 8, 1963.

From this dispatch, he quotes the following:

"The FBI attempt to recruit Oswald as an informant, an informed law enforcement source said, was made in September, just before he moved to Dallas from New Orleans.

"Oswald's mother said 'an agent named Hosty' came to the Irving house and talked to the young man at length in his car.

"An FBI agent named Joseph Hosty handles investigations of subversives from the Dallas field office.

"The source said he did not know if the FBI succeeded in hiring Oswald; and the federal agency would not discuss the matter."

[5] *Hearings Before the President's Commission on the Assassination of President Kennedy*, Vol. XV, p. 640.

Thus, Feldman's second witness for the prosecution is Mr. Anonymous: "an informed law enforcement source." But what type of law enforcement source would be both "informed" with respect to an FBI recruiting effort and ready to talk about it to the press? On the face of it, this "revelation" is implausible.

Moreover, if the attempt was made in *New Orleans*, what importance are we supposed to attach to the statement, later proved untrue, that Hosty and Oswald talked *in Dallas* about an unspecified subject?

Feldman's third witness is Lonnie Hudkins, whose article in the *Houston Post* on January 1, 1964—"Oswald Rumored as Informant for U.S."—turned out, when scrutinized by the Commission, to be remarkable for the sleazyness of its evidence. Here again Mr. Anonymous appears—in the guise of an unnamed "sheriff's deputy" who allegedly explained the FBI's not having kept Oswald under surveillance by saying that "you wouldn't think to check up on your own stoolies." But how would a "sheriff's deputy" know who was or was not an FBI informant?

Feldman also accepts as reliable a report in the *Dallas Times Herald* of November 30, 1963, to the effect that Oswald had, over a considerable period, received by Western Union sums of money from an "unidentified sender." He calls the FBI "secretive" about this and "reticent" about an improvement in Oswald's finances—and thus reaches a conclusion, called logical, that the moneys had come to Oswald from a governmental source.

The Commission could find no evidence of Oswald's having received mysterious sums by Western Union. Neither could it find any greater improvement in his finances that would come from his being employed after a long period of unemployment.

Finally, Feldman contrasts the literary styles of two letters sent by Oswald: one to his mother, from the Soviet Union; the other, and much better composed, to the New York Fair Play for Cuba Committee. "Who and where," he asks, "is the invisible scribe?" The mystery would be solved if "Oswald was employed by the FBI to operate in 'Castro groups,' as the news report suggests . . ." It could then be assumed that in the second letter his "pen was guided by the FBI."

But this is the last thing that could be assumed. No experienced intelligence body would help an informant so to misrepresent his capabilities, on any score, that he would be rendered vulnerable to later exposure. Had FBI agents had any part in the composing of the second letter, *it would have been in a style that Oswald could duplicate on any occasion*: which is to say, in the one that came naturally to him.

The Nation seems not to realize that to feature materials of this character is to underwrite, not undercut, the FBI's reputation. Since it has been trying for years to build a case against that agency, the fact that it is reduced to treating as important the "revelations" of Levine and a Feldman verdict of probable guilt based on obtrusively rumor-laden and implausible materials would seem to indicate that the Bureau cannot be doing too bad a job.

FIFTEEN

WHO THINKS HE WANTS WHAT?

O NE THING that bothers us about certain confirmed critics of the FBI is that they pronounce fervent judgments that seem to be based on principle—and reverse themselves when a different cause is at issue. Moreover, we doubt that they would like to live with the end results of what they seem to demand.

They are consistent about wanting Hoover to get out or be put out. What they say on this score goes far beyond the casual remarks of those who acknowledge that he as an individual gets on their individual nerves; and far beyond what is said by those who feel that he has been Director too long: that no one in our system should be made to seem indispensable. The closest parallel to their intense anti-Hooverism is, perhaps, the John Birch Society's campaign to impeach Earl Warren.

It resembles this in its unrelenting virulence, and also on a more serious count. The Birchers have wanted not only to get Mr. Warren out but to have him replaced by a Chief Justice whose standards of constitutionality would match theirs. In like fashion, the virulent anti-Hooverites want to have the Director replaced by someone less "legalistic" and "reactionary"—which, in context, seems to mean someone who would use the FBI to do the type of thing, and only the type of thing, which they want to have done. This is why their demands must be scrutinized: to make sure that we do not let ourselves be persuaded to want an investigative body that would soon be intolerable.

What made the Bureau of the Palmer-Flynn era such a menace was chiefly its responsiveness to tides of public emotion. When Palmer was called upon to explain the excesses of the "Red raids," he took refuge in the fact that the public had demanded action against radical bomb-throwers:

I was shouted at from every editorial sanctum . . .; I was preached upon from every pulpit; I was urged—I could feel it dinned into my ears—throughout the country to do something and do it now, and do it quick, and do it in a way that would bring results to stop this sort of thing in the United States.[1]

His responsive action did not lead to the arrest and fair trial of anyone identified as having had a part in the 1919 rash of bombings. But it turned the Bureau into the executor of hysteria's short-sighted will.

Far from wanting a return to the Palmer era, today's anti-Hooverites want the FBI to be responsive to "liberal" value judgments. But it would be in the fact of *responsiveness* that danger would lie.

During Hoover's directorship, we have all been oddly protected by the "rhinocerous" skin which he says he has had to develop. The post-Hoover Bureau could promptly become a menace if its Director were to let *any* pressure group influence his decisions. It would become intolerable if he were either to ally himself with any one cause or to let the Bureau

[1] Cummings and McFarland, p. 429.

be turned into a prize to be contended for by advocates of rival causes.

We have spoken about "confirmed critics": plural. In this chapter, however, we shall concentrate on statements made by James A. Wechsler of the *New York Post*. The demands and charges that he directs at the FBI and also the ambiguities in which these are shrouded are both individual and representative.

In his *Post* column of July 15, 1963, he writes that the "debilitated" CPUSA is kept alive by the work which FBI undercover agents do for it in the course of maintaining their "masquerade." Do not informants, he asks, have to act like super-dedicated Communists to reach positions where they can learn what they want to know? Does it not follow that their activities strengthen the Party?

His example is a man named Scarletto who, having served for years as press director of the Communist El Sereno Club, in Los Angeles, dropped his disguise to testify for the Government in a deportation case. "How many innocent boys and girls were bewitched by the anti-American tracts that rolled off his mimeograph machine? How many faltering comrades derived inspiration from his manifestoes?"

Wechsler follows his charges with a demand that Hoover be required to explain his use of public funds to strengthen a subversive body that he claims to oppose.

We will grant that any undercover agent must, when in Rome, do with consummate skill what the Romans do. Thus, there can be no guarantee against his lending some increment of strength to the penetrated group. What, then, does Wechsler want the FBI to do "in areas of racial violence"? *He wants it to practice on a massive scale the type of infiltration about which he waxes indignant in his column on Scarletto.*

In his column of June 13, 1963, he denounces the Bureau for showing "no capacity for infiltrating the racist mobs

. . . ." In that of September 18th, he writes that it "has systematically failed to infiltrate the racist mobs . . . ."

Actually, FBI infiltration of the Klans has been continuous for decades, and it was swiftly expanded after the Supreme Court's 1954 ruling on school desegregation had stimulated a new period of Klan growth. Far from being a failure, the program has been so successful that the work of an informant is now both harder and more hazardous than it once was.

In self-defense, the Klans now assign most illegal activities to super-secret units of from six to ten men whose identities remain unknown to the general membership: units variously known as "Terrors," "Knock off Groups," "Killer Squads," and "Secret Sixes." To work himself into a position where he can hope both to prevent violence and to collect evidence of criminality that will stand up in court, an informant must earn admission to one of these "inner-terror" groups.

Would Wechsler care to say how an informant could do so without performing any actions that might exert a pro-Klan influence? Does he feel that here, too, Hoover should be required to explain his use of public funds for purposes that may add some measure of strength to a subversive body?

If not, his indignation about Scarletto looks either synthetic or arrogant. Is he, in fact, saying anything more in that column than that the FBI Director, regardless of his national-security assignment, should have to explain why he pays more attention to the CPUSA than he, Wechsler, thinks necessary?

Persons who can handle the informant role within a Klan, and live with its hazards, do not come in quantity lots. Many, like their counterparts within the CPUSA, were the real thing before they became imitations of it. They are defectors who have concealed their defection.

Moreover, an informant who has worked for months to reach a strategic position may have abruptly to end his usefulness—and invite his own murder. Since he is cooperating with a federal law enforcement body, he is obligated to "surface," at whatever risk to himself, if *the only alternative* is to participate in the commission of a felony.

When informants can prevent crimes of violence by getting word to the proper authorities, they do not rise and take a bow, making sure the press is on hand. They try to maintain their "masquerade" and stay on the job—while Wechsler denounces the FBI because they are not there.

Or he says, "One often wonders how much more effective the FBI might be (especially in areas of racial violence) if so many of its operatives were not giving their all for the Communist Party . . . ." Does he regard informants as interchangeable parts of an infiltrating machine? Does he think that a Scarletto could be pulled out of a Los Angeles Communist club and inserted into a Klan terror-squad in rural Mississippi?

The Liuzzo murder case pinpointed the very complexities that Wechsler ignores. Gary Thomas Rowe had been serving as an FBI informant within the Klan for three years when Wechsler wrote the above columns. As a prerequisite to assuming the informant role, he had, in 1960, taken the Klan oath.

In 1965, at the awful cost of being present at a murder he could not prevent, he was able to give eyewitness testimony against the killer of Mrs. Liuzzo. An all-white jury failed to convict: various of its members set Rowe down as a liar because he had broken the "solemn oath" without which he could not have penetrated the Klan. When he testified at a second trial, history repeated itself.

Wechsler gets in an extra dig at Scarletto by saying that, after all his long service to the CPUSA, his testimony was "futile": the Supreme Court reversed the conviction which it helped to secure. Does he rate Rowe's testimony as also futile, and his five years of undercover work as just so much free service to the Klan, because a split jury in the Liuzzo case failed to convict?

In a full-scale article—"The FBI's Failure in the

South"—which *The Progressive* included in a 1964 publication called *Toward Civil Rights Now*—Wechsler renews a demand made in his column about the murder of Medgar Evers: namely, that all federal activity in the civil rights field be taken away from the FBI and given to some agency "that would 'offer real protection' to the freedom fighters of our country."

He says that on the testimony of "countless men and women who have been pushed around in the battle for equal rights," FBI agents have not given protection to "embattled Southern Negroes—and their white supporters": not even when these have appealed for protection. Therefore, it is "utterly clear" that law enforcement in the civil rights field "should be taken out of the hands of the FBI."

No matter how emotionally involved we are with the Negro cause, we cannot afford to make an unthinking Yes-response to this thesis. What Wechsler's demand comes to is that a duly assigned part of the FBI's work should be taken away from it *because it does not, in behalf of a good cause, trespass beyond the limits of its assignment to perform a police function.*

The Bureau could not *both* stay within the limits of federal law—and certainly not within the limits of such laws as were on the books in 1963, when this article was written—and meet Wechsler's terms. We have checked and re-checked to make sure of this. Congress has passed no statute under which the FBI could give any such protection as Wechsler demands; and, under the Constitution, police power belongs to the states.

United States marshals have seemed to us, at times, to be performing police functions. We have seen photographs, for example, of their walking with Negro children to newly integrated schools in areas beset by mob violence. Not knowing under what precise authority they render such service, we turned for information to the office of the Chief Marshal, James J. P. McShane, in the Department of Justice.

The marshals, we learned, have two roles. They perform, under the supervision of the Attorney General, certain specified tasks for which Justice is responsible—chiefly in relation to accountancy matters. But they are also officers of the federal courts. Only in the latter capacity would a marshal walk with Negro children in the manner described or perform any similar activity; and he would do so only as part of his task of executing a federal court order.

Could the marshals protect "freedom fighters" if they were asked for help? The answer was a categorical *No*: that would constitute a trespass upon the police power of the states. Even with the school children, the assignment was not to give protection—although the children had the benefit of their presence—but to insure compliance with a court order. Back of every such instance was a civil action that had served as the basis for a court order.

Could FBI agents protect "embattled Southern Negroes—and their white supporters"? Again the *No* was categorical. The FBI's job, we were reminded, was to conduct properly authorized investigations and to arrest on warrant persons for whom the Government was prepared to seek indictments for alleged violations of federal law.

Among the persons whom we asked about the matter was Senator Paul H. Douglas, who, on February 10, 1966, introduced into the Senate the Civil Rights Protection Act of 1966. In doing so, he took solemn account of the Medgar Evers case and of multiple other instances of violence. Also, the text of the Act—which did not become law—reveals an earnest wish to provide firm safeguards for the exercise of civil and constitutional rights. But when we asked the Senator whether the FBI could have provided the type of protection called for by Wechsler, the answer was *No*.

Is Wechsler assuming that Congress would give to the alternative agency that he proposes a broader power than it has ever given to the FBI? Is he anticipating a transfer to it, by constitutional amendment, of certain police powers now vested in the states? Or is he visualizing an agency that would not, when a good cause was at issue, let itself be inhibited by law?

In neither his column nor his *Progressive* article does he give any clue as to how he would answer such questions. In framing his charges against our chief federal law enforcement body, he does not discuss law at all.

In Part IV, we shall be devoting several chapters to the FBI's role in the civil rights field. Most of our examples will relate to federal efforts to secure the rights of Negroes. At this point, therefore, we shall take a single example that has to do with a different issue: that of religious freedom.

No so long ago, as history moves, the Jehovah's Witnesses were under hysterical attack because they saw a salute to the flag as an obeisance to a "graven image." Towns, and even states, pushed through hastily-conceived restrictive legislation, and violence against the Witnesses broke out in a host of places.

Drawing on what they had learned as members of the Justice Department, Victor W. Rothnem and Fred J. Folsom, Jr. reported in the December 1942 issue of the *American Political Science Review* that in the brief period of June 12–20, 1940, "hundreds of attacks" upon persons who belonged to this minority sect took place. They gave specific examples of violent action in Kennebunk, Maine; Rockville, Maryland; Litchfield, Illinois; and Jackson, Mississippi. Other examples, as well as much information about the handling of cases, can be found in Robert Carr's *Federal Protection of Civil Rights: Quest for a Sword.*

The response of the Witnesses is described by Milton R. Konvitz, in his *Expanding Liberties*, p. 15:

They tested the laws, passed or interpreted to thwart their efforts, by peacefully, but intentionally, doing the acts they were prohibited from doing (preaching and distributing literature). In fact, they practiced non-violent resistance in the 1930s and 1940s in scores of American cities and towns, and ... they went to the courts for the vindication of their constitutional liberties.

The results comprise a vital chapter in the history of civil liberties in the United States:

From 1938 to 1946 the Supreme Court decided fifteen cases dealing with this sect—more than the total of all cases in religious liberty decided by the Court in its first 150 years ....

The Witnesses' manner of approach to their problem, according to Konvitz, "prepared the ground for the later civil rights movement to develop along the line of non-violent resistance." The resultant Supreme Court rulings, which "firmly established the Constitution as a fortress of protection against persecution of, or discrimination against, unpopular sects or cults," introduced a new pattern of pro-test: one which revitalized the concept of liberty *under law*.

The type and extent of FBI involvement in all this was determined by the Justice Department's new Civil Rights Section. In line with policies laid down by the CRS, the Bureau made preliminary investigations, when complaints were received by the Department, to enable the lawyers of the CRS to determine whether or not a federal law had been violated. If their conclusion was affirmative, FBI agents made an intensive investigation and reported their findings. If the CRS decided to prosecute, the agents went at the job of assembling evidence and testimony on which an indictment could be sought from a federal grand jury.

In many cases, particularly after it had Supreme Court rulings to which it could refer, the CRS used the data provided by the Bureau as a means of persuading local and state authorities to change their attitude and assume their proper responsibilities. Where it could be made to work, the CRS preferred this approach to the multiplying of prosecutions.

Whether the type of action it decided to take was prosecutive or persuasive, it had at its command evidence painstakingly gathered by Bureau agents. But these agents did not provide—and could not legally have been instructed to provide—protective surveillance for beleaguered Witnesses. By Wechsler's standards, then, work in the civil rights field should have been taken away from the FBI.

It is not that Wechsler objects to the FBI's being kept within strict legal bounds. Rather, it is that he extends and contracts these boundaries to fit his own concept of what should and should not be done.

In addition to writing his column, Wechsler is in charge of the *New York Post's* editorial page and writes much of the material for it. An editorial in the issue of May 19, 1965, declares that "FBI Director J. Edgar Hoover has again trespassed into dubious areas"—the chief area in question being the University of California campus at Berkeley. "Campus radicalism is not the proper province of heavy-handed FBI vigilance; that is the way student rebellion is treated in a police state."

No province would be a proper one for *heavy-handed* FBI vigilance. But we confess to a twofold skepticism about its having been exercised in this instance.

For one thing, as graduates of the University of California, we made a special effort to keep posted during the campus demonstrations. Several persons who relayed to us their versions of events felt a strong emotional tie with the rebelling students. The maximum activity which any one of them attributed to FBI agents was that of "looking on."

For another thing, when we first began, around 1954, to appraise FBI procedures, we undertook to check up on several charges that were then going the rounds about agent high-handedness or outright misconduct in relation to campus events. In every instance, evidence that had been offered to us as conclusive evaporated under scrutiny.

Moreover, we were moved to conclude that Mr. Hoover exercises to the farthest limit consistent with the FBI's national-security assignment a hands-off policy where educational and religious institutions are concerned. This policy does not, however, imply that an American campus is, in the medieval sense, a *sanctuary*—a place where a criminal is immune to arrest.

"I know of no legal principle," wrote Associate Justice Abe Fortas, in his *Concerning Dissent and Civil Disobedience*, "which protects students on campus from the consequences of activities which would be violations of law if undertaken elsewhere."[2] But such laws as have been broken in campus riots have not, for the most part, been federal.

If the FBI was keeping tabs on what took place on the campus at Berkeley, as it probably was, it is a safe bet that it was making an estimate of the role played by subversive agitators; and it is doubly obligated to perform this task—even if the *New York Post* does not approve. Since 1939, the Bureau has been responsible for intelligence work in the national-security field. Since 1964, it has been under a Presidential order to estimate and report on the degree of subversive influence in riot situations.

The fact that it makes such an estimate does not mean that it is seeing Communists everywhere. In the summer of 1964, for example, in response to instructions from the President, the FBI prepared a report on a survey made of race riots in New York City, Rochester, and Philadelphia. Its report indicated that these riots were neither Communist-instigated nor Communist-controlled; but that certain Communist elements—most particularly, the Maoist Progressive Labor Party—had moved in to try to exploit them.

The FBI's job is not to satisfy the Far Left or the Far Right—with their ever-ready demands that their preconceptions be given support. It is to conduct investigations when it has been instructed to do so by an appropriate authority; and to report its findings. Because it deals in specifics, it can

[2] New York, Signet Books, 1968, p. 47.

both help us to distinguish between what is and what is not Communist-inspired and cut down to size irresponsible charges of Communist control.

A pointed compliment was paid the FBI in June 1968 by a man who emphatically did not intend it as such: J. B. Stoner, vice-chairman of the National States Rights Party. Stoner's hatred of Bureau agents—"Federal Bums of Integration"—is unbounded. When the NSRP comes to power, he repetitiously declares, it will "try them all for treason and hang them."

Expressing his venom, in the course of one of his diatribes against Negroes, Jews, and the FBI, he accurately defined, however, the Bureau's role in relation to civil rights and testified to its having been well performed: "Without the FBI there wouldn't be any integration in the South in my opinion. Enforcement has brought it about."[3]

The FBI would scarcely claim such exclusive credit. Before it could act, Congress had to put the civil rights statutes on the federal books. To move Congress to do so, a myriad persons, Negro and white, had actively to engage in the shaping of public opinion.

Yet Stoner pronounced a sizeable truth—and, for him, a thoroughly unpalatable one—when he said of integration in the South, "Enforcement has brought it about." Unenforced laws are just so much dead verbiage.

It seems a pity that Wechsler, with his passion for civil rights, has so consistently ignored the Bureau's performance of its duly assigned task and belabored it for not having done what it could not do. In his *Progressive* article, he lets his hostility to Hoover and the FBI carry him to a point where he renders negative service to the very cause he cares about.

[3] Jack Nelson, in the *Los Angeles Times*, in a report on an NSRP gathering in Georgia; reprinted in the *Washington Post*, June 13, 1968.

When his article was written, the vitally important Civil Rights Acts of 1964 and 1965 were not yet on the books— much less that of 1968. Yet instead of urging the passage of such laws, he says that it would do no good unless the FBI was taken out of the civil rights field. Most strangely of all, he concludes by asking Congress, not to enact needed legislation, but to investigate the FBI's failure to do that for which Congress has never given it a license.

SIXTEEN

THE FBI ACCORDING TO
LOWENTHAL

M AX LOWENTHAL'S *The Federal Bureau of Investi-gation,* published in 1950, is probably the longest and most elaborate criticism of the FBI yet to appear in print. It may also be the most influential—because of the extent to which other critics have relied upon it as a source.

It appears to be a product of meticulous scholarship. Its makeup is dignified. The 465-page text is vouched for by 80 pages of notes. Even to glance at these is to be assured that the source materials to which they refer have substance: chiefly, they are official documents.

Thus, we think it fair to say that the book must stand or fall on the reliability of its documentation. We do not mean that Lowenthal is to be denied that reasonable margin for error which we grant to any author who copes with a host of details. We mean that he invites us to assume a trustworthy correspondence between what the text conveys and what is to be found in the materials to which the notes point the way.

Our contention will be that this trustworthy correspondence is lacking. There are more—very many more—discrepancies between what the text implies and what the sources reveal than any reasonable margin for error could accommodate.

We will contend further that, in his quoting, he abuses the privilege of selection. As a rule, the words he quotes can be found in his sources. But he omits data that are indispensable to the reader's proper evaluation of what he puts in.

His opening passage deals with the events which surrounded the forming of the Bureau of Investigation in 1908. The sources listed for his Chapter I—"The Bureau Is Created"—are basically those from which we quote in our Chapter II. His first two pages plus eight lines of text establish the thesis which he carries forward and rounds out on the book's final page.

In order that the reader may know exactly what we are talking about, we shall quote his first five paragraphs in their entirety:

The Federal Bureau of Investigation had a somewhat unorthodox beginning. First proposed in 1907 by Attorney General Charles Joseph Bonaparte and repeatedly requested by him, authorization of the Bureau was withheld by the Sixtieth Congress in 1908.

The temper of the times was unfavorable to Mr. Bonaparte's proposal, in spite of the fact that the Treasury and Post Office Departments had long maintained special forces to protect their activities in minting money and carrying mail. The grounds for opposition were expressed in Congressional debates and committee hearings on the subject and in comments of the press.

James A. Tawney of Minnesota, chairman of the House Appropriations Committee, to which Attorney General Bonaparte made his request, warned on the floor of the House against the danger of setting up any additional Federal police force. Another member of the Committee, Congressman Fitzgerald of New York, told the House that though past efforts to create a general

police system under the Federal Government had never succeeded, and though it had "never been the policy to establish a
central police or spy system in the Federal Government," he was
now fearful that "we will have in time a Federal secret police."
Reporting for the Senate Appropriations Committee, Senator
Hemenway of Indiana said, "It has never been the intention of
any Congress to build a spy system of that character." Congressman Walter I. Smith of Iowa, veteran member of the House
Appropriations Committee, added that "Nothing is more opposed
to our race than a belief that a general system of espionage is
being conducted by the General Government."

Congressman Waldo of New York told the House: "The only
question here before the House is whether we believe in a central secret-service bureau, such as there is in Russia today I
believe that it would be a great blow to freedom and to free
institutions if there should arise in this country any such great
central secret-service bureau as there is in Russia."

Congressman Smith of Iowa warned that "No general system
of spying upon and espionage of the people such as has prevailed in Russia, in France under the Empire, and at one time in
Ireland, should be allowed to grow up."[1]

If this passage means anything by normal standards of
communication, it is that the statements quoted in paragraphs 3-5 illustrate those "grounds for opposition" to Bonaparte's proposal of which Lowenthal speaks in paragraph 2.
We do not see how any reader could think otherwise—
unless, by some odd chance, he was familiar with the hearings and debates in question.

Chairman Tawney, as we noted in our Chapter II, *was*
opposed to the creation of any new federal investigative
body. But not even one of the statements quoted from Fitzgerald, Hemenway, Smith, and Waldo was directed against
Bonaparte's proposal—*and Lowenthal's own source materials show this to be the case.*

In the spring of 1908, we would recall, Congress had
before it two different but related matters. One was the

[1] Max Lowenthal, *The Federal Bureau of Investigation* (New York, William
Sloane Associates, 1950), pp. 3–4.

Attorney General's request that it authorize "a small permanent detective force" for the Justice Department—*not* a general police system" or "central secret service bureau." The other was the question of whether or not to continue letting the various departments hire operatives as needed from Treasury's Secret Service.

The passages from which Lowenthal quotes were all directed against the use of the Secret Service as a central or general source of investigative manpower. *No one of them expressed opposition to the type of departmental force that Bonaparte wanted to establish.*

The fragments quoted from Fitzgerald are from two speeches made more than eight months apart: one on May 1, 1908 (*42 Congressional Record,* p. 5558); the other on January 8, 1909 (*43 Congressional Record,* p. 678).

In 1908, Fitzgerald urged the passage of the amendment which forbade the various departments to use moneys appropriated for fiscal 1909 to hire Secret Service operatives. He was particularly disturbed by the Secret Service's keeping on its payroll, to hire out to other departments, men not provided for in its appropriation or needed for its own work.

In quoting what he said—in 1908, and also in 1909—we shall italicize the fragments which Lowenthal invites us to believe expressed opposition to Bonaparte's proposal:

There has been an effort once or twice to create a general police system under the Federal Government. It has not been successful. But if the practice be continued . . . of having carried apparently upon the rolls of the Secret Service twenty more men than are necessary or are required for that work . . . then *we will have in time a Federal secret police.*

In 1909, he defended the amendment against the President's charge that it has been of benefit only to criminals. After reviewing the funds granted to the several departments for the prevention and detection of crime, he declared it to be apparent "that it has *never been the policy to establish a central police or spy system in the Federal Government."*

He went on to say, "Every department has been given and is given ample funds and authority to procure evidence and detect criminals . . . ."; and he called "wise and proper" the policy of their having separate investigative bodies.

The next sentence which Lowenthal quotes is from *Senate Report 970,* which was read into the *Congressional Record* of February 11, 1909, at the request of Senator Hemenway. Here are three consecutive sentences from this *Report,* with the one used by Lowenthal italicized:

The scope of the work of the Secret Service Division of the Treasury Department might be enlarged so as to enable them to investigate violations of the law under the jurisdiction of that department, but to give them authority to conduct all governmental investigations would, in the opinion of your committee, be very unwise and would result in much conflict and friction between the departments.

It has never been the intention of any Congress to build up a spy system of that character. The Department of Justice, to which ultimately all prosecutions of violations of federal law must be referred should have secret service agents to enable that department to properly conduct such prosecutions.[2]

How could Lowenthal possibly believe that the italicized sentence was directed against the Attorney General's request for an investigative unit in the Justice Department?

Next, Lowenthal writes that Congressman Walter I. Smith of Iowa "added that 'Nothing is more opposed to our race than a belief that a general system of espionage is being conducted by the General Government.'"

To remind himself of the original context of that statement, the reader can turn back to p. 24. It was Congress-

[2] *43 Congressional Record,* p. 2183.

man Smith's response, on April 2, 1908, to what Attorney General Bonaparte said about the danger of employing an *agent provocateur.*

Lowenthal's second quotation from Mr. Smith is from his speech in the House on January 8, 1909. In the original, it does not begin with a capital letter, as it does in Lowenthal's text. It is the last part of the second clause of a sentence. The passage in which it appears reads thus—with the italics added to show what Lowenthal extracts from the whole:

There is no limit whatever upon the power of any department in the selection of its numerous special agents and inspectors who are authorized by law to appoint as many detectives as its appropriation will cover. I think we ought all to be able to agree that some detective force is necessary to the enforcement of the criminal laws; and that, on the other hand, in a free country, *no general system of spying upon and espionage of the people, such as has prevailed in Russia, in France under the Empire, and at one time in Ireland, should be allowed to grow up.*[3]

In the next paragraph—to repeat part of a statement which we have quoted more fully in Chapter II—Smith said that he was "wholly at a loss to know why the Attorney General has not full power to organize a detective force under the numerous appropriations now at his disposal . . . ."

Congressman Waldo also favored departmental investigative units. The passage from which Lowenthal quotes two fragments, which we are italicizing, shows this to be the case. During a debate on February 25, 1909, Waldo said that no one was suggesting any reduction of the funds to be appropriated for the detection and prosecution of crimes:

The only question here before the House is whether we believe in a central secret-service bureau, such as there is in Russia today, or whether we believe the separate departments should

[3] *43 Congressional Record,* p. 672.

investigate the violations of law in those departments by a trained force of their own. That is all there is to the question. *I believe it would be a great blow to freedom and to free institutions if there should arise in this country any such great secret-service bureau as there is in Russia. We do not need it . . . .* Crimes are amply prosecuted. They are much better investigated and detected by the several departments of government . . . .[4]

Since Lowenthal is a lawyer, we can assume his familiarity with the rules of evidence. Yet within the space occupied by his first five paragraphs, he transports three members of Congress and a Senate committee to positions approximately 180 degrees removed from those which his own source materials show them to have occupied. This would seem to set a record of some sort—and matters do not improve as he goes on.

When, for example, he belatedly introduces the subject of Congress's vote to end the use of Treasury's Secret Service as a "central secret-service bureau," he presents this as a result of the legislators' having been "aroused and alarmed" by Bonaparte's wish for a small departmental detective force. By this excursion into non-history, he gives himself room to pronounce solemn nonsense: "Thus, the Sixtieth Congress made doubly clear its intention that the Attorney General should not employ detectives."

It did nothing of the sort—as the above passages make plain. It voted the Attorney General the full amount that he asked for their employment. Had it wanted to keep him from hiring detectives, it would scarcely have done so; and it would have amended, not the Sundry Civil Appropriations Bill for 1909, but the Department of Justice Act of 1870—which it left untouched. Lowenthal puts the Sixtieth Congress into the absurd position of wanting the Justice Department to take cases to court *with no prior investigation*; no gathering of evidence on which to base a prosecution.

[4] *43 Congressional Record*, p. 3132.

His odd version of events provides a background, however, for his saying:

On July 1, a month after Congress adjourned, Attorney General Bonaparte quietly established in the Department of Justice the force of secret police which Congress refused to authorize. Thus the Bureau of Investigation, renamed in 1935 the Federal Bureau of Investigation, was born.

When a reader has gone this far—through two pages and eight lines of the book—he has been told in capsule form what its thirty-eight chapters elaborate. He has been told that a "force of secret police" was smuggled into our system after the representatives of the people had denied it entrance; and, by implication, that the FBI is both lineal descendant of this unwanted bureau and heir to its dubious character.

By the book's final page, FBI policy has become the "realization" of the fear of the Sixtieth Congress "that the newly established Federal police force at the Department of Justice might some day adopt practices habitual to political police systems in Europe but abhorrent to a democracy." This is the conclusion toward which Lowenthal's whole creation moves.

He starts it toward this goal in his opening paragraphs by the means we have illustrated. He keeps it moving by one application after another of the formula by which he ties together these first paragraphs and his final conclusion. This formula consists of first reporting the pre-Hoover Bureau to have been nefarious in this or that respect—illegitimate, to begin with; and thereafter, publicity-seeking, power-seeking, inefficient, lawless, reactionary—and then, far more briefly, ascribing these same traits to the FBI under Hoover's directorship.

The theme which appears to be the book's *raison d'être* is introduced at the point where Hoover entered the Justice Department in 1917—and is progressively developed from that point on. It is to the effect that the very types of investigations which are, in aim and method, most dangerous to our liberties are those that come most naturally to J. Edgar Hoover.

Having portrayed the original Bureau as unwanted, Lowenthal proceeds in his Chapter 2—"Survival in the Early Months"—to portray it as unneeded:

What Federal work there was—for example, tracking down smugglers or counterfeiters, checking tax evaders, and protecting the mails—was in the hands of the long-established Treasury, Post Office, and other departmental forces. Chief Finch acknowledged that his portion of the nation's crime detection work would be primarily what was left over.

That last sentence would appear to be a remarkably free rendition of the fact that, under the terms of the Department of Justice Act, any federal law which Congress did not specifically assign to some other department would come under Justice's jurisdiction. Only in this sense would that Department's work be "primarily what was left over."

Lowenthal continues:

The Bureau's first criminal cases were of a somewhat makeshift character. The Justice detectives investigated crimes committed on Indian and other Government reservations; they prepared some District of Columbia cases involving false purchases and sales of securities; and they handled a few peonage and bankruptcy fraud cases. In addition some accountants who worked on antitrust cases were transferred to the roster of Chief Finch's Bureau.

Is this the most accurate account he was equipped to give of the Bureau's early work? Our answer is a categorical *No*. Seven of his notes for Chapter 1 cite as a source the portion of the Hearings of the House Appropriations Committee on the Sundry Civil Appropriations Bill for 1910 which was given over to Attorney General Bonaparte's testimony. Surely, then, we can assume his familiarity with what Bonaparte said.

The Attorney General was asked (*Hearings,* p. 969) about antitrust cases that were currently being handled. His answer does not suggest that this 40-man detective unit would have had much time for thumb-twiddling even if antitrust work had been—as it emphatically was not—its only concern:

We have one against the Standard Oil Company which is going to be tried below on the 23rd of March. We have one against the Tobacco Trust, which is in the Supreme Court. We have one against the Powder trust in which the Government's testimony has been taken .... We have a case against the Union Pacific and the Central Pacific, against the Harriman system generally, in which they are taking testimony .... The testimony is very voluminous. Then we have one against the anthracite coal carriers in Pennsylvania in which they are taking testimony .... There is another, that against the Naval Stores trust in Savannah .... There are seven or eight very large cases, and there are a certain number of small ones ....

After reporting that Congress passed various statutes under the "commerce clause" of the Constitution, and thus gave the "Justice detectives" a chance to busy themselves with interstate crimes—most of them "mere odds and ends"—Lowenthal writes as the final sentence of his Chapter 2:

In 1910, when the Bureau was two years old, Congress passed the Mann Act, which gave the Bureau of Investigation its first big push toward an important place in the detective world.

In Chapter 3, which deals with the Mann Act, the allegedly unwanted and unneeded Bureau acquires a third characteristic: namely, an exaggerated taste for cases that let it grab the limelight and make the headlines:

The Mann Act became law; but no particular Federal detective unit was given responsibility for its enforcement. It was clear that this detective assignment might involve one of the most spectacular tasks in police history. Mr. Finch's Bureau took it.

With the innuendo removed, what this says is that Congress put the Mann Act under the Justice Department by not assigning it elsewhere. Finch exercised no choice in the matter: jurisdiction over the Act was not left up for grabs.

One of the notes for this passage cites as a source the Attorney General's *Annual Report* for 1910, p. 26. But this source does not suggest that the Bureau was interested in the "spectacular" possibilities of the Mann Act. It indicates that "especial attention" was given in that year "to the investigation of violations of the national banking laws, antitrust laws, peonage laws, bucket shop laws, and laws relating to fraudulent bankruptcies, the impersonation of government officials with intent to defraud, thefts, murders, and other offenses committed on government reservations or with respect to government property." Far from being emphasized, Mann Act cases are lumped with "a great number of other matters."

An account of the enforcement of the Mann Act which is strikingly different from Lowenthal's is that in Edward H. Levi's *Introduction to Legal Reasoning*, pp. 33 ff. When he wrote this book, Levi, now president of the University of Chicago, was Dean of that university's Law School.

He deals with the Mann Act at some length, for two reasons. First, he uses it to illustrate the problems that can follow from Congress' including in a statute a phrase so vague that no one knows what it covers: namely, the phrase "any other immoral practice." Secondly, he analyzes a number of Supreme Court decisions by which the Act's coverage was progressively broadened: decisions which set certain precedents that have influenced rulings on other "commerce clause" statutes.

Levi indicates that the Justice Department was a firm practitioner of moderation in its enforcement of the Act. In a long footnote on pp. 50–51, he quotes from a policy statement issued by Attorney General Wickersham on July 28, 1911 (Department of Justice File 14582565). In this, the Attorney General took the position that not every case which a Supreme Court decision had given the Department a technical right to handle should be taken on. The focus was to be kept strictly on cases involving commercialism.

Wickersham instructed United States Attorneys to weigh each alleged violation of the Act to determine "what reasons, if any" existed for thinking that the ends of justice would be better served by a federal prosecution than by leaving the case to "the state having jurisdiction." The investigative activities of "Mr. Finch's Bureau" were geared to this departmental policy.

Lowenthal's account of the enforcement of the Mann Act is like his account of the Bureau's "unorthodox beginning," *preparatory*. It paves the way for his making Hoover seem to share, across the years, that absorption in snooping and headline seeking which allegedly marked "Mr. Finch's Bureau."

The Mann Act, he writes, p. 401, "engaged Mr. Hoover still early in his career as Chief of the Bureau, in what he described as 'an intensive effort to correct vice conditions.'" The source given in his notes is the Attorney General's *Annual Report* for 1925, p. 119. When we turn to this source, however, we find that the cases about which Hoover had been concerned were precisely of the type which Attorney General Wickersham, with his policy of restraint, would have instructed Finch's Bureau to investigate. They involved commercialized vice and flagrant offenses against minors.

Among the victims of those who, in 1925, were convicted

under the Mann Act were twenty-seven girls under 18 years of age, twenty-one under 15, three under 12, and one under 10. A high percentage of these minors had been forced into commercialized vice. For some reason, Lowenthal never gives such examples to illustrate Mann Act cases. He gives only ones that can be so presented as to make the Bureau seem to have been an officious intruder into the privacies of grown men and women.

On another front, also, he exaggerates the Bureau's interest in private misconduct. Writing of the enforcement of the prohibition laws, he says, p. 24, "The Justice Department's men found the work so absorbing that one year after their job of enforcing prohibition was officially transferred to the Treasury Department in 1920, they were still able to report to Congress that 'we also dip into the prohibition business.' "

His source shows the quoted statement to be incomplete. A representative of the Justice Department, John D. Harris, told the House Appropriations Committee, "We also dip into the prohibition business *so far as violations of the Reed Amendment are concerned.*"[5] The italics are ours. The Reed Amendment had to do with the sale of liquor around armed services installations. The enforcement of the prohibition laws in these areas was not transferred to Treasury, but remained with Justice.

On pp. 319–320, Lowenthal reports an "incident of early 1940" which, he says, raised doubts as to whether the FBI "had been successful in indoctrinating its lawyer-detectives in the true meaning and purpose of the Constitution and the Bill of Rights." But his handling of the "incident" raises doubts as to whether lawyer-reporter Lowenthal has been successfully indoctrinated in the true meaning and purpose of rules of evidence.

The "incident" was the arrest, on February 6, 1940, of certain "residents of Detroit and Milwaukee for alleged crimi-

[5] *Hearings of the House Appropriations Committee on Secondary Deficiency Appropriations for 1921*, p. 263.

nal action in recruiting people in the United States, for participation in the Spanish War some years earlier." FBI agents, Lowenthal writes, made "simultaneous raids on eleven residences in [Detroit] at 5 A.M. . . . , broke in doors where necessary to effect entrance, declined to let the lawyer of the arrested persons see them when he made his appearance at the Federal Building and submitted his request, and held the prisoners incommunicado until shortly before their arraignment in court in the afternoon." In response to press reports which alleged a denial of due process and the use of "third-degree" methods, many persons, including Senator George W. Norris, denounced the FBI.

Here is Lowenthal's version of what followed: "Attorney General Jackson sent an investigator of his own to inquire into the facts; the latter reported that FBI agents had engaged in conduct that might constitute a violation of the Constitution. The Attorney General quashed the indictments as dealing with matters which, even though criminal, were stale."

This account invites us to conclude, certainly, that the investigator's findings supported the charges made against the agents; and that Jackson's dismissal of the indictments was, in some measure, at least, conditioned by these findings. But Lowenthal's own source materials tell us what he has left out.

One such source is 86 *Congressional Record*, pp. 5645–5649. Here we learn that the investigator sent out by the Attorney General was Harry J. Schweinhaut, Chief of the Justice Department's Civil Rights Section; and also the nature of his report. He spent three intensive weeks checking up on specific charges of agent misconduct; and he secured signed statements from 98 persons, with most of the defendants and many of their relatives among the signers. No one was forced to make a statement; and a few defendants chose not to do so.

The findings completely exonerated the Bureau's agents of having used brutal or illegal methods of arrest and questioning and of having denied the prisoners prompt access to counsel. The United States Attorney in charge had decided upon simultaneous arrests, and had instructed the FBI agents accordingly, because of information he had received that at least some of the defendants, if they had any advance warning, would flee to Mexico—where various members of the International Brigade were in residence. Four of the sixteen persons indicted by the federal grand jury could not, in fact, be found.

The 5 A.M. hour was set—again, by the United States Attorney—because investigation had shown it to be the time when all the wanted individuals were most likely to be at home. Their "daily routine . . . fitted into no regular pattern . . . . Few remained at fixed places all day; all arrived home at different hours of the night . . . ; each left home at a different hour in the morning." In cases where entrance had been made by forcing the door, agents had properly identified themselves; had warned that they would have to force the door if it was not opened; and had been denied admission.

With respect to the interrogation, all the defendants except one said that no attempt was made to compel them to make a statement. "The evidence is conclusive that [they] were adequately informed of their right not to incriminate themselves and that no compulsion was used to make them do so."

The finding that agents had, in Lowenthal's terms, "engaged in conduct which might constitute a violation of the Constitution" referred, not to the treatment of persons, but to the seizure without a warrant of certain evidential items. Here, the agents had again acted on the advice of the United States Attorney, who had acted on instructions from Washington:

. . . there can be no doubt that the agents believed their procedure was entirely proper . . . . An examination of [Supreme

Court] decisions demonstrates that it is by no means clear to what extent an arresting officer, without a search warrant, may go.

Mr. Schweinhaut felt that one recent decision might have rendered illegal the seizures in Detroit; but he was not sure. It would take, he felt, a further Court decision to clarify the issue.

Attorney General Jackson made plain to the press his reasons for dismissing the indictments; and they had nothing to do with the FBI. One reason was the lateness of the decision to prosecute: a decision made by his predecessor, Attorney General Frank Murphy, in December 1939—some nine months after the Spanish Civil War had ended. The other key reason was that the statute violated by the recruiters—then Section 22, Title 18, U.S. Code, but now renumbered as Section 959—had been violated during the same 1936-1938 period by persons involved with the Italian-Ethiopian and Japanese-Chinese conflicts:

Unless we proceed with all the cases arising during that period, it would be manifestly unjust to single out the Detroit indictments.[6]

Far from being disgusted with the Bureau agents, the Attorney General held that Mr. Schweinhaut's report completely exonerated them. Further, he wrote to Senator Norris, in a letter which was released to the press at the same time as this report, on May 5, 1940:

I am of course anxious, as you are, that in law enforcement we do no violence to our traditional civil liberties. I am convinced that if those liberties are generally endangered in this country it is not by the F.B.I.

In weighing the general attitude of the Bureau, it is important to bear in mind that every agent acts under the probability that

[6] *Milwaukee Journal*, February 16, 1940.

his conduct will be examined by shrewd lawyers for defendants, every confession will be challenged, and every act exposed in open court. The Bureau is thus under continuous and hostile examination.

Under this severe test of cases investigated by the Federal Bureau of Investigation and prosecuted as a result of its investigations, convictions are had in 96%. In the years since Mr. Hoover became head of the Bureau not one case has been reversed by an appellate court because of "third degree" or other improper treatment of defendants. These, to me, are very impressive facts, not only by themselves but in comparison with any law enforcing body anywhere.

In an agency as large as the Federal Bureau of Investigation errors of judgment and of overzeal will from time to time occur, and criticism is helpful both to the Director and to the Attorney General in avoiding repetition. But I am confident that the more the operations of the Bureau are explored the more it will appear that its vigorous and effective work for law enforcement is conducted with a fundamental purpose to observe the rights of defendants.[7]

In his role as lawyer, Lowenthal would doubtless agree that a show of bias disqualifies a witness. By this standard he would have to move that his own book be stricken from the record. But in his role as author, he presents it as evidence in the court of public opinion—and for two decades other critics of the FBI have relied upon it as a prime source of data.

Its persuasiveness comes from its seeming to be scrupulously documented. Its fatal weakness is that the documentation cannot stand scrutiny. Its singularity is that Lowenthal provides the reader, by means of his notes, with guideposts to the materials that disprove his text. Thus, we are almost forced to conclude that those 80 pages of notes are designed, not to encourage research, but so to impress the reader as to make it appear to be unnecessary.

[7] Department of Justice, Washington, D.C. Press release to Sunday papers, May 5, 1940.

SEVENTEEN

THE FBI ACCORDING TO COOK

T HE TITLE of Fred J. Cook's *The FBI Nobody Knows* tacitly promises a wealth of unfamiliar data. Yet as materials critical of the FBI go, the book is pretty standard fare. While there are some references to personal interviews, most of Cook's evidence comes, as his footnotes indicate, from secondary sources. What turns the already published into what "nobody knows" is not the book's substance, but its exposé style.

Cook's account of the Bureau's formation is not new. In a chapter called "Strange and Stormy Beginnings," we read that it was "created in secrecy, by executive order, in defiance of the will of Congress." Unsurprisingly, his footnote, p. 70, says, "For much of the material about the Congressional debates that raged around the creation of the Bureau and its early history, I have relied upon Max Lowenthal's *The Federal Bureau of Investigation*."

His portrayal of Hoover as an arch-enemy of dissent and a determined exploiter of the Communist issue is not new.

Neither is his portrayal of Congress as intimidated by the FBI's "dossiers." These themes had been worn threadbare before his book appeared.

Precisely because his acknowledged debt to the already published is so great, we must ask who his chosen authorities are. Also, we must take stock of what it is that he adds to a collection of familiar charges to produce a "shocker."

Indubitably, Cook gives top place on his roster of authorities to Lowenthal. In the footnote from which we have quoted, he affirms his confidence in *The Federal Bureau of Investigation* and says that while this book was "denounced," when it came out, it "was not factually discredited in any respect."

We take it that he has not compared Lowenthal's text with his source materials. One of many reasons for our making this assumption is the way he uses the passage from Congressman Smith's speech of January 8, 1909. Lowenthal quotes the last part of the second clause of a sentence, we would recall, as though it were a full sentence, and makes it seem to have been directed against Bonaparte's request. Cook carries forward both inaccuracies and goes his mentor one better: on his p. 51, we meet the quoted fragment as a full paragraph:

Congressman Walter I. Smith, of Iowa, a veteran member of the House Appropriations Committee, put it this way:

"No general system of spying upon and espionage of the people, such as has prevailed in Russia, in France under the Empire, and at one time in Ireland, should be allowed to grow up."

Cook's chapter on the creation of the Bureau abounds not only in uncorrected Lowenthalisms but also in examples of what he adds to make the style his own. Thus, while Lowenthal describes Congress as "disturbed" by Bonaparte's formation of the Bureau, Cook describes it as "shaken by righteous outrage."

He says, p. 52, that when the Sixtieth Congress met for its Second Session, Bonaparte was "called upon to explain his conduct"; and that his explanation "enraged the legislators further." This combines the Lowenthal and Cook approaches; but as history it is farcical. The only testimony which the Attorney General gave with respect to his new detective force was at the regular hearing, on February 8–9, 1909, on Justice's budget for 1910; and the text does not suggest that the House Appropriations Committee sat in angry judgment.

In the published *Hearings* on the Sundry Civil Appropriations Bill for 1910, Bonaparte's testimony begins on p. 945. Not until most of the Department's work has been covered is the subject of the detective force brought up, on p. 1007. It is then discussed at some length, but not with any such "righteous outrage" on the Committee's part as Cook implies.

When Chairman Tawney introduced the subject, he emphasized that Bonaparte had, in his previous Annual Report, recommended the establishment of the detective unit. Then:

Chairman: I understand that you have organized such a force since July 1, last?
Mr. Bonaparte: I was obliged to.
Chairman: You have organized such a force?
Mr. Bonaparte: Yes, sir.

Cook describes as "sophistry" Bonaparte's statement that he was "obliged" to create the force and says that it "enraged" Congress; but he does not quote what follows. The Chairman, after re-emphasizing that the Attorney General's recommendation had *preceded* Congress's vote to end the hiring out of Secret Service men, said:

In other words, the provision carried in the sundry civil bill limiting the use of the secret service force of the Treasury De-

partment enabled you to do what you had recommended in
your latest annual report?

Bonaparte replied:

I suppose I could have done that under the previously existing
law, since the law is unchanged, but that provision made it indispensable for me to do so.

No Committee member either questioned his need for
investigative manpower or took issue with his statement that
he had a legal right to create the force. That he possessed
that right was precisely what Congressman Smith had
emphasized on the floor of the House a month earlier, on
January 8th.

One passage in the text suggests, indeed, that Congress, in
May 1908, may simply have taken it for granted that its
ending of the use of the Secret Service was *equivalent to* its
authorizing Bonaparte's "permanent detective force":

Congressman Smith: Did you anticipate starting with any more
of a nucleus of experienced men when you made your recommendation?
Mr. Bonaparte: No, sir. What I had in mind, and I substantially
expressed it, was to have a small force that would at first be very
moderate in size and that we would be quite certain to need all
the time, and then to have the secret-service force to call on for
special occasions until my force could gradually be organized
up to its normal number.
Congressman Smith: Of course, you unfortunately did not state
that you expected to use the Secret Service as a secondary reserve in either your report to Congress or in your hearing before
the committee?
Mr. Bonaparte: I had no idea that Congress was going to cut me
off from it.

Smith felt that what the Attorney General had
"impressed" upon the Committee was his wish to stop

relying on the Secret Service. Bonaparte felt that he had indicated his wish to have his use of it phased out gradually. Nothing in the text makes this exchange seem to have been an angry one.

We stress this because Cook's attitude, not that of Bonaparte or that of the Sixtieth Congress, is at issue here. Congress, we must recall, had made the Attorney General head of the Department of Justice—and therefore the man responsible for the "detection and prosecution of crimes against the United States." At no point did any member of Congress even remotely imply that he should have halted all investigations of such crimes when he could no longer use the Secret Service men.

It is Cook who makes his failure to halt them seem villainous. Had Bonaparte acted as Cook implies that he should have acted, the May 1908 amendment would quite emphatically have been "of benefit only to criminals." They would have had everything their own way, without being subject to investigation.

We might as well state, here, that we find Cook's attitude toward Attorney General Bonaparte hard to understand—in view of the causes to which he has himself professed a commitment. Bonaparte's whole adult life was spent fighting political corruption. His money and skill were spent far beyond any routine call of duty on the legal defense of the impoverished. He staunchly defended the rights of minorities. He could not be bribed or intimidated by the giant trusts that were establishing an octopus hold upon our economy. During his brief term as Secretary of the Navy, he made history—and friends and enemies—by refusing to let plain sailors be used as scapegoats when officers blundered.

Cook mentions none of these facts. He simply describes Bonaparte as having "the typical mental bias of the prosecuting official." What he cannot forgive, it would seem, is the Attorney General's use of his quite proper authority under the Department of Justice Act to provide for the investigation of "crimes against the United States"— employing for this purpose funds which the Sixtieth Congress had voted for their "detection." The type of judgment he brings to bear upon Bonaparte does not seem irrelevant to that which he brings to bear upon Hoover.

Like Lowenthal, indeed, he repetitively uses a derogatory description of the early Bureau to preface a matching description of Hoover. His passage on the Mann Act is a case in point. He writes, p. 56, that the Act gave the Bureau "its first eye-catching national assignment" and was "an invaluable windfall for the bureaucracy-building purposes of the new Bureau":

Finch quickly saw the Mann Act as a golden opportunity to apply to Congress for ever more funds and ever more agents. The technique he developed, it is interesting to note, is virtually the same technique that J. Edgar Hoover has employed during the long years of his directorship. First, there needs be a Menace. Next, this must be such a tremendous Menace that the entire nation is convinced it stands at a crossroads, shuddering and trembling in need of succor. And who can save it? Only the Bureau.

What cuts the ground out from under this report on Finch's exploitation of the Mann Act? Only the record.

Cook is indebted to Lowenthal for far more than his version of particular events. Beyond his first chapter, which is a unit in itself, the pattern of his book is strikingly like that of *The Federal Bureau of Investigation*—even to the fact of the FBI's being presented on its final page as the realization of the fears of the Sixtieth Congress. The spirit of Lowenthal, we might say, broods over *The FBI Nobody Knows*.

As measured by the attention given his statements, the second place from the top on Cook's roster of authorities is held by Jack Levine. Not only is he the hero of the 48-page opening chapter—"An Agent Talks"—but he is quoted in various later passages.

Levine enters the text in the first paragraph as a young man with "close-cropped dark hair, bright dark eyes, and that thoroughly clean-cut, all-American-boy look that one almost automatically associates with a Special Agent of the Federal Bureau of Investigation." Yet he may not have been altogether the FBI type—this young ex-agent who resigned within a year *either* because his parents needed him, as he told Hoover, *or* as he said later on WBAI and as Cook reports, because he was "disillusioned."

Our sampling of Special Agents must differ markedly from Cook's. It would never occur to us to describe those whom we have known as having an "all-American-boy" look. To the very limited extent that they have had any common appearance, they have looked like fairly seasoned adults. More important, they have been far less talkative than Levine's own report shows him to have been, and less prone to dramatize themselves.

Even Cook grants that Levine, as a trainee, was "a bit obdurate and intractable." But we would have to add a further reason why we cannot think of him as an FBI type: namely, the extent to which the pronoun *I* looms large in his vocabulary. The Bureau is, and must be, a *we* organization; but Levine seems to have cast his relationship to it in the first person singular.

In the letter, for example, in which he applied for reinstatement as a Special Agent, he made his brief period of service in the Detroit office seem to have been one of almost single-handed accomplishment:

During the course of my assignment in the Detroit office, investigations which I conducted led to the conviction of eight bureau subjects for fraud against the government and for violations of Federal laws relating to Federal Housing Administration matters . . . . Through my efforts the Government is recovering large sums of money on its claims.

To keep unsmudged the image of Levine as a young man who was "lured" into the FBI by his idealized conception of it, and who was "revolted" by the reality, Cook must subdue three recalcitrant facts.

The first is that Levine urgently tried to secure a reappointment. Here, Cook reports Levine's own explanation: that "he had hoped to get a post in the training division where, he thought, many of the flaws in the organization might be most easily corrected." Apparently, Cook sees nothing incongruous in Levine's having felt qualified for this reforming role.

The second recalcitrant fact is that Levine's record was judged to be "substandard." Cook does not even weigh the possibility of this appraisal's being justified. He simply attributes it to the Director's "vengefulness" toward agents who resign. It was, he says, p. 39,

naive of Levine to suppose that, once he had resigned, he would ever be reinstated, much less given a more responsible post in the training division. The FBI does not work that way, and Levine should have known it.

But the FBI *does* work that way, so far as reinstatement is concerned; and Cook could have learned as much by asking. After we had, without success, sought in the public domain some policy statement relevant to this issue, we sent a letter of inquiry to J. Edgar Hoover. His answer, from which we quote by permission, declares it to have been

a long-standing policy of this Bureau that all appointments to the position of Special Agent are based entirely on the current needs of the service and on the qualifications of the individual applicant. In the past some of our Special Agents who have resigned for personal reasons have been reinstated at their request when these prerequisites existed.

On the theme of appointments to the training division, he states that it has been "a matter of normal procedure" for

Special Agents to have "extensive experience in the field prior to reassignment to headquarters as training instructors or for supervisory duties." In addition, men who are thus reassigned "have special abilities and have maintained a quality performance over a prolonged period of time."

The third recalcitrant fact with which Cook must deal is that Levine carried his assault upon Hoover and the Bureau to extremes that do not fit the image of a selfless young idealist. Here again Hoover's alleged vengefulness is called into service—to make the virulence of Levine's attack seem like an understandable form of "retaliation for jobs lost, doors closed to him."[1] But Levine's own words seem to provide a rather different chronology of events.

Cook does not quote at all from Levine's letters to Hoover; but in the last of these, dated October 1, 1961, Levine wrote, "I wish, once more, to express my affection for and loyalty to the Bureau."[2] When he wrote this, he knew that his request for reappointment had been conclusively denied; so that its denial cannot logically be included among the "jobs lost" that moved him to "retaliation."

Yet on WBAI, he said that "shortly after [he] had gotten out of the FBI," he was offered a position in the Criminal Division of the Justice Department; and by his account, what recommended him for this post was his report on what was wrong with the FBI. Those with whom he had interviews, he said, "had no idea what the internal operations of the Bureau were like"; and what he revealed about FBI investigations of organized crime—a field in which he had never worked—appeared to "startle" the Chief of the Organized Crime Section.

Common sense would suggest that the Chief might well have been startled, not by Levine's revelations, but by his patent readiness to tell all. This could scarcely have recommended him as a person with whom the confidential affairs of *any* agency would be safe.

[1] Cook, p. 39.
[2] *Hearings of the House Subcommittee on Appropriations on Sundry Civil Appropriations Bill for 1964*, p. 500.

The Chief might well have been startled, also, by the discrepancy between what Levine "revealed" about the work on organized crime and what he himself knew. On the record—which we shall be exploring in Part IV—the very year when Levine was in the FBI was one of greatly intensified effort against the crime syndicates; and the Organized Crime Section was presiding over a broad new inter-agency drive, in which the FBI played a leading role, to secure both more complete intelligence data about organized crime leaders and more convictions.

Hoover testified with regard to this stepped-up campaign against the syndicates at a hearing on March 1, 1961.[3] Yet Levine exhibits no knowledge of his testimony. In spite of what he does not seem to have known, he affirms that he was "offered a job" *because he could, as an ex-agent, instruct the department on aspects of the FBI's work of which it was wholly ignorant.*

The field of organized crime, moreover, was not the only one about which he was ready to give information—without having worked in it. He said on WBAI that members of the Civil Rights Commission were "interested" in what he could reveal about the Bureau's handling of civil rights matters.

"And then I wanted to discuss some aspects—some very, very confidential aspects—of the FBI's penetration of the Communist Party with people over at the White House." He suspected that the White House did not know "the extent to which the FBI had penetrated the top levels of the Communist Party." When he talked with "a staff director of the National Security Council," his suspicions were confirmed: "the National Security Council had not gotten this information."

As his story goes, the offer of the post in the Criminal Division was later withdrawn. When he asked the head of the Division, Assistant Attorney General Herbert J. Miller,

[3] *FBI 1962 Appropriation*, p. 15.

Jr., for a reason, he was given to understand that its employment of him might lead to "strained relations" with the FBI.

If he had complaints against the Bureau, Miller told him,
they should be put in writing. Levine interpreted this as a
request to provide the department with a report on the
FBI's shortcomings. He wrote up a full "report"—which was,
he said on WBAI, given a "non-committal" reception. It was
this report which he later offered to the press; and it served
as the basis for his radio interview.

Cook writes, pp. 39–40, that Levine's carrying of his
"retaliatory" campaign to extremes "does not necessarily
mean that the items of which he spoke from personal
experience were untrue." Neither does it mean that they
were true—and Cook suggests no standard by which the
evidential wheat can be separated from the chaff.

Instead, he exempts Levine from any obligation to
substantiate his charges and puts the burden of proof upon
the accused. They cannot clear themselves, he asserts, by
"generalized" denials; and he deplores their failure to con-
test Levine's charges "fact for fact."

But why—and how—should Hoover and his associates
have contested "fact for fact" Levine's version of what was
in a "very confidential memorandum" circulated to Bureau
officials; or his charge that the Director had, "for political
reasons," been withholding from the National Security
Council and the White House "very, very confidential" data
which he, Levine, was able to provide; or his statement that,
within the confines of the FBI, Negroes are regularly called
niggers out of deference to the prejudices of Hoover and
Southern agents? And so on—*ad infinitum.*

Cook comes closer here than he may realize to adopting
an old and dishonorable tactic of the Far Right. "If X isn't a
Communist," say the Rightists, "let him prove that he isn't."
"If Hoover and the FBI are not guilty as charged," Cook

says, in effect, "let them prove that they aren't."

How, then, does Cook choose his authorities? His rating of Don Whitehead, author of *The FBI Story*, provides one kind of answer. Cook on p. 30 designates Whitehead not as an authority but as an "apologist." Finding it necessary to downgrade a statement of Whitehead's favorable to Hoover, he calls *The FBI Story*

a glowing account published under the aegis of the FBI, with a foreword by Hoover and a replica of the FBI shield on a cover sporting the colors of the American flag.

But on p. 117, where Cook makes use of one of Whitehead's statements, the latter is granted more authority than he possessed: he becomes a person "who had access to the FBI files."

Whitehead had no such access. We have his word for this. He enjoyed a remarkable—and, so far as we know, unique—measure of FBI cooperation. Many letters and other documents which the Bureau had *on file*, and which we have not found duplicated in the public domain, were put at his disposal. But to say that he "had access to the FBI files" is to suggest his having been turned loose to explore the records of a host of his fellow citizens. He was given no such freedom—and would not have wanted it.

Cook's standard for evaluating testimony would be ruled out in any court committed to due process. Yet in the world of the exposé, it has an invincible logic. In that ruthless and overmotional world, normal rules of evidence have no function. Rules of evidence are geared to the task of distinguishing between innocence and guilt. In the world of the exposé, the villain has already been identified. An *authority* is a person who helps to build the case against him.

Thus, a useful witness is not disqualified by a show of bias. His charges may not be literally true and may reflect a spirit of "retaliation." But they are taken to be *of the same order* as that which would be proved true if the villain were not insulated against exposure. They suffice, therefore, to shift the burden of proof from the accuser to the accused: if the latter does not like what is said, let him discard his "bullet-proof shield." Since the FBI is forbidden by the nature of its work to make a public disclosure of all its evidence, it is a well-nigh perfect target for exposé writing.

Cook's application of his standard is further illustrated by his handling of what Lowenthal called "an incident of early 1940": the arrest of the Communist recruiters in Detroit. The key document to be evaluated in relation to this "incident" was the report of Harry J. Schweinhaut, head of the Civil Rights Section of Justice. But Cook neither quotes any key passages from it nor summarizes the findings.

He dismisses it by saying that Senator Norris called the investigation ordered by Attorney General Jackson a "whitewash" and "launched into a four-hour denunciation of Hoover and the FBI." He quotes from this—to the effect, for example, of Hoover's being "the greatest publicity hound on the American continent today." This statement may accurately have expressed the Senator's feelings; but it was irrelevant to the question of whether or not certain FBI agents had employed improper or illegal methods in making certain arrests in Detroit—which was the question at issue.

When two staunch civil libertarians like Schweinhaut and Senator Norris disagree about a case, it makes sense to give more weight to what is said by the one who has investigated it than to emotionalized statements made by the one who has not; and Senator Norris did not claim to have looked into the Detroit events at first hand. He had talked with one of the arrested Communist recruiters and received letters from several others. They had convinced him that they had been subjected to "third-degree" methods.

His views, however, he said, were chiefly derived from an editorial in *The New Republic*—"An American OGPU"— which he read into the Congressional Record on February

26, 1940. "I am not alleging these matters as facts of which I have personal knowledge, for I have not." The Senator, moreover, was rather jumping the gun when he applied the term "whitewash" in February to an investigation the results of which were not available until early May.

While Cook gives no space to Schweinhaut's findings, he devotes the better part of a page to anti-FBI diatribes by Westbrook Pegler—ostensibly to show that "[s]ome of the severest criticism came not from Communist-tainted or liberal sources but from writers usually deemed conservative in their orientation." Thus, Pegler is quoted as saying:

"The FBI has more dirt on more Americans, including Senators, Representatives, labor leaders, Governors, Mayors, and members of the political families of the New Deal government, than the foulest whelp of an open-air grand jury bred of a professional blackmailer of the press, radio, and screen could reefer up in a thousand and one nights under the goofy spell of the toxic weed."[5]

With respect to what is in the FBI files Pegler is, of course, exactly as much of a non-authority as is John Doe—or as we are. But aside from this fact, the passage, as an example of either responsible criticism or responsible conservatism, is about as illuminating as Pegler's attack on Mrs. Eleanor Roosevelt in the November 1963 issue of the John Birch Society's *American Opinion*, p. 17:

Her career was notoriously immoral in her hypocrisy, and cruelty, and her insensate greed for money. Lehman promoted her imposition upon millions of franchised fools to the extent that on her demise, and for a long time before, she was often described as the First Lady of the World. This was managed idolatry. In the first place, she was not a lady . . . .

In one key passage, Cook's authorities are anonymous. To show the extent to which official Washington is intimidated

[5] Cook, p. 239.

by the FBI Director, he writes that, in 1959, when the *New York Post* planned a series of articles on the FBI, its publisher, Mrs. Dorothy Schiff, "discovered that some of the most distinguished figures on the Hill simply will not be quoted on the subject of Hoover."

Among them was an unnamed "veteran liberal Senator" who purportedly said that he "didn't like a police state." This would not make him unique. But if he defined the term or specified the counts on which it could rightly be applied to the FBI, Cook does not say so.

Another figure was an unnamed "important member of Congress who had intimate dealings with the FBI in the course of his official duties." He purportedly said, "It is true that the FBI has detailed dossiers on everyone in Washington." But *any* Congressman, however "important," who claimed that his "official duties" gave him the type of access to FBI files on which such a generalization could be based would impugn the reliability of his own word.

A third figure—"a liberal Senator promised anonymity by the *Post*"—purportedly said:

"Hoover is not *vulnerable*. In politics you do not attack Santa Claus and you do not attack God. If it got back to my district that I attacked J. Edgar Hoover, I would be pilloried. Those who were concerned with the growth of the federal police—men like Senator Norris and others—are dead now, or back home. Those who are here cannot afford to speak up.[6]

This sounds horrendous—until we ask what we are supposed to conclude from this example of moral and intellectual mediocrity. By quoting these men, Cook is trying to make Hoover responsible for an atmosphere in which "only he is safe who keeps his mouth shut, or if he opens it, opens it but to agree." Yet what he chiefly does is to make various unnamed Congressmen *called* liberals seem like feeble car-

[6] Cook, pp. 417–419.

riers of the liberal tradition—which did not become splendid in history by people's sniping at other people's reputations from safe ambush.

Senator Norris did not thus play safe. His judgment was not infallible; but his courage was not open to question. If the Congressmen who talked to Mrs. Schiff belong to a lesser breed, we do not see how Hoover can be held accountable.

We have not ourselves found any sufficient reason to rate the present FBI as a police-state menace. But this is not the point. The point is that various Congressmen, according to Cook, do rate it as such—and would rather let it get an ever-stronger hold on our country than run the risks which they think would attend the act of speaking out. How do such wishy-washy minds know that they are *liberals*?

Furthermore, since all that Cook tells us about them is that they are afraid to say what their consciences dictate, why should we be impressed by their testimony? We recognize that the press has an established right to protect its sources. But in this age of the anonymous smear, it does well to use this right sparingly; and it should not be surprised if the lay citizen protects his own mind, by skepticism, against the impact of what is said by those who refuse to stand up and be counted.

Cook's last chapter is called, with apocryphal overtones, "The Final Judgment." Having portrayed Congress, Justice, the Supreme Court, and the press as so intimidated by Hoover that the free discussion "essential to a democracy" is stopped at its source, he ends thus his chapter and his book:

No man wishes to court the scowl of the FBI. No man dares to suggest that it would be helpful for the country if the FBI could be curbed a bit, restricted from investigating the thoughts and associations of men, and confined to its proper task of fighting crime. The fears of the Sixtieth Congress—fears that we might create a federal "secret police" force like the French ministry of police under Fouché—seem to have been justified.

Since *The FBI Nobody Knows* was published in the midst of a clamor of free discussion on virtually every aspect of our national life and policy—with a fair share of the clamor coming from critics of the FBI—there is something about this melodramatic climax that recalls a passage in *Through the Looking Glass*:

" 'I can't believe that,' " said Alice in response to one of the White Queen's more spectacular exaggerations.

" 'Can't you?' the queen said . . . . 'Try again: draw a deep breath, and shut your eyes.' "

Alice protested: " 'There's no use trying . . . : one can't believe impossible things.' "

" 'I daresay you haven't had much practice,' said the Queen . . . . 'Why, sometimes I've believed as many as six impossible things before breakfast.' "

EIGHTEEN

THE TURNER STORY

WILLIAM W. TURNER was in the FBI for ten years. Unlike Levine, he did not resign; he was discharged in July 1961. Availing himself of his veteran's privilege, he appealed his dismissal to the Civil Service Commission. It ruled against him in his effort to be reinstated.

He took his case to the courts: to the United States District Court of the District of Columbia; the Federal Court of Appeals of the District of Columbia circuit; and, finally, the Supreme Court. Each in turn ruled against him.

Our own acquaintance with the Turner story came by way of the 1962 radio interview on KPFA. On this, he said that he was fired for exercising his constitutional right to appeal to members of Congress for redress of grievances; but that this reason was concealed by a charge that he had made false statements in his letters:

Of course, the funny part of it all is that after ten years of being entirely truthful and entirely accurate, as soon as I made certain statements which were critical of the Bureau and certain of its policies all of a sudden I lost this truthfulness and accuracy.[1]

Later, we saw press items about the court decisions. But had it not been for Turner's articles "The FBI Could Have Saved President Kennedy's Life!" and "Crime Is Too Big for the FBI," we might not have gone any further into the case than his KPFA broadcast had taken us. These articles reactivated our interest because they seemed so unlike anything that would be authored by a man with legal training and ten years of FBI experience.

At the top of one page of the former article, it says in very small print "By William W. Turner, as told to Bruce Lee." The editorial note, however, calls Turner the author; so we shall do likewise.

In *Saga*, Turner tells of exploring the circumstances of President Kennedy's death. "As I went about my private investigations in Dallas, I used FBI techniques to find out what went wrong." The trouble is that his "FBI techniques" yielded him only what John Doe could have pulled out of the rumor-laden air.

He attributes the FBI's not having transmitted Oswald's name to the Secret Service to "rivalry" between the two agencies. Then he says that he learned "that the FBI eventually did give the Secret Service a 'risk list' of people the Bureau thought might harm the President. But Oswald's name was not on it." He does not explain how a spirit of "rivalry" would have been serviced by the omission of one name—Oswald's—when others were transmitted.

Rumors about a last-minute "risk list" were all over the place. But as Chief Rowley made plain in his testimony before the Warren Commission no such list was transmitted "eventually" or otherwise; and Turner would not have

[1] *Report of Former Agent Turner*; transcript, p. 2. KPFA, Pacifica Radio, Berkeley, California, October 1962.

needed the Chief's word to this effect. He had operated for ten years under the FBI's policy of *immediate* transmission of every "risk" name "by the most expeditious means." Why, then, would he present as something that he had learned by applying FBI techniques a rumor which he was in a position to scotch?

The FBI does not deal in last-minute "risk lists." For it to wait until a Presidential trip was planned and *then* go through its files and compile "lists" for particular cities would be intolerably dangerous. It would give the Secret Service no time to process names—and would be altogether useless if the President made a sudden decision to go here or there.

The Secret Service had on file in its Protective Research Section (PRS) every name which the FBI or any other federal agency had, up to that time—and we might say up to that moment—had reason to identify as a possible "risk." Turner could not have failed to know this, by reason of what he knew about relevant policies.

Again, he says that he "soon learned that a Dallas FBI agent had especially interviewed Oswald only ten days before the assassination." No investigative skill would have been needed to ferret out such a rumor; but later testimony established the fact that Oswald was not interviewed by the FBI after his return from Mexico. Turner, in short, promises the fruits of professional competence and delivers grab-bag rumors.

A mildly amusing footnote may be in order: Turner has now repudiated, it would appear, the conclusions of his own "private investigation." He says in *Saga*:

My investigation confirms that Oswald was indeed the assassin, and that he killed on his own; there was no plot by left-wingers, right-wingers, or the crime syndicate.

More recently, however, he has been supporting, through a series of articles in *Ramparts*, the effort of New Orleans District Attorney Jim Garrison to prove a massive conspiracy. Thus, he writes in the June 1967 issue, in an article called "The Inquest":

The truth, according to Garrison, is certain to rock the republic as it gradually unfolds in court. He is convinced that Lee Harvey Oswald was not a triggerman.... He is equally sure that the working level of the conspiracy was composed of rabid anti-Castro Cuban exiles in league with elements of the American paramilitary right.

In a long article in the January 1968 issue—"The Garrison Commission on the Assassination of President Kennedy"—he elaborates the conspiracy thesis. The motive attributed to the conspirators is that of preventing a détente with Castro which President Kennedy was allegedly planning. Just as in the case of the Far Right's conspiracy thesis, the federal "establishment" is presumed to have been deeply implicated in the crime.

Turner's thesis in *The Nation* is that the FBI avoids coming to grips with organized crime and has "pet crimes"—bank robberies, kidnappings, and car thefts—in which it "specializes." These, he asserts, are for the most part "amateurish capers that can be wrapped up without much fuss."

This passage is one to ponder. If Hoover were to decide to investigate fewer bank robberies, how would he proceed? Turner says that the FBI "takes its authority from a wisp of technicality: federal money partially insures deposits." But this "technicality," as Turner must know, is a very substantial "wisp." Congress has repeatedly expressed in law its will to have broader, not narrower, federal coverage of bank robberies; and the FBI has no license to treat as unimportant laws which Congress has put under its jurisdiction.

In 1934, Congress amended the National Bank Act to make it cover any bank "organized or operating under the laws of the United States"; and in 1935, to cover "financial institutions insured by the Federal Deposit Insurance Corporation." Since then, coverage has been extended to federally insured savings and loan associations and, in 1959, to Federal Credit Unions.

Again, Turner writes that the "federals plunge into kidnappings on the 'rebuttable presumption' that the victim has been taken from one state to another . . . . " In exactly the same manner, as we noted in Chapter XI, they "plunge" into bombing cases on the "rebuttable presumption" that the explosives were transported across a state line. But there must be a strange gap in Turner's knowledge of the law if he thinks that the presence of a presumptive clause in a statute gives the FBI a right to choose whether or not to enforce it—up to the point, if there is one, where evidence rebuts the presumption.

Besides, what does he think it contributes to a respect for law to have an ex-FBI agent catalogue car thefts, kidnappings, and bank robberies as being, for the most part, "amateurish capers": *playful tricks*; *frolicsome acts*?

Amateurs do steal cars—and often kill themselves and others in their getaway racing. But professionals also steal cars: at the end of fiscal 1968, the FBI had 75 active car-theft rings under investigation; and their networks spanned the continent.[2]

Amateurs do rob banks. Turner cites a young bride who did so, and a Los Angeles grandmother. A third example would be that of Duane Earl Pope, the football star who was convicted and sentenced to death in 1965 for one of the bloodiest bank robberies of modern times. On June 4, 1965—six months before Turner's article appeared—Pope killed three bank employees and wounded a fourth in the course of robbing the Farmers State Bank in Big Springs, Nebraska.

Professionals also rob banks. John Franzese, for example, a New York labor racketeer, was convicted on March 3, 1967,

[2] *FBI Annual Report* for fiscal 1968, p. 14.

of masterminding a series of bank robberies in New York, Massachusetts, and Utah; and several members of his gang were convicted with him.[3]

Turner speaks *only* of amateurs and conveys no sense of how dangerous an armed amateur can be, because of his tendency to panic and start shooting. Moreover, it is not accurate to imply that most crimes committed by amateurs can be "wrapped up without much fuss." Often they are singularly hard to solve, because the amateur has no criminal record and is not known to law enforcement personnel.

Hoover, when he writes about the bank-robbery problem—as in "Profile of a Bank Robber," in the November 1965 *FBI Law Enforcement Bulletin*—is considerably more realistic than Turner. He deals with *both* the amateur and the professional.

Turner's own estimate of bank robberies and kidnapping as being, for the most part, "capers" must be of recent origin. On KPFA, in 1962, he was asked about his work as an agent. He had not, as a rule, he said, handled cases of types involved in organized crime, "although I have worked on kidnapping cases and major criminal investigations, bank robberies, extortions, things of that nature."[4]

Turner, in his *Nation* article, writes contemptuously of the Bureau's war on the gangs in the 1930's: "G-men donned their snap-brim hats and entered the fray. Rashly, they decided to meet gunfire with gunfire; skirmishes erupted all over the country, causing considerable hazard to innocent bystanders. In the ill-fated raid on Little Bohemia resort, from which Dillinger and his cronies fled by a rear entrance, two taxpayers were winged by federal guns and one of them died . . . .

"When the smoke settled, however, these mishaps had barely dented the FBI shield . . . . With an entire nation watching, flinty-jawed G-men mowed down Public Enemies,

---

[3] *FBI 1969 Appropriation*, pp. 73, 83.
[4] KPFA transcript, p. 7.

one by one." Hoover, a new public hero, "disported himself at the Stork Club and signed autographs with Shirley Temple."

Recalling the arrogant, law-corrupting power of the gangs of that era, we can only say, "We are not amused." The tragedy at Little Bohemia—a roadhouse fifty miles from Rhineland, Wisconsin—took place in the dark early morning hours of April 23, 1934. It was probed and reprobed; but "when the smoke had settled," no reason had been found to charge the FBI agents with trigger-happiness. Turner omits the fact that they were under fire from machine guns which the Dillinger gang had mounted on the roof of the roadhouse when the citizen-victim—one of three men from a nearby CCC camp, who had emerged from the house a few minutes earlier—was caught in the cross fire.

He is silent, also, about the aftermath of the events at Little Bohemia: an aftermath involving a not-yet-reported car theft. The *St. Louis Post-Dispatch* carried the following report, under an Ironwood, Michigan, dateline of April 24th:

"The car looked innocent enough. It belonged to one of my neighbors. But there were gangsters in it. We never had a chance. They shot us down like dogs."

Choking for breath because of bullet wounds, Constable Carl Christensen, 34 years old, of Spider Lake, Wis., thus summed up today the story of his encounter Sunday night with members of the Dillinger gang (at Koerner's resort, three miles from Little Bohemia).

In this encounter, Christensen was seriously wounded; one FBI agent, W. Carter Baum, from the Chicago field office, was killed; and another, J. C. Newman, was wounded.

Turner's charge that agents indulged in reckless gunfire "all over the country" recalls one made by Senator Kenneth McKellar of Tennessee at a hearing of the Senate Appropriations Committee in 1937. The Senator asked how many gangsters had been killed since the Bureau's agents had, in 1934, been given permission to carry weapons.

Hoover said that from 1934 to 1936 inclusive—the period within which the Dillinger gang, and other similar gangs, had been broken up and virtually eliminated—eight had been killed. Each had fired before he was fired upon. Four agents had been killed—three by Baby Face Nelson of the Dillinger gang.

McKellar professed to see no excuse for so much gunfire: "I doubt very much whether you ought to have a law that permits you to go around the country armed as an army would, and shoot down all the people you suspect of being criminals, or such as you suspect of having guns, and having your own men shot down."

This odd interpretation of the record moved Senator Harry Truman to ask, "How would you catch them, Senator, if they commenced shooting at you?"[5]

One explicit charge which Turner makes is that Mr. Hoover would not cooperate with a Special Group on Organized Crime which Attorney General William P. Rogers created, in response to a public demand for action, after a 1957 gathering of Mafia leaders at the home of Joseph Barbara, Sr., at Apalachin, New York.

"The response of most federal agencies was enthusiastic; they gave unstintingly of men and materials. But Hoover turned a cold shoulder to the Group, supplying only token cooperation. A 'super-duper Dick Tracy outfit,' he snorted."

But it was not Hoover who used this phrase. It was Congressman John J. Rooney of New York—at a hearing on March 6, 1961. He may or may not have "snorted"; but he was exasperated. The Special Group, he said, claimed not to have received cooperation from "the courts or the Congress or the FBI or any government agency." Yet Congress had voted it all the funds for which it had asked. Rooney wanted

[5] *1937 Hearing of the Senate Subcommittee on Appropriations on the Justice Department's Appropriation*, pp. 199–202.

to know about Mr. Hoover's experience with the leaders of the Group.

Hoover said that they had, at first, expressed satisfaction with the help given by the FBI. Their later criticisms, he felt, stemmed from his not having granted a request that he assign them "a substantial number of special agents" to work under their direction "without any special target in mind, but to be used for 'fishing expeditions.' "[6]

Turner contends that Hoover should have loaned the agents and could well have spared them if he had been conducting fewer "fishing expeditions" in the car-theft field. To appraise his contention, we must take account of what the FBI Director—whoever he may be—must consider when such a request is made.

Congress has never licensed the FBI to act as an agent-lending bureau. The agent force represents the Director's best estimate of the minimal number of men needed for its legally assigned work. At the time of the request, the average workload of an agent was around 20 investigative matters; and Hoover has testified that he regards any load heavier than this to be "excessive." Some investigations can no doubt be quickly handled; but others are sure to stretch out over months and to require the patient development of sources of information.

To have granted the Group's request, Hoover would have had to relieve "a substantial number of agents," for an undefined period, *of their total workloads.* Even if we take a "substantial number" to be as few as a dozen, this would have meant that some 240 investigations, at all stages of development, would have had to be added to the workloads of other agents or put aside till someone could take them up.

Moreover, the FBI Director—whoever he may be—must be able to say, at any point of challenge, "*This* investigation is being conducted under *this* federal law—or under *this*

[6] *FBI 1962 Appropriation,* p. 61.

order from the Attorney General or the President." The rigidity of this formula is a basic safeguard against abuses.

Had the agents been loaned to the Special Group, they would have gone out of the FBI's frame of discipline and into the very type of setup that Hoover has always rated as a threat to constitutional rights: namely, one in which investigative assignments are so vaguely defined that their terms do not constitute a barrier against trespasses outside the law.

FBI agents cooperate with many law enforcement and intelligence bodies, federal, state, and local; but only for the Secret Service, with which he is allegedly "feuding," does the Director make an exception to his non-lending policy. If Chief Rowley asks for a given number of men to supplement his force during a Presidential visit to a city, Hoover, as he told the Warren Commission, lends them if he possibly can.

This policy of helping out the Secret Service was established long before the passage, on June 6, 1968, of *Public Law 90-331*: the *Resolution* to "authorize the United States Secret Service to furnish protection to major presidential or vice presidential candidates." *Section 2* of this law reads:

Hereafter, when requested by the Director of the United States Secret Service, Federal Departments and agencies, unless such authority is revoked by the President, shall assist the Secret Service in the performance of its protective duties under section 3056 of title 18 of the United States Code and the first section of this joint resolution.

Section 3056 is the one that spells out the protective responsibilities of the Secret Service as these were amended in 1967.

Finally, Turner charges that the "inert FBI" has had abundant jurisdictional authority to wage a massive campaign against organized crime, but has turned "legalistic" to avoid having to do so. He then reels off a list of laws—within a context that invites us to think that they were on the books while he was in the FBI and was restive under its policy of "inertness." Among the statutes that he mentions, however, those of key importance were sponsored by Attorney General Robert Kennedy and passed by Congress in September–October 1961—after Turner was out of the Bureau.

Moreover, they represented a type of legislation *that Hoover had suggested.* On June 10, 1960, in a memorandum to Assistant Attorney General Malcolm R. Wilkey, then head of Justice's Criminal Division, he had recommended ten items of legislation designed to cope with organized crime; and on February 16, 1961, he had written to Attorney General Kennedy recommending "Federal legislation to prohibit interstate travel of individuals in aid of racketeering, [and] transmission of wagering information and paraphernalia."[7]

This was the type of legislation that was enacted in the fall of 1961 and supplemented in 1962. Testifying before the Senate Permanent Subcommittee on Investigations, on September 25, 1963, Robert Kennedy said that these statutes had given the FBI "for the first time" a jurisdictional right to investigate large-scale interstate gambling, the number one source of wealth for the crime syndicates.

To indicate the results of their passage, he said that for the first six months of 1963 "we secured indictments of 171 racketeering figures—compared with 24 for the same period 3 years ago."[8] This report does not suggest that the FBI is "inert" when it has laws under which to act; and Kennedy's testimony was in the public domain for two years before Turner's article appeared.

It is not uncommon for an author to claim more knowledge of a subject than he can convincingly deliver. But it is uncommon for one glaringly to exhibit less knowledge than his training and experience tell us he must possess.

[7] *FBI 1968 Appropriation,* pp. 90-91.

[8] *Hearings of the Senate Permanent Subcommittee on Investigations, on Organized Crime and Illicit Traffic in Narcotics,* Vol. I, p. 8.

Patently, Turner has not given us in *Saga* and *The Nation* the best products he could deliver. Instead, he has done a hatchet job on the FBI—at the cost of making himself appear grossly uninformed in a field in which he worked for ten years.

It was when we began to ponder this fact that we decided to look further into the story of his relationship to the Bureau; and we found the relevant documents to be available at the United States District Court, where his case is identified as Civil Action #3160-62—*Turner vs. Kennedy*, et al. In addition to copies of such evidential items as Turner's letters to Congressmen, the docket contains three key documents—which can be found, also, at the Court of Appeals:

I. "Appellant's Brief" signed by Attorney Vincent J. Fuller, for the appellant (Turner), and filed with the Board of Appeals and Review of the Civil Service Commission.

II. Brief of the FBI filed with the Board of Appeals and Review of the U.S. Civil Service Commission in rebuttal of "Appellant's Brief." FBI Brief signed by J. P. Mohr, Assistant to the Director.

III. U.S. Civil Service Commission, Appeals and Examining Board, decision of December 20, 1961, upholding the FBI dismissal of William W. Turner.

We have added the numbers above, so that we can use them, in the following account, to identify the source of quotations.

In October 1960, Turner was transferred from Seattle to Oklahoma City, where Special Agent in Charge (SAC) Grapp had asked for an expert in sound-equipment. Turner qualified and was in line for transfer.

"A cornerstone of the FBI's personnel policy is the requirement that Special Agents be available for assignment anywhere their services are needed . . . . If Mr. Turner had any reservations about the transfer, he did not make them a matter of official record prior to his reporting to his new office of assignment" (II).

Once there, however, he made his dislike of Oklahoma and his contempt for "Okies" so obtrusive that SAC Grapp had to explain that his attitude made it hard to use him for certain interviews. Turner continued to "scowl" and "pout," stating that he just did not like that rural area, preferring a large city office with more night life. He would do his work but would not pretend to like Oklahoma (II). He told other agents that his assignment "might have been made in error": that Oklahoma was not a city of his "preference" (I).

When he was put on a four-county road-assignment, he protested that it interfered with his sound-work and cast doubt upon the honesty of the reason given for his transfer. Yet his predecessor had handled both jobs. In the smaller field offices, such double assignments are a necessary commonplace.

In a memo which he asked SAC Grapp to forward to Washington, he said that if he was not to have any supervisory work, he wanted to request transfer to an office where he could have it: "I am primarily interested in and qualified for administrative advancement . . ."(II). Grapp did not feel that Turner had made himself familiar enough with the territory to qualify for the role of Saturday supervisor; and that his uncooperative attitude disqualified him for regular supervisory work. Washington headquarters rated Turner's memo, in view of his attitude, as "incongruous, bordering on insolence." But Turner decided to submit through Grapp a request for transfer.

Grapp told him that when it went to Washington, it would have to be accompanied by a "special performance rating"—which would report his work as satisfactory, but his attitude as deficient. When the rating was shown to Turner, he "requested four changes which were made exactly as he requested." He initialed the final draft; and both SAC Grapp and Assistant SAC Onsgard testified that he seemed to accept it as accurate (II). When his request led, however, not to his being transferred to a metropolitan office, but to his being put on probation, he launched a retroactive campaign against the rating.

So tenacious was this campaign that Chief Inspector Roy K. Moore was sent down to conduct an inquiry. His findings revealed a determined effort by Turner to discredit Grapp—by means of hearsay evidence, statements allegedly made by persons whose names he could not "recall," statements attributed to persons who flatly denied having made them, and charges that collapsed under scrutiny.

Washington headquarters concurred in these findings. On February 3, 1961, Turner was advised "that he was being censured, continued on probation and suspended without pay for 30 days" because of his "inexcusable judgment" in making charges against Grapp that he could not substantiate (II).

It was at this point that Turner began writing letters appealing for redress of grievances: to Senator Javits, on April 3, 1961; to Senator Kefauver, on April 30th; to Congressman Celler, on May 21st; and to Attorney General Kennedy, on May 24th. His father, a Buffalo business man, wrote on his behalf to Senators Keating, Javits, Jackson, and Magnuson.

The FBI contested neither "Mr. Turner's right to petition for redress of grievances, nor his right to include in such petition language objectively critical of appellant's supervisors and the FBI's employment practices." It did not contend that a petition, to be valid, must be accurate in every detail.

It did contend that neither Turner's constitutional right of petition nor his statutory right cloaked him "with immunity for the use in his petition of language unnecessarily defamatory of both his supervisors and the employing Agency, or for the making of charges so widely at variance with the facts as to indicate a malicious desire to destroy the target of attack rather than to conscientiously state a reasonable petition for redress of grievances" (II).

Turner contended that appeals for redress of grievances enjoy unlimited privilege and cannot be used as evidence against the sender, whether their contents be true or false; and, further, that certain of the statements which the FBI designated as *false* were *expressions of opinion*, and were thus protected by the First Amendment. He held that what was in his letters to Congressmen "was none of the Bureau's business" (I, III).

On KPFA (transcript, p. 3), Turner said that two of the four charges brought against him by the FBI were *thrown out* by the Civil Service Commission. This should not be taken to mean that it found them lacking in substance.

It set aside number two on the ground that it was not presented as a charge, but as the FBI's "narration" to Turner "of a past record." In it, the Bureau explained to Turner that, almost from the start, his record had been marred by his tendency to reject "administrative decisions" that did not fit his "preferences"; and that this trait had gradually developed to a point where it had become a "disruptive influence."

Charge number four stated that Turner had, in his letters to Senators Javits and Kefauver, made "unauthorized disclosures" about a security investigation. The Commission indicated that such a matter lay outside its province: that a "separation action" based on a national security charge would have to be instituted "under Public Law 773" (III).

The Commission's final holding in favor of the FBI was based on items in number one relating to the falsity or irresponsibility of statements in the letters; and in number three relating to manifestations of disloyalty and hostility that could only militate against good employer-employee relations. A bare sampling will have to indicate the types of statement that became matters of issue.

In his letter to Senator Kefauver, Turner said that morale in the Bureau was "at an all-time low"—because agents knew that any "untoward incidents" that embarrassed the FBI would be held against them even if they were victims of circumstance. For the purpose of judging them

there is assembled in Washington headquarters the greatest army of Monday morning quarterbacks in the world. Their presence there has been gained by complacency and blind adherence to a set of rules and regulations, not by forthright dedication to the solution of the tasks at hand. The past few years has seen an increasing difficulty in recruiting qualified agents. The reason is obvious, competent men refuse to work under these conditions. New agent training classes have been constantly postponed for lack of applicants and the qualifications have been so lowered that clerks are now filling these classes. Many new agents quit their first few days in a field office.

The Civil Service Commission, in its ruling, noted that the FBI had introduced statistics that refuted the appellant's statements about the number of applicants and the extent of the turnover. It had also introduced evidence to show that the "clerks" whom Turner disparaged were former clerks who had wanted badly enough to become agents that they had qualified themselves for training. At the Commission's hearing, Turner said that he "had no reason to believe the persons formerly employed as clerks did not possess the required qualifications to become agents" (III).

At this hearing, Turner also said that he based his statement that qualifications had been "lowered" on the fact that the Bureau, which formerly accepted only applicants trained in law or accountancy, was now accepting "science graduates, language students and persons with Theological degrees." The FBI indicated that the standards had been broadened, not lowered, because it found itself needing a greater diversity of experts.

Turner wrote Congressman Celler that SAC Grapp's "own enthusiasm" for his work was shown by the fact that "he was not in his office on time once during the month of December 1960 which speaks for itself." FBI records showed that

Grapp had, because of urgent family problems, used up part of his unused annual leave by taking off certain morning hours on 14 days in December 1960; and that on all other working days of the month, "he was on duty at or before the starting hour." He had ended the year with some of his leave still unused. Turner told the Civil Service Commission that he had based his statement on hearsay (II, III).

The Commission made note of Turner's contention that the letters were "none of the Bureau's business" and that "as a matter of law" he was immune to any action based on their contents; and it gave its own "short answer": namely that "tenure in government employment is not a right of person or property protected by the Constitution." Further, it cited *Keystone v. Anderson*, 1956, to the effect that "the right to file a grievance does not carry with it the right to make false statements."

It weighed the FBI's statement that Turner was suspended because it considered his "retention on duty contrary to the best interests of the United States"; and it decided that there was "a reasonable basis" for this decision—in view of "the powers and duties of a Federal Bureau of Investigation agent and the fact that he must be available as a credible witness . . . ."

Finally, it stated its conclusion:

In the light of all the evidence and the foregoing analysis, we find that the personnel action of the Federal Bureau of Investigation in effecting the removal of Mr. Turner was warranted and was for such cause as will promote the efficiency of the service as prescribed by Section 14 of the Veterans' Preference Act of 1944, as amended, and that such action was not arbitrary, unreasonable, or capricious (III).

On May 10, 1963, The United States District Court upheld this judgment. On April 2, 1964, the Federal Court of Appeals did likewise. On November 14, 1964, the Supreme Court closed the case by declining to rehear it.

The most astonishing aspect of all this is the limited character of Turner's effort to defend as true, or to support with evidence, the statements by means of which he had sought to discredit Hoover, SAC Grapp, and the FBI. His basic claim was that of *immunity* to any action based on these statements.

To return from an encounter with this fact to the *Saga* and *Nation* articles is to realize why they fall so disappointingly below the level of what a man of Turner's experience could be expected to produce. They are less like serious efforts to discuss federal law enforcement than like a continuance in public print of the campaign he launched against Mr. Hoover and the Bureau in his letters to Senators Javits, Kefauver, and Congressman Celler.

For what he thus puts into public print, in these articles and others that have appeared more recently, he can, in practical terms, enjoy the immunity which he sought in vain to establish in the eyes of the Civil Service Commission and the federal courts. But likewise we can claim the right to suspect that much of what these articles ask us to believe is on a par with his statements that training classes were filled with "clerks" and that SAC Grapp "was not in the office on time once during the month of December 1960 which speaks for itself."

NINETEEN

THE EXPLOITATIVE ADULATORS

T HE FARTHEST-OUT sector of the Far Right breeds anti-FBI propaganda no less virulent than that of the Communist Left. Imperial Wizard Robert Shelton of the United Klans of America accuses Bureau agents of employing " 'police-state' tactics."[1] And the terms "political police" and "secret police" are applied to the FBI by the National States Rights Party precisely as they are by the CPUSA.

Thus, a headline in the April 1964 *Thunderbolt*, organ of the NSRP, screamed in oversized type: "FBI CONSPIRACY TO FRAME JACKSONVILLE WHITES—ACCUSE FBI OF TERROR TACTICS!" Had this read, "FBI CONSPIRACY TO FRAME JACKSONVILLE NEGROES...," it would have fitted neatly into the CPUSA's *Worker* or the Trotskyite *Worker's World*.

The most common stimulus to such outpourings is the Bureau's enforcement of the civil rights acts. The November 1967 *Thunderbolt*, for example, really let itself go on the

[1] *Atlanta Constitution*, September 3, 1965.

subject of the conviction of seven of the defendants charged with the 1964 murder of the three civil rights workers near Philadelphia, Mississippi. Its article was headed "F.B.I. FRAME UP IN MISSISSIPPI"; and three Bureau informants who testified at the trial were labeled as "lying paid pimps!"

The authority cited to the effect that "FBI agents are trained to lie—so are their pimps!" was Norman Ollestad, whose *Inside the FBI* has been hailed also by the Far Left. It is advertised as the book "that may force J. Edgar Hoover to retire!" And it is credited by *Ramparts* with providing "a profound analytical look at the Man and the Myth."

Like Jack Levine, Ollestad is a "disillusioned" ex-agent. He, too, we are assured, went into the FBI as a young idealist who saw it as "an awe-inspiring organization made up of men of purity, virtue and courage" and who wanted only "to dedicate his life to fighting crime and subversion." His "sad disillusionment" began on his first day of training; and it eventually led him to resign—and write an exposé.

To return to *The Thunderbolt*, Bureau agents and informants made up only a small part of its gallery of villains. It declared that whenever John Doar, head of Justice's Civil Rights Division, "is sent to take over a case, one can be assured that a frame up is in the works." The jury which convicted the Klansmen "was loaded with the Chamber of Commerce element"; and its foreman was a member of the state's industrial commission:

A man like that would always be against people who fight to maintain our traditions and heritages from being destroyed by enemies in New York City.

The civil rights issue is not the only one that has inspired the National States Rights Party to denounce the FBI. Its June–July 1961 *American National Bookstore News* carried an article headed "FIRST FULL-DRESS EMERGENCE

OF TURNCOAT J. EDGAR HOOVER"; and here the stimulus was Hoover's having given Chief Inspector William
C. Sullivan—now Assistant Director and Head of the Domestic Intelligence Division—the task of making various
speeches to pinpoint as invalid charges about massive Communist influence over the churches of America.

"Since the late 1940's," said Sullivan, "Communist influence within the churches and among the clergy has
waned . . ." It could be stated "without equivocation" that
any charge to the effect that "there has been and is, on a
national scale, an extensive and substantial infiltration of the
American clergy" is false.[2]

This Sullivan thesis, said an NSRP spokesman called "The
Trumpeter," is " 'straight up the alley' for the Communist
Party U.S.A.—as it is for THE NATIONAL AND WORLD
COUNCIL OF CHURCHES—Communist-led and Commu-
nist-saturated . . . .

"It just goes to prove that even J. EDGAR HOOVER,
Director of the Federal Bureau of Investigation—CAN BE
BOUGHT—and WAS BOUGHT!"

We are less interested here, however, in this most extreme
sector of the Far Right than in that which fills the wide gap
between it and the outer edge of responsible conservatism.
To an undefinable extent this broad sector—which holds
such groups as the John Birch Society and Christian Crusade—merges with that which it touches on either side.

This sector's listings of what it is against show a considerable overlap with those of the more extreme sector. But
it does not openly proclaim itself to be anti-Semitic; and
whereas the NSRP is made up almost wholly of poor, unedu-
cated whites, a group like the John Birch Society seeks to
identify itself with money, "scholarship," and respectability.
Symbolic of this difference is the fact that, far from criti-

[2] Chief Inspector William C. Sullivan, *Communism and Religion in the
United States* (FBI, Washington, D.C.), pp. 18–19.

cizing Hoover, groups of the Birch Society type praise and quote him to the point of tedium. This fact might seem to validate the Far Left's contention that the Director is an "extreme reactionary." But when we study the pattern of their fulsome praise, we realize that these adulators of the Right are no more just to Hoover than they are to liberals and conservatives whom they call Comsymps or Communist agents. They are simply unjust to him in a different way.

They have everything to gain by making their anti-Communism seem to be cut from the same cloth as his. Thus, they quote . . . and quote . . . and quote. But when the chips are down, they seem chiefly to be latching on to the FBI Director's prestige.

These Rightists were, for example, as jolted as was "The Trumpeter" by Chief Inspector Sullivan's speeches. But while it was obvious that Sullivan had not decided on his own to go out over the country and make these speeches, and while this fact was underscored by his being promoted to the rank of Assistant Director in the midst of the furor which the speeches created, the Rightists sought ways to exempt Hoover from responsibility.

The Church League of America, of which Edgar C. Bundy is Executive Secretary, tried unconvincingly to dissociate Hoover from the whole issue and to make Sullivan appear to be contradicting the Director. It did so by issuing to its members a special *Report* in which it contrasted a statement made by Hoover *in 1948* with what Sullivan said *in 1961*—ignoring the latter's assertion that Communist influence within the churches had waned since the late 1940's.

Carl McIntire did not question Sullivan's having spoken with the Director's consent; but in the *Christian Beacon* of May 21, 1961, he undertook to explain away this consent. His theory was that the Kennedy Administration, urged on by the National Council of Churches, had put heavy pressure upon Hoover to have the speeches made.

Robert Welch, blandly ignoring the furor, continued to retail the Far Right's time-worn estimate that three percent of the Protestant ministers in this country are *Comsymps*. Converted into figures, this would come to 7,931 individuals, since there are, according to the National Council of Churches, 264,373 Protestant ministers. By his own account, he used this percentage, which he called "no wild surmise," in twenty-seven speeches between April and October 1961.[3]

The fact that the Rightists' quoting of Hoover is more of a ritual than an effort to make his viewpoints known is evidenced by their matching policy of not quoting him. His unpalatable statements are smothered in the cotton wool of silence—and are thus turned into "un-statements."

Hoover told the Warren Commission, "I think the extreme right is just as much a danger to this country as is the extreme left." Going beyond generalities, he spoke of those who make "disparaging references to the Chief Justice" and who "allege that General Eisenhower was a Communist agent . . . ."[4]

This could only be "memory-hole" material. For the Birchers to have taken issue with it would have meant their taking issue with the FBI Director. For them to have referred to it and not taken issue with it would have meant their leaving undefended both Robert Welch and their "Impeach Earl Warren" campaign. But why speak of it at all? It was hidden away in a 24-volume set of *Hearings* which Birch Society members had been warned to discount as "liberal," and therefore untrustworthy.

Again, Hoover told the Commission, "I have been unable to find any scintilla of evidence showing any foreign conspiracy or any domestic conspiracy that culminated in the assassination of President Kennedy."[5]

[3] Letter from Robert Welch to Monsignor Francis J. Lally; *The Pilot*, Boston, Massachusetts, October 21, 1961.

[4] *Hearings Before the President's Commission on the Assassination of President Kennedy*, Vol. V, P. 101.

[5] *op. cit.*, pp. 98–99.

But Far Right dogma requires the assassination to have been the result of a Communist plot directed by persons within our own Government. Thus, we have here an almost perfect test case by which to determine how much weight these Rightists give to Hoover's words when they go counter to their own line; and how ready they are to give him a hearing in the court of public opinion even when they disagree with him.

The September 1965 issue of the John Birch Society's *American Opinion* has in it an article by Martin Dies called "Warren Report: *The Strange Conclusions*." Dies says that he recognized from the start that the Commission would be unlikely to publish facts and "logical deductions" that would "darkly reflect upon the attitude of 'Liberals' toward the International Communist Conspiracy."

He does not claim to have had any intimate access to evidence in the case at issue. He claims a generalized capacity to set forth the facts by reason of what he learned about Communism as Chairman of the Dies Committee—some twenty years earlier.

Bypassing Hoover's testimony, he takes Secretary of State Rusk to task for having expressed doubt that the USSR wanted President Kennedy removed. He mentions the FBI only to say that "an honest examination" of its files would reveal many unsolved assassinations by Communist agents in the United States. He does not say how he knows what the files contain.

Billy James Hargis, founder-director of Christian Crusade, declares in *The Far Left*—with what seems like bated breath—that on "November 16, 1963, just one week before the assassination of President Kennedy, J. Edgar Hoover, head of the Federal Bureau of Investigation, identified these satanic forces at work in America as 'hate mongers.' "[6]

Such respectful quoting would seem to suggest that Hargis would be quick to give weight to the Director's testi-

---

[6] Billy James Hargis, *The Far Left* (Tulsa, Oklahoma, Christian Crusade, 1964), p. 17.

mony. But we find no evidence of his having done so. He has held fast to the Far Right's conspiracy thesis and has provided a platform for those who do likewise. A featured speaker at his Crusade's Anti-Communist Leadership School, in Miami, Florida, January 18–20, 1965, was Samuel Blumenthal—who has, on one platform after another, called the assassination a "deliberately planned act of the Communist conspiracy."

Just as Feldman, in *The Nation,* charged the FBI with doing a cover-up job to hide its use of Oswald as an informant, so Blumenthal charged the Warren Commission with doing a cover-up job to protect Communist conspirators within the Government. Hargis' respect for Hoover seems not to have moved him to inform the audience of the Director's different view.

Only highly selective quoting and non-quoting can make Hoover's anti-Communism and that of the Far Right appear to be cut from the same cloth; for they are not. Hoover's expresses his commitment to liberty under law. That of the Far Right expresses itself in a determination to downgrade any person or policy that cannot be made to support the Rightist line.

The November–December 1963 issue of Kent and Phoebe Courtney's *Independent American* had four boxed quotations from Hoover, each a general dictum about the aggressive tenacity of international Communism. Under the longest, on p. 1, was an article called *A National Police Force?* Since Hoover often warns against letting such a force develop, our first thought was that the Courtneys were reporting some statement of his. But not at all: what they said, he would never conceivably say:

"If the Liberals and pro-Communists in this country ever succeed in registering or taking away our guns, it will be the end of a free United States." Also: "The registration of guns owned by individuals is one of the goals of the International

Communist conspiracy"—the aims of which are "revealed" in gun-control bills pending in Congress.

On January 29, 1964—some two months after this article appeared—Hoover was asked at an appropriation hearing to give his views on these same bills. In his opinion, he said, one bill had "excellent provisions" but might be too narrow: it would not cover the type of rifle "which came into this country from Italy and was later used to kill President Kennedy."

He did not think that a properly worded gun-control law would be unconstitutional—in spite of the constant presence of a lobby to call it so. "I have felt for many years that there should be some statute enacted by Congress, with some steps taken to have the enactment of State laws to supplement and buttress it, that would restrict the obtaining of guns without some type of ownership registration."

He would not want us to place all our reliance on a federal statute; for such a statute would be almost unenforceable without local and state support. Besides, good state laws had proved their effectiveness, and should be strengthened:

The percentage of murder in Dallas during 1963 by the use of a gun was 72%. In New York City during the same period a gun was utilized in 25% of the willful killings . . . . New York has rather strict laws concerning firearms . . . .[7]

Significantly, during this extended discussion of gun-control problems, Hoover did not mention Communism. He is accused of being obsessed with the subject. But one thing that distinguishes his approach from that of the Far Right is that he neither drags in "the Communist menace" with irrelevant abandon nor blames all our ills on the "International Communist Conspiracy."

At another point in this hearing, he reported on current

[7] *FBI 1965 Appropriation*, pp. 60-61.

Communist activities—in specific detail. He ticked off the domestic issues that had been singled out by the CPUSA for exploitation, discussed the Party's finances and membership, explained the character of some of its recent campaigns, and listed the main publications used as outlets for the Party line.

It is by their approach to the civil rights movement, however, that the Rightists most clearly reveal their capacity to exploit Hoover's words and ignore his overall viewpoint. An article in the February 1964 issue of *American Opinion* and a brochure put out by the Birch Society front called *TACT* (*Truth About Civil Turmoil*) well illustrate their methods.

The article, "Communist Betrayal of a Good Cause," is by John Rousselot. He quotes Hoover as having said, "The Communist Party's objectives are not to aid the negroes—but are designed to take advantage of all controversial issues on the race question so as to create unrest, dissention, and confusion in the minds of the American people."

This sentence from the *FBI 1959 Appropriation,* p. 29, is correctly quoted except that in the original *negroes* is capitalized. It can be taken as both a statement of fact and a warning to the unwary. But Rousselot uses it to bolster a thesis which Hoover has explicitly rejected: namely, that all the major organized groups "in the 'civil rights' fight" are Communist-dominated; and that federal legislation in the civil rights field is a "ruse" to extend federal power.

Rousselot says that the "*decisive leadership*"—that which can "call the shots"—in the NAACP, as in other Negro groups, is "beyond reasonable doubt" pro-Communist. Hoover says:

Let me emphasize that the American civil rights movement is not, and has *never* been, dominated by the Communists—because the overwhelming majority of civil rights leaders in this country, both Negro and white, have recognized and rejected communism as a menace to the freedom of all.[8]

The FBI's Domestic Intelligence Division keeps track of both the CPUSA's current activities in relation to civil rights matters and its plans for the future. Hoover summarizes such data at his annual appropriation hearing. He did so, for example, on February 16, 1967, and made note of a significant change in the CPUSA's policy and program—one which reflects its belief that Negro unrest is now expressing itself in ways that give the Party a new chance to extend its influence.

Hoover reported that at the CPUSA's 18th National Convention, held in New York City in June 1966,

Claude Lightfoot, the party's vice-chairman, presented the resolution on the Negro question . . . calling for the broadest linking of the civil rights struggle with the struggle for peace. He emphasized that the Communist Party must be known as the 'best fighter' for Negro rights in the United States.

Although the Communist Party has always been active in the field of civil rights, it has done very little in its own name. Based on the action taken at the convention, the keynote now is that the party will boldly step forward and lead its own movement for civil rights as well as infiltrating into all civil rights struggles and joining with more militant elements.

He again stressed that "legitimate civil rights organizations" have, for the most part, warded off the Communists' efforts to penetrate them, but expressed concern about the current readiness of some groups to accept Communist members—and advice.[9]

It is out of such factual reports that the Communist and

[8] J. Edgar Hoover, "Our Heritage of Greatness"; Remarks Before the Pennsylvania Society and the Society of Pennsylvania Women, New York, December 12, 1964, p. 7. FBI, Washington, D.C.

[9] *FBI 1968 Appropriation*, p. 57.

non-Communist Left manufacture "proof" that Hoover is a "racist" and is "obsessed" with Communism. And out of such reports the Far Right extracts "useful" fragments to which it can attach its own implications.

The *TACT* brochure asserts, "Tact agrees with Hoover"—and quotes him as saying, " 'I am greatly concerned that certain racial leaders are doing the civil rights movement a grave disservice by suggesting that citizens need obey only those laws with which they agree.' " But Hoover would not agree with *TACT*—for it ties onto his statement the thesis that the whole organized civil rights movement is a "fraud."

At the hearing on the FBI's 1968 budget, Congressman Mark Andrews of North Dakota brought up the subject of a *Newsweek* article which had said that the John Birch Society

"plans to expand its nationwide campaign to link the civil-rights movement and communism. The society already is supporting some 454 local TACT (Truth About Civil Turmoil) committees, which use booklets, films and public speakers (usually billed as ex-FBI undercover agents) to spread the word . . . ."

This, said the Congressman, "looks more or less like a deliberate attempt on the part of an extremist organization to capitalize on the high regard in which the FBI is held."

Hoover called it "an improper attempt to capitalize on the name of the FBI" and said that he in no way condoned "the use of the name 'ex-FBI undercover agent' in such endeavors."

"I am very glad to make that clear for the record," Congressman Andrews replied.[10]

Of all the examples we have seen of Far Right exploitation of the Director's prestige, the most bald-faced is on p.

[10] *op. cit.*, p. 101.

14 of a 16-page "Advertising Supplement" called *The John Birch Society: A Report*. This elaborate, patently expensive publication—distinguishable from a regular Sunday supplement only by a small-type notice that it was an advertisement—came from the *San Francisco Examiner and Chronicle* of October 7, 1964.

Its introductory distribution had been in September, with the *Los Angeles Times* and the *Los Angeles Herald-Examiner*; and it seems, altogether, to have gone out with key papers in sixteen cities. By November 1965, according to the *John Birch Society Bulletin* of that month, newspapers with a total circulation of more than 7,000,000 had been vehicles through which it had reached the public; and the Society itself had distributed half a million copies from its headquarters.

At the top of p. 14, we read in boldface type: "NATIONAL LEADERS SAY." Photographs of five men, each accompanied by a quotation, fill the rest of the space. In the order presented, they are J. Edgar Hoover, Ezra Taft Benson, Strom Thurmond, Reverend J. L. Ward, and W. Cleon Skousen.

Nothing that readily meets the eye of a person turning the pages puts Hoover in a different category from the others. The visual implication is that the five national leaders are all addressing themselves to a common theme; and the subject of Communism does, indeed, figure in each quotation. All the statements except Hoover's, however, are, from one or another angle, about the John Birch Society. His is not.

Benson and Ward warmly endorse the Society. Thurmond says that he does not belong but is "for" any group that is against Communism. Skousen deplores the Society's being "dishonestly ridiculed and smeared at the instigation of the International Communist Conspiracy." Hoover's statement, which has to do with our need to understand "Red Fascism," is from a 1947 hearing of the House Committee on Un-American Activities.

PART FOUR

UNFINISHED BUSINESS

TWENTY

ONE FEDERAL SUIT

"THIS IS AN action of the Nation against a klan." Thus, Circuit Judge John Minor Wisdom began the reading of an *Opinion* handed down, on December 1, 1965, by a three-judge Federal Court panel. An appended note said, "Although this order is cast in the form of an opinion, it represents the Court's findings of fact and conclusions of law."

The action was a civil suit which Justice had filed, on July 19, 1965, in the United States District Court for the Eastern District of Louisiana, New Orleans Division. The defendants were the Original Knights of the Ku Klux Klan, the Anti-Communist Christian Association, and thirty-eight named individuals who resided in and around Bogalusa, Louisiana.

The suit was a response to months of Klan-inspired terrorism in that area. It sought from the court an injunction to prevent the designated organizations and individuals from interfering with persons who sought to exercise rights guaranteed to them under the Constitution.

"In deciding to grant the injunction prayed for," Judge Wisdom stated, "we rest our conclusions on the finding of fact that, within the meaning of the Civil Rights Acts of 1957 and 1964, the defendants have adopted a pattern and practice of intimidating, threatening, and coercing Negro citizens of Washington Parish for the purpose of interfering with [their] civil rights . . . . The compulsion within the klan to engage in this unlawful conduct is inherent in the nature of the klan. It is its ineradicable evil."[1]

Only a "broad decree," the panel declared, could afford protection against the Klan-fostered terror that had raged almost unchecked throughout Washington Parish. On December 22nd, the court handed down an injunction deemed to have the requisite coverage; but it also retained "jurisdiction of this cause to grant such additional relief as may be required . . . ."[2]

The court enjoined the defendants, "their agents, employees, officers, members, successors, and all those in active consort or participation with them" from assaulting, otherwise injuring, or terrorizing any of four categories of persons: Negroes who sought to exercise their constitutional rights; public officials and employees who sought to accord Negroes "equal treatment in the use of public facilities"; businessmen who sought to employ Negroes on an equal basis or to accord them equal treatment in the "use and enjoyment" of restaurants, theaters, and places of public accommodation; and persons who participated in legal and orderly picketing or other civil rights demonstration.

Further, the injunction ordered the defendant bodies and their "unit or group heads" to maintain membership records

[1] Civil Action No. 15793, in the U.S. District Court of the Eastern District of Louisiana, New Orleans Division. *Opinion of Circuit Court Judge John Minor Wisdom and District Judges Herbert W. Christenberry and Robert A. Ainsworth*, p. 2. Dec. 1, 1965.

[2] Preliminary Injunction; United States of America, *Plaintiff, vs. Original Knights of the Ku Klux Klan*, et al. Civil Action No. 15793, December 22, 1965.

"during the pendency of this action"; and to post "at all meeting places . . . a copy of this Court's decree." Since the order covered all persons "in active concert or participation" with the defendants, the injunction carried a list of some two hundred "non-defendants for whom proof as to Klan-ACCA membership is in evidence."

The Federal Government's right to "pray for" an injunction of this type is one of the most constructive and least remarked products of the passage of the series of Civil Rights Acts which began with that of 1957. Obviously, no court injunction could end racial tensions in the Bogalusa area—or in any area. But it provides, nonetheless, one sort of answer to those who say that changes of mind and custom cannot be legislated into existence.

What the above injunction has done has been to help redress the balance of power between rational and irrational forces in Washington Parish. Forces of both types are present in every community. But where clandestine, brutal irrationality has achieved a strength that no individual can challenge without inviting disaster, men of good will, and of plain good sense, have the cards stacked against them. What the court's ruling has done has been to give good will and good sense a fresh chance to be heard in the court of public opinion.

Furthermore, *custom* is what people are accustomed to. In Washington Parish—as in a host of other places, North and South—white people were wholly unaccustomed to having Negroes accorded "the equal use and enjoyment of public facilities" and "public accommodations." They were wholly unaccustomed to seeing them working with whites on an equal basis or lined up with whites at polling places, waiting to cast their votes.

We can assume that, by and large, they are still unaccustomed to all these things; and that many are determined to remain so. Yet the injunction, by helping to insure the

Negro's right to enter new situations without overt harassment, has initiated at least a small change in that to which people are accustomed—which is to say, a change in local customs.

Also, the Court stripped away, very decisively, the trappings of secrecy and pseudo-respectability behind which the Klan had been wont to operate. "Seeking refuge in silence and secrecy," said the *Opinion*, "the defendants objected to the admission of any evidence as to klan activities. We hold, however, that what the klan is and what the klan does bear significantly on the material issues and on the appropriate relief." The court proceeded, therefore, to catalogue the types of "violence and crime [that] follow as the night the day when masked men conspire against society itself."

The court's "findings of fact" were based on an extraordinarily solid body of evidence presented by the Justice Department; and this evidence was, in turn, the product of a long, patient, thorough FBI investigation. It was the FBI that had, in the first instance, to amass proof of what had been happening throughout Washington Parish: proof that would stand up under any type of cross-examination and that would establish beyond reasonable doubt the fact that the Klan had violated specific prohibitions set forth in one or more of the Federal Civil Rights Acts.

It was the FBI that had had to locate—within an atmosphere charged with terror—persons who could and would testify with respect to Klan harassment and violence. It had had to check and double-check all stories, including those of its own undercover agents, to protect the Justice Department against being in the predicament of calling witnesses whose testimony could be broken down by defense attorneys.

Still further, working with the Civil Rights Division of the department, it had had to try to anticipate every maneuver to which the defense might resort and to assemble, then, types of evidence by which each such maneuver could be blocked.

The FBI performs such tasks, of course, in every case where the Government challenges the Klan; and, more broadly, in every civil rights case. On March 28, 1966, for example, thirteen members of the White Knights of the Ku Klux Klan of Mississippi were arrested by the FBI in connection with the death of Vernon Dahmer, a Negro civil rights worker who lived near Hattiesburg. Dahmer had suffered fatal burns and smoke inhalation when attackers had forced him by gunfire to stay in his house after they had set it ablaze. A fourteenth man, Sam Holloway Bowers, Jr., imperial wizard of the White Knights, was arrested later.

In announcing the arrests, Attorney General Katzenbach said that, "as in past civil rights cases," the taking of suspects into custody culminated "thousands of hours of exceptional and painstaking investigative effort by the FBI."[3]

The Bogalusa case was remarkably informative, however, because the Justice Department was bringing a civil suit and "praying for" an injunction rather than a criminal indictment, so that the range of admissible evidence was unusually broad. In a criminal suit, each defendant is accused of having committed or been accessory to a specified illegal act. The question at issue is whether or not he is guilty as charged. The only evidence the prosecution can relevantly introduce is that which bears upon this question.

In this civil suit, however, what had to be established beyond reasonable doubt was not only that the defendants had engaged in a long campaign of terrorism but also that they would, if not stopped by a federal injunction, project this campaign into the future. Their past actions, in brief, had to be established as *characteristic expressions* of "what the klan is and what the klan does."

In assembling evidence on this point, the Bureau had the advantage of a vast store of accumulated knowledge. It had

[3] *Washington Evening Star*, March 28, 1966, pp. A-1, A-6.

been investigating and infiltrating the Klan since the mid-1920's. Hence, it had far more data about the secret body than Justice could ever use in a criminal case. In this suit, where both specific past actions and the basic nature of the Klan were at issue, the department could draw upon the FBI's full store of information.

The course which the defense adopted at the Court hearing was a tribute to the thoroughness with which the Government's case was prepared. The defendants did not try to prove themselves innocent. They concentrated on a series of maneuvers to keep the full body of evidence against them and against the Klan from being introduced in court.

They succeeded and they failed. They were able to keep a host of witnesses off the stand—by admitting what these witnesses would have been called upon to prove. But they were not able to keep basic facts out of that durably public document, the judges' *Opinion*, which was read in court.

In the *Opinion*, p. 7, we read,

An unusual feature of this litigation is the defendants' damning admissions. The defendants *admit* that the klan's objective is to prevent Washington Parish Negroes from exercising the civil rights Congress recognized by statute. In their pleadings, the defendants concede that they furthered their objectives by—

(a) assaulting, threatening, and harassing Negroes who seek to exercise any of their civil rights, and assaulting, threatening and harassing persons who urge that Negroes should exercise or be accorded these rights;

(b) committing, threatening to commit, and urging others to commit acts of economic retaliation against Negroes who seek to exercise these rights, and against any persons who urge that Negroes should exercise or be accorded these rights, or who permit open, free and public discussion of the issue;

(c) threatening and intimidating public officials and businessmen who accord or seek to accord Negroes their rights without regard to race or color.

The reason for the admissions was evident at the trial and is evident in the defendants' brief. The United States subpoenaed over a hundred witnesses and, no doubt, was prepared to prove every allegation in the complaint. Because of the defendants' admissions, the disputed issues were few and only a few witnesses were called. As a result, the klan avoided an airing of its activities that necessarily would have occurred had a large number of witnesses testified.

Thus, the defendants achieved a limited success at the cost of putting on record the types of activities in which they had engaged in order to make the law of the land inoperable in Washington Parish. In order to keep off the stand witnesses who could report the horrible specifics of their conduct, they made generalized "damning admissions."

In so doing, they took a chance that they could escape the logical consequences by squeezing the Federal Government out of the case. The Attorney General, they contended, could not, under the terms of the civil rights acts, sue for an injunction against "a private organization and private persons." Here, they failed: "There is no merit in this contention," the panel concluded.

As a further maneuver, "the defendants objected to the introduction of 'any evidence pertaining to the activities of the Ku Klux Klan' on the grounds that (a) the Klan had ceased to exist and (b) 'delv[ing] into these unrelated matters' was solely 'to expose' the Ku Klux Klan, an invasion of the 'privacy and individual freedoms of all these defendants.' "

The *Opinion*, p. 8, gives the judges' response: namely, that "the nature of the klan's activities bears on the existence of a pattern and practice of unlawful conduct and also on the sort of decree that should be issued."

Had the defendant Klan—the Original Knights of the Ku Klux Klan—"ceased to exist"? The FBI had provided Justice with definitive evidence to the contrary. This evidence, the *Opinion* affirms, "clearly establishes that the Anti-Communist Christian Association is not a bona fide, independent organization, but is the defendant klan thinly disguised under a respectable title. At an earlier time, the klan's dummy organization was called the Bogalusa Gun and Rifle Club."

The story goes on: "The Government subpoenaed membership lists and records of the klan. The defendants ... explained that all the records of the klan had been destroyed as a matter of klan policy after suit was filed."

That this maneuver did not, and could not, succeed is made clear by the presence of the list of almost two hundred "non-defendants" attached to the injunction. The FBI's informant system proved to be more than a match for the Klan's policy of destroying its records.

The *Opinion* was drawn up, of course, not just to expose the Klan but to make plain the court's reasons for granting the injunction. The document, which runs to 39 legal sized pages, with six added pages of footnotes, spells out these reasons in explicit detail.

Some of the data given have to do with Klan activities in Washington Parish; others relate more broadly to the nature of the organization. The former appear in a section called "Specific Findings of Klan Intimidation and Violence." (*Opinion* pp. 13ff.). Here, we find eleven diverse examples of such activities.

(1) Former Congressman Brooks Hays of Arkansas was to speak in Bogalusa, on January 7, 1965, "at the invitation of religious, business, and civil leaders." The meeting, to be held in the parish house of St. Matthews Episcopal Church, was to be desegregated. Hays's subject was to be "community relations." The Klan, "by means of threats of civil disorder and economic retaliation against local businessmen who supported the meeting, caused the withdrawal of the invitation to Hays."

Before it was withdrawn, "over 150 hooded Klansmen"

held a meeting, on December 18, 1964, to show their power. Mayor Cutrer of Bogalusa and Police Commissioner Arnold Spiers went to this meeting "in an effort to head off possible civil disorder." The Mayor was later called as a witness by the Government. "On the stand, [he] admitted that he was 'frightened when he looked into 150 pairs of eyes.'"

(2) From at least January 1965 on, various of the defendants "and other members of the defendant Klan" had "made a practice of going to places where they anticipated that Negroes would attempt to exercise civil rights, in order to harass, threaten, and intimidate Negroes and other persons."

(3) "William Yates and Stephen Miller, two CORE workers, came to Bogalusa in January 1965." The Grand Dragon and Grand Titan of the Klan—defendants Charles Christmas and Saxon Farmer—called on the Mayor to ask that he tell the CORE workers to get out of town. The Mayor said that he could not send them away. The Klan took things into its own hands. On February 3rd, three of its members, "with two others persons," followed the CORE men and assaulted Yates.

(4) On February 15, 1965, "defendant Virgil Corkern, Klansman, and approximately 30 other white persons attacked five Negro citizens and damaged the car in which they were riding . . . because the Negroes had sought service at a gasoline station in Bogalusa." On that day, also, Corkern and another person entered a restaurant "brandishing clubs" because Negroes were there seeking service. They ordered the Negroes out and "threatened to kill Sam Barnes, a member of the Bogalusa Voters League, who had come to the restaurant with six Negro women."

(5) On March 29, 1965, two of the defendants "threw an ignited tear gas cannister at a group of Negroes standing near the Labor Temple."

(6) On April 7th, two other defendant Klansmen had "threatened Negro citizens during the course of a meeting at

the Labor Temple by brandishing and exhibiting a gun . . ."

(7) On April 9th, five of the defendant Klansmen "went to the downtown area of Bogalusa where Negro citizens were participating in a march to Bogalusa City Hall to protest denial of equal rights." Three of them, "Pounds, McClendon, and Burke, in a group, moved out to attack the marchers. Pounds assaulted the leader of the March, James Farmer, with a blackjack . . ." McClendon and Burke, having been deterred from making an assault, turned on a newsman and an FBI agent, assaulting them.

(8) On May 9th, "Virgil Corkern, Klansman," two of his sons, and several other persons went to Cassidy Park, where a group of Negroes and white CORE workers were using the facilities of the park "for the first time on a non-segregated basis." The Corkern group "entered the park and dispersed the Negro citizens with clubs, belts, and other weapons."

(9) "Negro members of the Bogalusa Voters League, unable to exercise their civil rights and unable to obtain from police officials adequate protection from the Klan, filed suit June 25, 1965, in the case of *Hicks v. Knight*, Civil Action No. 15,727, in this Court." The complaint asked for an injunction that would insure the plaintiffs and other Negroes adequate protection against " 'physical assaults, beatings, harassment, and intimidation' " when they sought to exercise their rights.

A preliminary injunction was handed down on July 10th. But even with it "in full force and effect," the defendant Klansmen continued to harass Negroes and to interfere with law enforcement officers who tried to enforce the injunction.

(10) On July 11th, "during a Negro march," two of the defendants, H. A. Goings, Jr., and Franklin Harris, "passed out 23–30 2 x 2 clubs to youths"; and a third defendant, Randle Pounds, "stationed the youths along the march route."

(11) "Included in the exhibits are a number of handbills bearing the caption, 'Published by the Original Ku Klux

Klan of Louisiana.' These are crude, scurrilous attacks on certain Bogalusa citizens who advocated a moderate approach to desegregation." Sometimes the attempted intimidation was by threats of violence; sometimes by character assassination.

One handbill said, " 'As the people tried to preserve our Southern way of life, the Mayor and Council were slowly selling the people out at every turn.' " Further on, we read, " 'Here is the list of elected officials who COULD & SHOULD have helped the People of Bogalusa. All these should be tarred and feathered.' " Those named were Mayor Cutrer, Representative Sheridan, Senator Sixty Rayborn, Sheriff Dormer Crowe, Congressman Jimmy Morrison, Governor John McKeithen, and Senator Russell Long. The handbill asks, " 'Why have these men elected by the WHITE people turned their back on us in our time of need?' "

" 'Is Communism so close? Who bought them? Who bought their HONOR and FOR HOW MUCH?' "

Another handbill, issued at the time when Brooks Hays was scheduled to speak, affirmed that the Ku Klux Klan was " 'strongly organized' " in the area; and that it would know who was invited to the Hays meeting and who did and did not go:

" 'Accordingly, we take this means to urge all of you to refrain from attending this meeting. Those who do attend this meeting will be tagged as integrationists and will be dealt with accordingly by the Knights of the KU KLUX KLAN.' "

In a section called "Out of Their Own Mouths," the court's *Opinion*, pp. 9ff, appraises the nature of the defendant Klan by taking stock of what its own documents say. These leave no doubt whatever about its being a secret body that claims the right to take the law into its own hands and to interpret the law and the Constitution to fit its own views and purposes.

" 'The Konstitution of the Original Ku Klux Klan embodies 'The Supreme Law of the Realm.' " Article I states that one object of the organization "is to 'protect and defend the Constitution of the United States' "; but another "is to 'maintain forever Segregation of the races and the Divinely directed and historically proven superiority of the White Race.' " Article II "limits the membership to 'mature, Native-born, White, Gentile Men who profess and practice the Christian Faith but who are not members of the Roman Catholic Church.' "

A Proclamation printed with the Konstitution states that it must be " 'STRICTLY ADHERED TO' " and that " 'ALL REALM work is carried on by a chain of command' " set up along military lines. It also "defines the duties of officers and committees, and describes 'The Way of the Klavern.' "

" 'All Klaverns will have at least five armed guards with flashlights posted during regular meetings.' However, 'No one will be allowed to carry a gun inside the Klavern during regular meetings except the Knight Hawk (Keeper of the Klavern).' "

One of the tasks assigned to an officer called the Klokan is strange, indeed. Each Klan unit is obligated to " 'set up at least one team of six men to be used for wrecking crew' "; and the Klokan must appoint these men " 'in secrecy.' " In the Proclamation, quoted by the court, we read, " 'Any Klansman who is known to violate our rules, especially those that give information to any aliens (non-members) shall be expelled immediately, then is to be watched *and visited by the Wrecking Crew if necessary.*' "

The phrase is italicized in the court's *Opinion*; and the judges note that the defendants were "evasive" about "the purpose and functions of the wrecking crew." An ex-Klansman who appeared as a witness for the Government was clearly afraid of Klan reprisals when he was asked about the "wrecking crew."

The Oath of Allegiance "requires faithful obedience to the

'Klan's Konstitution and Laws,' regulations, 'rulings and instructions of the Grand Dragon.'" And it goes to fantastic lengths to bind the members to " 'keep sacredly secret'" all matters related to the Klan.

Finally, we come to the Klan's "Boycott Rules," which throw a sharp light upon its tactics of intimidation:

"The Boycott Committee (one member from each local unit appointed by the Exalted Cyclops) shall have exclusive investigative authority...
(1) No person or subject upon whom a boycott shall have been placed shall be patronized by any member . . . Boycotts shall be imposed upon subjects who are found to be violating our Southern traditions...
Boycotts shall be placed upon any merchant using Negro employees to serve or wait upon persons of the white race (Service Stations using Negroes to pump gas are excluded.)
Boycotts shall be placed against a subject who serves Negroes and whites on an integrated basis.
Boycotts shall be placed upon a subject who allows Negroes to use White rest rooms...
Any member who shall after a hearing have been found guilty of personally patronizing a subject listed on the boycott list shall be *wrecked by the wrecking crew* who shall be appointed by the Committee (Emphasis added)...
Second offense—If a member is found guilty of personally violating the boycott list he shall be wrecked and banished from the Klan."

After quoting from the Klan's documents, the judges remark in their *Opinion*, "It is not surprising that the attorneys for the United States had difficulty extracting from klansmen answers to questions." Various witnesses showed acute fear.

"It is not surprising . . . ." In view of all that was brought to light by this one civil suit, it is not surprising that the FBI's task of gathering evidence for Justice to use in court against a Klan defendant is one that calls for ingenuity, courage, and interminable patience.

It is not surprising that even witnesses who have professed their willingness to testify are often plunged into a state of panic when, on the stand, they find themselves under Klan scrutiny.

It is not surprising that many jurors, counting the cost of voting for a verdict of *guilty* where Klansmen are on trial, decide—irrespective of what the evidence indicates—to vote for a verdict of *not guilty*.

Yet more and more often, Klansmen find themselves cast in the role of defendants, with the Government of the United States in that of plaintiff. And the Klan itself is put increasingly on the defensive in the court of public opinion.

TWENTY-ONE

FBI vs. KKK

THE KU KLUX KLAN of the Reconstruction era was short-lived. A half dozen young men founded it in Tennessee in 1865, for their own amusement. They met in secret, had elaborate ceremonials, and wore white cloaks with hooded caps that hid all but their eyes. But they soon discovered that their white cloaks, seen at night, frightened the Negroes; and they recognized that they had, in the trappings of their organization, a weapon they could use against the latter.

White Southerners—impoverished, humiliated, and all but disenfranchised—felt the need of a weapon. Klan units multiplied swiftly, with many of the respected people of the region among their members. But the tactics adopted could not for long be kept within bounds. It quickly became standard practice for the Klan to ride at night for the deliberate purpose of striking terror into the ex-slaves and the carpetbaggers.

Within three years, the "Invisible Empire," as it had come

to be called, fell into disrepute. In 1868, its Grand Wizard, General Nathan Bedford Forrest, ordered it to disband and to burn its white cloaks and hoods. Federal action, by Congress and the courts, wrote *finis* to its organized existence.

Brief as it was, the 1865–1868 period was long enough to make apparent the nature of the "ineradicable evil." Men who cloak themselves in secrecy to take the law into their own hands are not likely to practice restraint. As acts of brutality multiplied, the more responsible Klan members dropped away. Those who took their place were ignorant and violent men.

By 1871 the Klan was dead. But its pattern was lodged in our history. In 1915, William S. Simmons of Atlanta, Georgia—preacher, ex-organizer of fraternal orders, and Colonel by courtesy—pulled this pattern out of the past and established the Knights of the Ku Klux Klan. It was anti-Negro, anti-Semitic, anti-Catholic, and xenophobic.

After a slow start, the Klan began, around 1920, to spread like wildfire across both the South and the North. By 1925, it was reputed to have 4,000,000 members. In a host of places, it controlled courthouses, police forces, and elections. In a number of states it could ordain the outcome of any vote.

Obviously, membership on this scale was not built solely out of standard Klan-type human material. In the 1920's, the Klan could draw to itself a multitude of persons for whom a klavern would not seem a natural habitat—because the sharp isolationist reaction after World War I was itself anti-Negro, anti-Semitic, anti-Catholic, and xenophobic.

The vast majority of the members practiced no violence. In many places, the klavern was more like a fraternity than a secret order of terrorists. In yet more, it was forged as a political weapon. Most of the 4,000,000 joined, not to destroy, but to exclude, the dark and different from social groups, residential areas, prestige occupations, public office, and, if possible, the United States.

But *the will to keep out* is too much like *the will to keep down* to exert a moderating influence upon it. The "respectable" majority did not change by one iota the basic character of the Klan. It merely spread the cloak of respectability over Klan-type terrorism—for a time.

In 1921, the Attorney General instructed the Bureau of Investigation to look into Klan activities. In *The FBI Story*, pp. 61–62, Don Whitehead gives a concise account of the first engagement in the Bureau's long war against the KKK.

In September 1922, Paul Wooton, Washington correspondent for the *New Orleans Times-Picayune*, delivered to Assistant Attorney General J. Edgar Hoover a letter from Governor John M. Parker of Louisiana. Wooton explained that he had brought it in person because the Governor dared not convey by regular means an appeal for federal help: " 'His mail is watched by the Klan and his phone is tapped by klansmen.' "

The Attorney General of Louisiana, when Hoover talked with him, confirmed this report; and it was decided that the Governor should appeal directly to President Harding. He did so on October 2, 1922, in a letter that read in part:

Due to activities of an organized body reputed to be the Ku Klux Klan . . . not only have the laws been violated, but men taken out, beaten and whipped. Two men have been brutally murdered without trial or charges . . . These conditions are beyond the control of the Governor of this State . . . a number of law officers and others charged with enforcement of the law in this State are publicly recognized as members of the Ku Klux Klan.

The Governor asked that Justice be instructed to take action under Article IV, Section 4, of the Constitution:

The United States shall guarantee to every State in this union a republican form of government and shall protect each of them against invasion; and, on application of the Legislature, or of the

Executive (when the Legislature cannot be convened), against domestic violence.

Here, the Government could move: the Constitution could not be ruled *unconstitutional*. The Justice Department instructed the Bureau to investigate. As Whitehead reports, "The agents began working under cover, themselves hunted by klansmen at times. But slowly they pieced the story together.

"The Klan controlled the whole of northern Louisiana by terror. The Klan's membership included law enforcement officers and leading townspeople. Persons considered undesirable were ordered out of their communities. Men and women were flogged or jailed on orders of Klan leaders . . . .

"One night, Dr. B. M. McKoin, a klansman and former Mayor of Mer Rouge, reported that his car had been fired on by would-be assassins." Skeptics believed that he had fired the shots himself for his own involved purposes. But klansmen seized two men—Watt Daniels and T. F. Richards—for questioning. Each had an alibi and was released, with a warning not to talk.

But they talked: they told friends that they had recognized some of their kidnappers. A week later, they were seized by hooded, armed men. No one saw them alive again, Lake La Fourche yielded the headless, mutilated bodies; and these yielded evidence that the torturing mutilations had been performed by a skilled hand.

"Murder charges were filed against Dr. McKoin and a deputy sheriff. But no indictments were returned." A majority of the grand jurors, said the *Times-Picayune*, were Klansmen.

Even in that year, however, with the Klan burgeoning, the failure to secure a conviction was accompanied by a small success in the area of citizen education about the nature of the "Invisible Empire." And other cases added to this education.

A determined collaborative effort by the Bureau, honest law enforcement officers, and crusading newsmen gradually broke both the power and the drawing power of the Klan. Its huge membership dissolved as swiftly as it had formed. By the late 1920's, only scattered hard-core units remained.

During the 1930's, the Klan was virtually dormant. During World War II it was inactive. In 1944, it went out of business as a corporate entity—because Internal Revenue brought claims against it for almost $700,000 in delinquent taxes. Its comeback was in the form of rival splinter groups—many of which fell apart, and most of which seemed, for some years, to have only a tenuous hold on existence.

Yet on March 4, 1965—a hundred years after the forming of the original Ku Klux Klan—Hoover told the House Subcommittee on Appropriations that the FBI was keeping tabs on fourteen Klan-type organizations. And he spelled out a grim warning: "During the past year there has been a marked increase in Klan membership."[2]

Klan leaders boast, "The Spirit of the Ku Klux Klan still lives. It was here YESTERDAY, and it is here TODAY, and it will be here FOREVER." Those whose arrogant prophecies have reached all the way to FOREVER have, as a rule, been cut down to size before many years have passed. But it would be folly to gloss over the fact that the "Spirit" of the Klan is dangerously alive TODAY; or the further fact that the Klan has shown itself to be possessed of a tenacious power of comeback.

It has shown no capacity to maintain either a high-level membership or a steady upward curve of growth. But it has shown a remarkable capacity to expand swiftly, overreach itself, decline swiftly, survive in an almost dormant state, and again expand swiftly when conditions are ripe.

When the Klan's membership is at low ebb, it is made up

[2] *FBI 1966 Appropriation*, p. 81.

almost wholly of true Klan-type individuals—just as the CPUSA's membership, when it is at low ebb, is made up almost wholly of hard-core Communists. But our population appears to contain an overabundance of persons whose fears, prejudices, and hostilities differ from those of the true Klansman in degree rather than kind. The *sine qua non* of resurgent Klan growth is some change in the objective world that tends broadly to activate such fears, prejudices, and hostilities, and lift them toward the Klan level of virulence.

In the Bogalusa case, the three-judge panel said in its *Opinion,* p. 2, that the Klan's coercive activities today are directed toward frustrating "the national policy expressed in civil rights legislation." Hoover's testimony at the March 4, 1965, hearing not only underscores this fact but suggests that the Klan's new members are persons who so ardently share its will to frustrate this policy that they are willing to close their eyes to Klan terrorism, or to become apologists for it.

The upswing in membership, the Director said, dates from March 17, 1954: the day when the Supreme Court ruled that public schools must desegregate. Further, the passage of each civil rights act has contributed to the Klan's power to exploit fears and prejudices—and mounting antagonism to the Federal Government. Finally: "Investigative experience has shown that Klan activity and membership have increased in those areas in the South where civil rights groups have been most active."

Speaking of the fourteen Klan-type organizations, he told the Subcommittee that the FBI had within all of them "highly qualified sources consisting of not only rank-and-file members but also individuals who are in a position to have access to plans and policies." On the basis of data provided by such "sources," he gave certain facts and figures.

"The largest and dominant Klan group is the United Klans of America . . . ." Its headquarters are in Tuscaloosa, Alabama. It has klaverns in eight states. Its estimated membership is 4,600. Its Imperial Wizard is Robert Shelton.

"Another prominent Klan group is the White Knights of the Ku Klux Klan of Mississippi, which was organized in February 1964, and operates solely in the State of Mississippi. Its membership is estimated at 2,000 persons and it is led by Imperial Wizard Samuel Bowers."

The next two in order of size are the Original Knights of the Ku Klux Klan, in Louisiana, with an estimated membership of 1,500 and the United Florida Ku Klux Klan, which operates only in that state and has a membership of around 900.

Hoover gave figures for only these four. Several of the smaller Klans, we understand, are strictly local and have only one klavern each. We have been told, when we have been in the respective states, that this is true of the Independent Klavern, St. Augustine, Florida; and of the National Knights of the Ku Klux Klan, Tucker, Georgia.

The membership figures given by Hoover may seem too small to qualify the Klans as a really dangerous force. They could tempt us to make the same error that we have been repetitively prone to make with respect to the CPUSA: namely, that of translating numerical weakness into intrinsic weakness. But the given figures are those of hard-core membership.

Where the established system is one of "terror squads" and "wrecking crews," it takes only a few persons to do enormous harm. As they now operate, indeed, the Klans do not want their lay members to be practitioners of overt violence—not with the new civil rights acts on the federal books and federal agents watchfully on the job. The function of the many is to provide a "respectable" cover for what the hard-core members do.

Exploiting the fact that the latent fears and hostilities of a great many persons have now become active, the Klan is trying to keep its terrorism invisible enough to let it build a

public image of patriotism, dedication to Christian principles, and ardent anti-Communism. Further, it is becoming
more and more skilled in operating through front groups.

Those who have the task of building its public image and
enlarging its "respectable" membership have learned to
choose their issues—and their language—to fit the standard
Far Right pattern. This practice could lead to a dangerous
amount of surreptitious cooperation between the Klan and
groups that would, in the open, continue to "despise" it.

Today's Klan advertises itself as against Communism, the
"so-called" civil rights movement, Big Government, foreign
aid, the "Communist-controlled" Supreme Court, the anti-
poverty program, and any form of federal gun-control legislation. This is standard Far Right dogma.

Here is a headline: "Communist Infiltration Into the
So-Called Civil Rights Movement." The item under it deals
with certain civil rights activities in Cleveland in April 1964.
In it, we read, "Thirty-one persons who had been active in
one or more subversive organizations were among the
so-called civil rights demonstrators . . . ." This item would fit
into any of a sizeable number of Far Right publications. But
it appears on the front page of the August 1964 issue of *The
Fiery Cross*—the official publication of the United Klans of
America.

We can assume that civil rights demonstrations will continue. FBI investigations of the Klan will continue—on the
broad front that federal statutes have opened up. After the
passage of the 1965 Act, there was a lull. The Acts of 1966
and 1967 failed to pass in the Senate. But the front has been
further broadened now by the 1968 Act.

The Justice Department will continue to prosecute cases
that stem from Klan atrocities. More, not fewer, such cases
will be tried in state courts on the basis of evidence gathered
by the FBI. Convictions will become more frequent. Every
case will further underscore the nature of the "ineradicable
evil" which the Klan represents.

But *also*—and we dare not close our eyes to this fact—these developments will lift to a higher pitch fears and hostilities that can be designated as of the Klan type—whether or not those in whom they are lodged are Klansmen. We are reminded of Robert Tristram Coffin's striking phrase, "Life and death upon one tether . . . ."

We have said that the Klan's basic character was not changed one iota, in the 1920's, by the fact that several million Americans became members. It was not changed any more than the character of the CPUSA was changed by the presence of those who, in the 1940's, brought its membership to an all-time high. What type of person, then, is the hard-core Klansman who benefits by, but is neither changed nor controlled by, an upswing in membership?

Repeatedly we have found the typical Klansman described, by those who have had occasion to observe him, as ignorant, prejudiced, hungry for power, frustrated, brutal, convinced that he is persecuted, and highly responsive to pseudo-dramatic oaths and rituals. He is commonly credited with a low-average or below-average intelligence. He has an obsessive interest in firearms.

The *Opinion* read by Judge Wisdom described him as having an arrogant need to be important and a gross lack of true leadership qualities. William Bradford Huie has provided thumbnail sketches of the four Klansmen arrested by the FBI for the 1964 murder of Lieutenant Colonel Lemuel Penn:

"Joseph Howard Sims, a machinist, father of eight, Navy veteran of World War II, and kladd (sergeant at arms) of the Klan. An avid gun collector and racing-car buff . . . . Known for his nasty temper, Sims suffered from migraine headaches."

"Herbert Guest, a 282-pound garage operator" whose schooling had ended with the first grade. "Also a gun collector, he kept shotguns and rifles hanging on the walls of his garage." Guest "frequently complained about his health."

"James S. Lackey, 28, father of one, a service-station

attendant. According to a defense psychiatrist, Lackey said he feared people were staring at him because of his 'misshapen head' and admitted that he spied on his fellow workers because he didn't trust any of them.

"Cecil William Myers, 25, father of three, yarn picker in a textile mill. Myers boasted of his Klan membership and habitually wore a pistol strapped to his hip."[3]

The composite Klansman whom we meet in these descriptions will be the true beneficiary of whatever strength the Klan may gain by drawing to itself, from the non-Klan community, recruits who share its hates and fears. Whatever tolerance is extended to the organization is tacitly extended, also, to the types of action that come naturally to the hardcore Klansman. The murder of Lemuel Penn provides an example.

For the materials out of which the following account is put together, we are indebted to Huie's article, press items—particularly from the *Atlanta Constitution*, and the *FBI 1966 Appropriation*, pp. 82–83. We shall quote, also, from a confession by James S. Lackey. The FBI agents in whose presence he signed it testified under oath that he had done so voluntarily. Lackey, however, later repudiated it, saying that the FBI had arrested him illegally and coerced him into confessing. The confession was accepted in evidence; but we shall indicate each point at which we have drawn upon it.

Just before midnight on July 19, 1964, Lieutenant Colonel Penn and two fellow officers, both Negro, left Fort Benning, Georgia, to drive home to Washington, D.C., after completing a tour of Reserve officer duty. It was a hot night, and they were not in uniform. As Huie reports, "They wore sport shirts. None of them had had a drink. There was no liquor in the car. The nearest thing to a weapon was a screwdriver."

---

[3] William Bradford Huie, "Murder: The Klan on Trial," *Saturday Evening Post*, June 19, 1965, p. 86.

In Athens, early that evening, Lackey, Sims, and Myers had gone out "on patrol" in Sims's station wagon. Lackey drove; Sims and Myers sat with sawed-off shotguns in their laps. Georgia law forbade such guns only if they measured 26 inches or less from muzzle to butt. Those carried by the Klansmen measured 26¼ inches.

Throughout the night, the three men cruised around, making three stops at Guest's garage and several at the Open House Café. At 4:10 A.M. while they were stopped at a traffic light, they saw a beige Chevrolet go by on the road which they were waiting to enter. In it were the three Negro officers, with Penn at the wheel. It bore a District of Columbia license plate.

According to Lackey's confession, Sims said "That must be some of President Johnson's boys. Let's follow 'em." They followed—for 22 miles before catching up with the car ahead. At this point, according to Lackey, Sims said, "Right here is where I kill me a nigger. Pass 'em!"

Something equivalent to this must have been said; for what happened next is spelled out in the testimony of Penn's two surviving companions, Major Charles E. Brown and Lieutenant Colonel John D. Howard. The pursuing car pulled even with the pursued, matching its speed. Penn was killed instantly by simultaneous blasts from two sawed-off shotguns.

In its sheer senselessness, this murder-on-impulse fits the pattern of a host of Klan crimes back through the years. Also, it points to one problem habitually faced by FBI informants within the Klan. They cannot give advance warning about the plans of men who have no plans. So long as it is tolerated practice for men who are armed with Klan-type hatreds and hairtrigger impulses to go armed, also, with guns, no informant can anticipate the random stimulus that will change a latent will to "kill me a nigger" into an overt act.

This murder provides, likewise, a classic example of the tenacity it takes on the part of the FBI and federal prosecutors to see a civil rights case through to the end. On August 6, 1964, FBI agents arrested Lackey, Sims, Myers, and Guest on the only federal charge that could be brought against them: that of conspiring to deprive a citizen of his civil and constitutional rights (Title 18, Section 241, U.S. Code).

As Hoover later told the Subcommittee on Appropriations, a detailed report of all the evidence gathered by the Bureau, "including some 800 pages of interviews with witnesses and subjects," was turned over to local authorities "so that they could proceed on the more serious murder offense . . . ."[4] Because of insufficient evidence, no indictment for murder was sought against Guest.

Lackey, Sims, and Myers were indicted by the Madison County, Georgia, grand jury on murder charges. Lackey got his trial postponed by charging the FBI with illegal arrest and coercion. Sims and Myers were brought to trial. On September 4th, a local all-white jury—after displaying a flagrant lack of interest in the evidence—brought in a verdict of *not guilty*.

The Federal Government thereupon reactivated its conspiracy charge. A federal grand jury indicted Sims, Myers, Guest, Lackey, and two men who had been arrested later—Denver Willis Phillips and George Hampton Turner—for conspiracy to injure, oppress, threaten, and intimidate Negro citizens in Georgia.[5] On December 29th, a federal judge in Georgia dismissed these October indictments. He claimed that the Government had failed to show a violation of *federal* law.[6]

The Government asked the Supreme Court to render a decision on this point. More than a year later, in March 1966, the court ruled that the suspects could be indicted and

[4] *FBI 1966 Appropriation*, p. 83.

[5] *Atlanta Constitution*, October 17, 1964.

[6] *Atlanta Times*, December 30, 1964.

tried in federal court for violating the civil and constitutional rights of Lemuel Penn. This decision automatically reinstated the Federal grand jury indictments of March 1964.[7]

In June-July 1966, Sims, Myers, and Turner were tried in the federal court in Atlanta. Turner was acquitted. Sims and Myers were found guilty and each was sentenced to a ten-year term in federal prison, the maximum term possible under the conspiracy statute. These convictions, on appeal, were upheld. In a separate trial before a different jury in the same court, Guest, Lackey, and Phillips were acquitted.

In Chapters XI and XV, we quoted certain charges made by James A. Wechsler in the *New York Post* to the effect that the FBI has shown neither will nor capacity to cope with anti-Negro violence in the South—charges that it has "systematically failed to infiltrate the racist mobs," that it "shrinks from doing battle with the segregationists," and that it is "engaged in a vulgar palship with the Southern police." In his column of September 18, 1963, he said that the Bureau's record of "total failure" reaches back to 1947.

Such charges seem ill-informed, for the record shows that the Bureau has been steadily engaged in seeking—and finding—the perpetrators of Klan atrocities. True, there have been a host of crimes that it has not been able to anticipate and prevent and a further host that could not be brought under any federal law. In the next chapter, we shall be exploring the law's coverage. But the record of tenacious effort and of many distinguished successes reaches back through the very span of years to which Wechsler refers.

On March 17, 1950, for example, Sheriff John William Lynch of Dade County, Georgia, and his Deputy Sheriff, William M. Hartline, were sentenced in federal court in Atlanta to imprisonment for one year and a fine of $1,000. This sentence was no match for their crime, but it was the

---

[7] *Washington Evening Star*, March 31, 1966.

maximum one allowed by the only federal statute under which the men could be indicted. Back of their convictions lay a story that began on the night of April 2, 1949, when a mob of robed Klansmen flogged seven Negroes in the town of Hooker, Georgia.

An FBI investigation led to the arrest of Lynch and Hartline on a charge of having arrested the seven victims and turned them over to the Klansmen. Lynch claimed that he had been forced at gunpoint to release them to the mob. FBI agents located witnesses who could testify that he had not been intimidated in any way. Hartline denied that he had even been present at the time. The FBI located witnesses to the contrary.

Justice prosecuted under Article I of the Fourteenth Amendment, which is to say, under the clause which reads:

... nor shall any State deprive any person of life, liberty, or property without due process of law, nor deny to any person within its jurisdiction the equal protection of the laws.

Its case was built, item by irrefutable item, out of evidence gathered by FBI agents and the testimony of witnesses whom these agents persuaded to go on the stand.

On December 14, 1949, the members of the federal grand jury which had indicted the men passed a *Resolution* commending Bureau agents who had worked on the case for "their great fidelity and singleness of purpose" in developing the evidence. The agents had, the *Resolution* stated, "gone far beyond the line of duty to aid, assist, and protect the citizens of the United States and to further the cause of equity and justice in America."

It was in the spring of 1953 that our own interest in the FBI "jelled" to a point where we began to note discrepancies between charges made against it and recorded facts. And it was on June 4th of that year that an organization of which we have long been members—the NAACP—put out a press release which is still in our files—a release which should, it would seem, have come to Wechsler's attention, since a number of papers based news items upon it.

This press release stated that the NAACP had, on that day, sent to Attorney General Herbert Brownell, Jr., a telegram of congratulation "upon the work of the Department of Justice in securing indictments of six Klansmen allegedly involved in acts of terror in Florida between 1949 and 1952." The telegram specifically commended "the splendid work of the FBI" in investigating crimes of violence in Florida.[8]

Walter White, Executive Secretary of the NAACP, who signed the telegram, expressed the hope that the "thorough work" would continue. It has continued—and expanded; and this fact constitutes one kind of promise that it will continue into the future for as long as may be necessary.

[8] *News from NAACP: NAACP Hails Indictments of 6 Florida Klansmen.* For Release: June 4, 1953.

TWENTY-TWO

FEDERAL LAW AND CIVIL RIGHTS

THE STATUTES under which the FBI operates in the civil rights field fall into two groups. There are the few survivors from among the civil rights acts of the Reconstruction era, the rest having been repealed by Congress in the 1880's and 1890's, or invalidated by the Supreme Court prior to 1906. And there are the Civil Rights Acts of 1957, 1960, 1964, 1965, and 1968.

The modern revitalization of the old statutes dates from 1939, when Attorney General Frank Murphy created within the Criminal Division of Justice a Civil Liberties Unit. Since this was soon renamed the Civil Rights Section (CRS), we shall employ this latter designation. In 1957, this section was replaced by a full-scale Civil Rights Division.

The department, in 1939, had a number of attorneys who were interested in civil rights, but it had lacked a policy for using them to good advantage. It had been prosecuting only such violations of rights as were urgently presented to it. Murphy wanted to establish a pattern of federal initiative.

To this end, he instructed the CRS to study the Constitution, federal laws, and court interpretations, to find out what legal weapons were at its command; and to formulate a program to fit "present conditions." Also, it was to "direct, supervise, and conduct" such prosecutions as it felt to be in order.

For an understanding of the problems faced by the CRS in its effort to build a civil liberties program on "certain fugitive and moribund statutory provisions, all nearly seventy-five years old," and also for multiple details about cases prosecuted in the 1940–1946 period, we are greatly indebted to *Federal Protection of Civil Rights: Quest for a Sword* (1947) by Robert K. Carr, Executive Secretary of President Truman's Committee on Civil Rights—and now president of Oberlin College. Unless we indicate to the contrary, we shall be drawing upon this book for what we say about policies and cases.

The attorneys of the CRS soon learned that the *United States Code* contained only three laws that could provide even a reasonably sound basis for invoking "criminal sanctions to protect traditional rights." These were Sections 51, 52, and 444 of Title 18; and even these were so ill-defined that it would take court tests to determine the extent of their usefulness.

The designations of all three have been changed since 1947; and, for convenience, we shall use the new ones. Sections 51 and 52 are now 241 and 242. Section 444, the old anti-peonage act, has been merged with 445 to create 1581. It is rarely invoked now; but Sections 241 and 242 are in constant use. Of the thirty-five criminal cases which the Civil Rights Division presented to grand juries in fiscal 1965, all except four came under one or the other of these two old statutes.[1]

Section 241—*Conspiracy against the rights of citizens*—was enacted on May 31, 1870, as Section 6 of the Enforcement

[1] Attorney General's *Annual Report* for fiscal 1965, p. 183.

Act of that year. Its present text, which differs only slightly from the original, reads as follows:

If two or more persons conspire to injure, oppress, threaten, or intimidate any citizen in the free exercise or enjoyment of any right or privilege secured to him by the Constitution or laws of the United States, or because of his having exercised the same; or

If two or more persons go in disguise on the highway, or on the premises of another, with intent to prevent or hinder his free exercise or enjoyment of any right or privilege so secured—

They shall be fined not more than $5,000 or imprisoned not more than ten years, or both.[2]

The meaning of this text seems clear enough. Yet Section 241 contains an ambiguity that has proved to be well-nigh incurable. The rights we commonly think of as guaranteed are those set forth in the Bill of Rights and the Fourteenth and Fifteenth Amendments. But these documents protect the rights which they specify only against actions performed by *federal or state agencies*. Section 241 protects against actions performed by *private persons*. To what rights and privileges does it, then, refer?

The only authoritative answer is one that has kept changing. It has been slowly compiled out of Supreme Court decisions—slowly, because the court can rule only with respect to a right that is at issue in a case brought to it on appeal. Rulings on this statute reach back to 1873. By 1939 the list of rights that had been specified as derivative from the Constitution or protected by it was fairly long. Other rights have been added to it since—as recently as 1966.

Usually, now, when Justice instructs the FBI to investigate an alleged infringement of rights or to arrest a suspect under Section 241, it is acting on precedent. Some Supreme Court decision which is already on the books establishes the propriety of the statute's being invoked.

[2] *United States Code Annotated*, Title 18, Sections 1–370, Chapter 13, "Civil Rights," p. 670.

Thus, on March 9, 1965, FBI agents arrested four white residents of Selma, Alabama, for an assault upon three white ministers who were active in the civil rights movement—one of them being the Reverend James B. Reeb, whose injuries proved fatal. The warrants specified that the arrests were made under Title 18, Section 241, and there were abundant precedents to justify the use of this law.

Sometimes, however, a case reminds us that in the world of Constitutional law, as in the physical world, "Every road was a new road once."[3] Unlike the three ministers, Lieutenant Colonel Lemuel Penn was not attacked for any civil rights activities. He was shot for being a Negro whom a group of Klansmen saw on a Georgia road in a car with a Washington, D.C. license.

After a local jury had acquitted the Klansmen on a murder charge, the Justice Department secured their indictment by a Federal grand jury on a charge of having conspired to deprive Penn of his rights. The judge of the United States District Court—who was by no means a racist—dismissed the indictments: he could not identify a *federally protected* right that had been violated. Justice appealed the dismissals.

In *United States v. Guest*, it asked the Supreme Court to affirm as protected under Section 241 the right *to travel interstate*. After long deliberation, the court, on March 28, 1966, ruled in the Government's favor. Thus, it both reinstated the indictments in the case at issue and made every citizen's right to travel interstate a constitutionally protected one.

On that same day the court delivered its unanimous opinion in *United States v. Cecil Ray Price* (et al): the case that grew out of the 1964 murder, near Philadelphia, Mississippi, of the three young civil rights workers. Here, too, Justice had appealed the dismissal of certain indictments by a District Court judge—who, in dismissing them, had done what legal precedent required.

[3] Clement Woods, from *New Roads*.

One indictment related to Section 241 and the court's ruling, which was in the Government's favor, reversed an earlier one. Thus, 96 years after the conspiracy statute was first enacted, the court held that it could be invoked to protect the Fourteenth Amendment right to "due process of law."

By decision after decision, the coverage of Section 241 has been expanding for almost a century. Justice can now instruct the FBI to make investigations and arrests under it that would have been out of bounds in 1939—or 1959. But the old law has not become an all-purpose weapon for the defense of rights. It has certain built-in limitations that no court ruling can reach. Only Congress could modify them—and to some extent it has done so by certain provisions of the Civil Rights Act of 1968.

For one thing, the Section, as originally worded, protects only *citizens*; not *persons*. Thus, Justice has never been able to invoke it to protect an alien. For another thing, it is a conspiracy statute; and its sanction, as Carr observes, "is useless in any situation where a threat to civil liberty comes from the action of one person." Here, it bears the mark of its origin: it was designed for use against the Ku Klux Klan.

Section 242—*Deprivation of rights under color of law*— dates back to April 9, 1866; but one key word—*willfully*— was inserted in 1909. The statute reads thus:

Whoever, under color of any law, statute, ordinance, regulation or custom, willfully subjects any inhabitant of any State, Territory, or District to the deprivation of any rights, privileges, or immunities secured or protected by the Constitution or laws of the United States, or to different punishments, pains, or penalties, on account of such inhabitant being an alien, or by reason of his color or race, than are prescribed for the punishment of citizens, shall be fined not more than $1,000 or imprisoned not more than one year, or both.[4]

[4] *United States Code Annotated*, Title 18, Sections 1–370, Chapter 13, "Civil Rights," p. 670.

When the newly created CRS undertook to study Supreme Court rulings under Section 242, it drew a blank. The statute, Carr writes, "had been invoked in only two reported cases, both in federal district courts." Yet local law enforcement officers, particularly in the South, were common violators of the rights of Negroes. Their compliance or cooperation was a determinative factor in many lynchings. To take the initiative against such offenders, the CRS would have to breathe new life into the old "under color of law" statute. This it proceeded to do by the prosecuting of cases.

While Section 242 is commonly called the police-brutality statute, the first Supreme Court test to which it was put—in *United States v. Classic*, 1941—did not involve brutality. It had to do with fraudulent ballot-counting in a Louisiana primary election in the turbulent period after Huey Long's death.

Classic was a double victory for the CRS. The Court upheld the use of Section 242 to prosecute state election officials who interfered with the voter's right to participate in a primary election in which candidates for federal office were on the ballot; and it interpreted the phrase "under color of law" as the CRS had hoped it would.

Did the phrase apply only to acts performed by an official in the course of his prescribed duties? Or did it apply also to unofficial acts which he could not have performed without the benefit of his official status? The court majority affirmed this latter broad interpretation:

Misuse of power, possessed by virtue of a state law and made possible because the wrongdoer is clothed with the authority of state law is action taken "under color of law."

Between 1941 and 1945, the CRS not only invoked Section 242 in several successful police-brutality cases that did not reach the Supreme Court but began to invoke, in connection with it, a statute which we have not yet mentioned:

Section 371, Title 18, commonly known as the general conspiracy statute. This law—*Conspiracy to commit offense or to defraud United States*—is not, in any specific sense, a civil rights act. It is framed to reach persons who willfully encourage and help to plan the commission of any federal crime, but who do not actually commit it.

The CRS was quick to recognize the utility Section 371 could have in cases where public officials and private persons had cooperated to deprive an individual of his rights. An official could be indicted under Section 242: he had acted "under color of law." If two or more officials were involved, each of them could be indicted, also, under Section 371, for *conspiring* to violate 242. Private persons who were in on the crime could likewise be doubly indicted: under Section 241, for conspiring to deprive the victim of his rights, and under Section 371, for conspiring to violate a federal law.

Such a multiplying of indictments serves a double function. It spreads out responsibility for a violation of rights over all who have connived to bring it about. And it makes the grossly inadequate penalties prescribed in Sections 241 and 242 slightly less inadequate. Persons indicted on two or more counts can, if convicted, be given the maximum sentence on each count.

In 1945 came *Screws v. United States*: a landmark case which evoked from the Supreme Court opinions that ran to a total of 25,000 words. The Government lost the case—but gained from it a revitalized Section 242. *Screws* provided the first Supreme Court test of the constitutionality of that Section.

In January 1943, M. Claude Screws, sheriff of Baker County, Georgia, aided by a policeman and a deputy sheriff, took into custody Robert Hall, a Negro, against whom Screws had a deep personal grudge. Hall was charged with stealing a tire; but, handcuffed and helpless, he was knocked to the ground and so severely beaten that he died.

When local and state authorities declined to act, the United States Attorney for the region, with Justice Department backing, secured from a federal grand jury indictments of the three officials under Sections 242 and 371. On October 9th, they were convicted in the United States District Court in Macon and were given the maximum sentence on each count.

They appealed. The Fifth Circuit Court of Appeals upheld the convictions. The Supreme Court did not: on May 7, 1945, it sent the case back to the District Court for retrial. The second trial ended with the acquittal of the defendants.

The Supreme Court's majority did not cast doubts upon the defendants' having killed Hall as specified by the prosecution. Its opinion related to a basic element of "due process": namely, the instructions given to the jury by the trial judge.

The judge had correctly instructed the jury that the defendants had acted illegally if they had applied more force than was necessary to make the arrest or to protect themselves from the prisoner's alleged assault. But, said the court, the jury should have been further instructed that, to convict *under the terms of the federal law*, the jury must find that the defendants had acted with the purpose of depriving the prisoner of a constitutional right, e.g., the right to be tried by a court rather than an ordeal. Because the judge had failed to charge the jury to consider the wilfullness of the defendants—which was an essential ingredient of the chargeable offense—the court said that the case should be retried.[5]

Among the justices, only Murphy contended, in a one-man dissent, that the convictions should have been upheld. Roberts, Frankfurter, and Jackson also dissented, but their contention was that the crime was so "patently local" that the court, instead of ordering a retrial, should have dismissed the federal charges. Douglas also felt that the charges should have been dismissed, but his emphasis was upon the

[5] *Screws v. United States*, pp. 8–13. May 7, 1945.

personal motive behind the crime. In the end, he voted with the majority.

On every issue other than the convictions, the majority upheld the Government's position. It ruled that Section 242 was constitutional; and it reaffirmed and strengthened the broad *Classic* interpretation of "under color of law."

Roberts, Frankfurter, and Jackson dissented on both counts. They held that the statute, by reason of its failure to specify the crimes covered, fell below the minimal standard for constitutionality; and that the phrase "under color of law" should be narrowly, not broadly, interpreted.

Thus, *Screws* brought into the open, to be argued and resolved, every dissent-breeding question resident in Section 242. Few cases have stimulated a more complex diversity of opinion. In the end, the old statute was not only left on the books but, with its constitutionality at last affirmed, was more securely there than at any time since its passage in 1866.

Yet eight years after *Screws*, and after the successful prosecution of various intervening cases, the Government's right to invoke Section 242 *under any circumstances* was again challenged. The site of the challenge was not the Supreme Court but the court of public opinion—in a case which led to one of the most widely publicized attacks ever made upon Hoover and the FBI.

In November 1952, young Robert Byers, an inmate of Pennhurst State School in Pennsylvania and a Negro, died under conditions which suggested extreme brutality. His father claimed that his body showed evidence of violent beatings. Attorney General Herbert Brownell, Jr. instructed the FBI to investigate under Section 242. It did—and abruptly became a storm center.

At the Governors' Conference, in Seattle, on August 23, 1953, Governors Fine of Pennsylvania and Battle of Virginia "joined in a public attack on the FBI, asserting that it had invaded the police power of the state." New York Governor Thomas E. Dewey agreed and "demanded repeal of the Civil-Rights law that would authorize such investigations."[6] Soon the furor was nationwide.

The NAACP, the American Civil Liberties Union, certain sectors of the press, and a number of key public figures strongly defended the Justice Department and the FBI. But supporters of Governors Fine and Battle charged the Bureau with having trespassed upon states' rights; and, in spite of *Screws* and other cases, held that the 1866 statute had died of disuse.

In a letter to *The New York Times* of August 26, 1963, Hoover met the challenge head on. He was moved to do so by an article by W. H. Lawrence which the *Times* had carried on August 4th. This gave the views of Governors Fine and Battle, and reported statements to the effect that if the Federal Government were to begin investigating all complaints made by inmates of state institutions contending that their rights had been violated, the states would soon "swarm" with FBI agents.

After expressing his surprise at the attitude taken by the two governors, and at Governor Dewey's apparent concurrence in their views, Hoover wrote:

It makes little difference whether the act of Congress was passed in 1866 or 1953. So long as it is the law of the land, the Attorney General has not only the right but the duty of establishing as a matter of policy that the FBI should investigate alleged violations of such acts of Congress . . . .

The FBI over a period of years has experienced difficulty in investigating alleged violations of civil rights. It has not been uncommon, in such investigations which do not meet with the public sentiment of the community wherein the act occurred, for the FBI to be singled out for attack . . . .

The record, I think, is clear and convincing. More progress has been accomplished in developing consciousness, understanding

⁶ *The New York Times*, August 24, 1953.

and respect for civil rights since 1940 than in any other period in our national history.

In the last thirteen years, for example, a total of thirty-six lynchings have occurred. This, of course, does not reflect credit either upon the communities where the acts occurred or upon the United States. In the thirteen years preceding 1940, however, a total of 157 lynchings occurred . . . .

The fact that the FBI investigates lynchings no doubt causes many would-be lynchers to stop and consider the consequence before engaging in mob violence. In such cases, or in others of the type which the Governors had in mind, it makes little difference whether the victim is the most lecherous type of criminal. He still is entitled to be treated as a human being. No one has the right in common decency or under our constitutional republic of taking unto himself the responsibility of inflicting punishment.

We of the FBI have no other choice but to do our duty as best we can. This we shall continue to do . . . .

No Supreme Court ruling between 1945 and 1966 brought any striking new interpretation of Section 242. Then came *United States v. Cecil Ray Price et al.*[7] We have spoken of this case in relation to Section 241; but it led, also, to a broadened interpretation of the phrase "under color of law." To put this interpretation into context, we must look at the manner in which the three young civil rights workers were killed.

On June 21, 1964, they were taken into custody by Cecil Ray Price, Deputy Sheriff of Neshoba County, Mississippi, and held in jail until after dark. According to charges in the indictments later handed down by a federal grand jury and quoted in the Supreme Court's decision, Price then released them and "proceeded by automobile on Highway 19 to intercept his erstwhile wards." At the point where they were to be intercepted, he was joined by two members of the Philadelphia, Mississippi, Police Department and fifteen private citizens.

---

[7] *United States v. Cecil Ray Price et al*, March 28, 1966, pp. 2–3.

Taken from their own car, the civil rights workers were put into one from the Neshoba County Sheriff's office, "and transported . . . to a place on an unpaved road." There "The defendants, it is alleged, 'did willfully assault, shoot, and kill' each of the three." Their bodies were taken to the site of an earthen dam that was under construction some five miles from Philadelphia and hidden where it seemed they would soon be buried beyond recovery.

A massive search ended on August 4th, when FBI agents located the bodies.[8] The subsequent investigation led to the arrest by the FBI, on December 4th, of twenty-one persons. The eighteen mentioned above—three law enforcement officers and fifteen private citizens—were indicted by a federal grand jury. The United States District Court sustained certain charges against all of them; but because it dismissed others on which Justice particularly wanted a ruling, for future reference, the dismissals were appealed to the Supreme Court.

The District Court had agreed that the officials had violated Section 242; and that the private citizens had violated Section 241 and had also, under 371, been guilty of a conspiracy to violate 242. But it had dismissed a charge that the private citizens, as well as the officials, had *violated* Section 242.

The Supreme Court reinstated the indictments based on this charge. The officers, it declared, had not merely committed an offense which prepared the way for a later, different offense by the private citizens. The case was not equivalent to one in which officers release a prisoner to a lynching mob—and let the mob carry on from there. The murders had been "a joint activity from start to finish." Thus, the private citizens had not taken over where the violation of Section 242 had left off, but had actively shared in its violation.

In a precedent-setting decision, the court held that private persons "jointly engaged with state officials" in a violation of Section 242 "are acting 'under color' of law for the purposes

[8] *FBI 1966 Appropriation*, p. 83.

of the statute." A person, in short, need not be an officer to violate 242. "It is enough that he be a wilful participant in joint activity with the State or its agents."[9]

The Supreme Court reinstated the dismissed indictments. But for one of the most ironic reasons on record, Judge Cox of the District Court had to dismiss *all* the federal indictments in the case: it turned out that they were defective because "Negroes and women had not been fairly represented on the grand jury . . . ." In a remark that tells a good deal about what it takes to be unswervingly for liberty under law, John Doar, head of Justice's Civil Rights Division, agreed that Judge Cox "had no choice but to dismiss the indictments."[10]

On March 27, 1968, Congress passed an act which should, when it has been implemented, and if it survives court tests, rule out the possibility of such defective juries: *The Jury Selection and Service Act of 1968*. But in 1966, the Government could only start to re-prosecute from scratch the case at issue.

Seven of the defendants—including Cecil Ray Price and Samuel H. Bowers, Jr., Imperial Wizard of the White Knights of the Ku Klux Klan of Mississippi—were convicted on October 7, 1967. They were convicted by an all-white jury—but not, in the opinion of the Government, by one that could be ruled defective: Negro members of the panel had been dropped on peremptory challenge. The verdict of guilty was the first ever brought in by an all-white jury in a major civil rights case in Mississippi. The convictions are now on appeal to the Fifth Circuit Court of Appeals.

To turn from the old civil rights acts to the new is to enter a different frame of reference. The old provide for the criminal prosecution of persons who have violated the rights of others. The new—except for scattered provisions and for certain major sections of the 1968 Act, are in the area of civil

[9] *United States v. Cecil Ray Price et al*, p. 7. March 26, 1966.
[10] *The New York Times*, September 28, 1966.

law. Their main purpose is to protect and promote the exercise and enjoyment of civil rights and basic opportunities.

The 1957 Act protects the right to vote in any general election in which candidates are running for federal office or in any primary "held solely or in part for the purpose of selecting or electing any such candidate." It forbids any person, "whether acting under color of law or otherwise," to intimidate, threaten, or coerce any citizen in order to prevent his voting in such an election; and it empowers the Attorney General to prevent or halt such interference by civil action: by applying to a Federal court for an injunction or other restraining order.

The stated purpose of the 1960 Act is to enforce "constitutional rights." Hoover, in an article called "The FBI's Role in the Field of Civil Rights," in the August 1963 *Yale Political,* indicates that the law prohibits:

(1) Willful interference with, or obstruction of, any Federal court order, judgment or decree—such as an order requiring a public school to desegregate.

(2) Interstate flight to avoid prosecution or confinement for willfully attempting to or actually destroying by fire or explosive any building, structure, vehicle, house, religious facility or educational institution—as well as interstate flight to avoid giving testimony in any criminal proceeding related to such offenses.

(3) Interstate transportation of any explosive with the knowledge or intent that it will be used to damage or destroy property for purposes of interfering with its use for educational, religious, charitable, residential, business or civil objectives— or for purposes of intimidating any person pursuing such objectives.

(4) Use of the mails, telephone, telegraph or other instrument of commerce to convey a threat—or to knowingly convey false information concerning a threat or attempted threat—to damage or destroy educational, religious, charitable, residential or civil property.

Further, the Act "requires that, following an election in which federal candidates appear on the ballot, state authorities must preserve the election records for 22 months and that they must on request make such records available to the Attorney General for inspection and reproduction purposes."

The 1964 Act forbids any state to employ discriminatory or double-standard qualifications for voting in an election where candidates for federal office are on the ballot. It provides injunctive relief against discrimination in places of public accommodation, defines the means which the Government can employ to bring about desegregation of public facilities and public education, establishes a policy of non-discrimination in federally assisted programs, and forbids, with certain exceptions, discriminatory employment practices. The exceptions protect, for example, the right of religious bodies to have working staffs made up of members of their own faith. Finally, the Act makes permanent the previously temporary Federal Commission on Civil Rights.

The Voting Rights Act of 1965 has as its stated purpose the enforcement of the Fifteenth Amendment. Section 2 forbids any state or political subdivision to establish voter qualifications or procedures that are designed to keep any citizen from voting by reason of his race or color. The other sections serve to implement this provision.

The covering aim of the 1968 Act is *To prescribe penalties for certain acts of violence or intimidation, and for other purposes.* Actually, it is an omnibus Act, with provisions so diverse that they can scarcely be compressed into a brief summary. The ten titles which it comprises fall, by subject matter, into several groupings—and they will have to be inserted under different Titles, criminal and civil, in the *United States Code.*

Moreover, at this writing, the Act has been on the books for only a few months; and no court cases have yet arisen under it. Obviously, therefore, no Supreme Court ruling has yet clarified any of several provisions that seem certain to breed controversy—and probably dissenting opinions.

The main provisions of the Act's Title I—*Interference with Federally Protected Activities*—will go into the *Code* under Title 18 as Sections 245 and 2101, the former into Chapter 13, "Civil Rights" the latter into Chapter 102, "Riots." They deal with strikingly different problems.

Section 245—*Federally protected activities*—does a vitally important job of supplementing the old criminal statutes, Sections 241 and 242. It enables the Government to prosecute an *individual*, not merely co-members of a *conspiracy*, who willfully prevents, or tries to prevent, any person's exercise of a constitutionally protected right. And it provides for a steep upgrading of penalties to match the results of intimidation or coercion: if death results, the offender "shall be subject to imprisonment for any term of years or for life."

Section 2101—*Riots*—prohibits, and establishes penalties for, interstate travel with the intent "to aid or abet any person in inciting or participating in or carrying on a riot or comitting any act of violence in furtherance of a riot."

Titles II–VII inclusive relate to the rights of Indians, being designed to insure their possession and enjoyment of civil and constitutional rights and to raise the level of court procedures in which Indians or their affairs are involved.

Titles VIII and IX form another unit. The former—*Fair Housing*—is designed to insure for all persons in the United States freedom from discrimination on the basis of race, color, religion, or national origin in the sale, rental, and financing of housing. The latter—*Prevention of Intimidation in Fair Housing Cases*—establishes penalties for interfering by threat or violence with persons who are seeking either to exercise their rights under Title VIII or to extend these rights to others.

Title X—the *Civil Obedience Act of 1968*—prohibits, and provides penalties for, certain activities that have as their aim the fomenting or carrying out of civil disorders. Chief among these activities are the teaching or demonstrating of how to make or use firearms, explosives, or incendiary devices "capable of causing injury or death" with the knowledge or intent that they will be used to foment civil disorder, the transportation or manufacture of such items for unlawful purposes, and interference with "any fireman or law enforcement officer" who is lawfully engaged in the performance of his official duties in a situation marked by or resulting from civil disorders.

Here, then, in capsule form, are the laws, old and new, under which the Attorney General, a United States Attorney, or the Civil Rights Division can instruct the FBI to conduct investigations or make arrests in the field of civil rights. While the Bureau's assignment in this field is obviously far broader now than it was prior to 1957, it is still limited. In no statute, for example, is there any wording in terms of which the FBI could provide, or be instructed to provide, the type of protection for individual civil rights workers which it is repeatedly denounced for not providing.

TWENTY-THREE

THE FBI AND CIVIL RIGHTS

B ASICALLY, the Justice Department's current policies
with regard to civil rights matters are those established
by the Civil Rights Section in the early 1940's. When the CRS
began to prosecute cases, it was at once confronted by two
touchy problems. Its policies were devised to insure the
fewest possible blunders with respect to these.

One problem, indigenous to our system, was that of drawing an accurate line between the federal and state domains.
The other was that of a vast discrepancy between the
number of complaints received and the number on which
prosecutions could be based. Carr estimates in his *Federal
Protection of Civil Rights*, p. 125, that three fourths of the
complaints received in the 1942–1944 period were "of such a
character that there [was] no possibility of federal jurisdiction or action . . . ."

In practical terms, the two problems were interrelated. If
a host of persons who made complaints became disillusioned
because no results were forthcoming, and if they became

agents of cynicism about the federal purpose, Justice's program of initiative would be blocked at the source. Yet only state and local authorities could act on most of the complaints received. Thus, it became a matter of the highest importance to develop with these authorities a relationship that would incline them to act on complaints referred to them by the Justice Department; and such a relationship could not be built upon repeated federal trespasses upon state prerogatives.

The persons responsible for defining the boundaries of federal jurisdiction and judging the legal merits of complaints were those attorneys in the Civil Rights Section who were schooled in constitutional law. But they were rarely the first recipients of the data to be judged. The vast majority of complaints, as Carr indicates, were made in the first instance to United States attorneys and FBI field offices.

We shall follow Carr's lead in describing the policies worked out in response to these complexities. The basic provision was that raw data regarding all complaints save those of an emergency character should be referred to the CRS before any investigative action was taken out in the field.

If the Section's attorneys decided that an alleged violation of rights might justify a federal prosecution, they instructed the FBI to make a preliminary investigation—the agents' first step being, as a rule, "to find the victim, if possible, and have him verify the complaint." If such verification could not be secured from the victim, or on his behalf, the case was usually dropped at this point.

It was dropped, also, if details provided by the complainant and transmitted to the CRS by the investigating agents took the case out of the federal field or showed it to be "factually and legally weak." And it had to be dropped if the complainant could not be persuaded to testify.

When, however, the facts contained in the agents' report suggested the existence of a case solid enough to warrant a prosecution, a full investigation was ordered. The FBI would then begin "to interview witnesses and assemble evidence which [might] be of possible use in a criminal prosecution." The Federal Government had as yet no statutory license to protect rights by means of civil suits.

In its essentials, the above policy still holds—because the problems to which it was geared have proved to be hardy perennials. At an appropriation hearing on January 24, 1962, however, Hoover told the Subcommittee that the FBI has been granted authority to take immediate action—but only *investigative* action—in police-brutality cases.

"When the FBI receives a complaint alleging police brutality, we immediately launch a preliminary investigation which includes the most thorough type of interview with the victim, the subjects and witnesses as well as a review of appropriate records." The results are transmitted at once to the Civil Rights Division, and it decides whether or not further action is warranted.[1] Here, in brief, the preliminary investigation precedes referral. In other types of cases, unless an acute emergency exists, the act of referral comes first.

But an exception to the above exception must be noted. It is the policy of the Civil Rights Division—as it was of the CRS—to give local authorities the right of way wherever they show a vigorous determination to act. Even in police-brutality cases, therefore, the FBI refers the complaint and awaits instructions if local authorities have initiated prompt action against the offender.

It was the conviction of the CRS, Carr emphasizes, p. 201, that "the locality must always be encouraged to solve as many of its own problems as it possibly can. The program of the Civil Rights Section has been directed toward this goal." So has that of its successor, the Civil Rights Division.

Such a goal is dictated by plain practicality. For one thing, a host of offenses against individual rights are still not

[1] *FBI 1963 Appropriation*, p. 70.

covered by federal law. For another, since police power is vested in the states, only local and state authorities can move in to prevent a crime or to protect those who stand in danger but whose rights have not yet been overtly violated. And, not least, federal authorities are bound, in many cases, to start what they cannot finish. A civil liberties case, Carr remarks, p. 127, "is apt to disintegrate at almost any stage . . . ."

It may do so because key witnesses suddenly refuse to testify; or, as in bombing cases, because the "rebuttable presumption" on which the Government has acted is rebutted by evidence; or for any of a variety of other reasons. What local and state authorities do after federal charges have had to be dropped is bound to reflect the degree of skill and pride they have developed in regard to the handling of civil rights matters.

For all these reasons, the FBI has, with the blessing of the Civil Rights Division, gone far beyond any routine call of duty in its effort to establish good working relations with local officers who have shown even a rudimentary will to do a responsible job in the civil rights field. It has drawn them into cooperative undertakings from which it might have excluded them, has made useful to them its informant system within the Klans, has transmitted to them in a host of instances leads that have helped to identify the perpetrators of non-federal crimes, and has made known its readiness to follow up out-of-state leads if they should develop in local cases.

But its main effort has been to raise the level of local law enforcement. Between January 1957 and February 1966, FBI specialists in the area of civil rights have taken part in more than 2,000 police training schools attended by 80,000 officers. They have clarified the provisions and constitutional significance of the civil rights acts, have shared their investigative know-how, and have discussed the control of mobs.

In the Attorney General's Report for fiscal 1965, pp. 168

ff., Assistant Attorney General John Doar discusses the problems and accomplishments of the Civil Rights Division and, within this context, the investigative work done for it by the FBI. The Division, he writes, is

charged with the enforcement of laws to prevent racial discrimination in voting, education, public facilities and accommodations, and employment; criminal statutes prohibiting deprivations of civil rights by persons acting under color of law or in conspiracy with others; certain federal custody and habeas corpus matters, and the Federal Youth Correction Act.

While the Division's responsibilities—and, therefore, those of the FBI—have now been expanded on several fronts by the Civil Rights Act of 1968, no prosecutions under this Act have yet been instituted. Hence, his report for 1965 is still, for our present purposes, up to date.

The number of "matters received," he writes, has, for each year from 1960 through 1965, "stayed fairly constant at the 3,000-plus level, with a slight upward trend." Civil matters have increased; criminal have decreased—although they still, by his figures, constitute a majority.

"Of the more than 3,318 matters received during fiscal 1965, 1,204 were concerned with public accommodation; 1,643 with Title 18 U.S.C. 241, 242; and 476 with federal custody. The categories 'due process miscellaneous' and 'equal protection miscellaneous' each contained more than 200 matters and 113 matters in connection with voting were also docketed."

In addition to the gradual shift from the criminal side toward the civil, the specifics of the work on both sides has changed through the years. The passage of each new civil rights act has brought a sharp increase in matters of the type that it covers. Enough compliance with various provisions of these acts has now been achieved to bring a decline in the number of complaints. Such fluidity has been most marked on the civil side.

On the criminal side, lynchings have become almost a thing of the past. Peonage cases, once so common, are now rare. Since the 1960 Act went on the books, destructive bombings have been a focus of intensive federal action. Crimes of violence against Negroes have declined in number—sharply, since the early days of the Civil Rights Section. This fact tends to be obscured by their now being publicized instead of ignored by the mass media.

Each civil rights case remains, however, obdurately hard to prosecute—in part, because of the limits of federal law; in other part, because juries continue to render verdicts that have nothing to do with the evidence.

"Thirty-five cases were presented to grand juries under Section 242 of Title 18, the police brutality statute; six under Section 241, conspiracy to deprive of rights; and four others involved miscellaneous due process, equal protection and unlawful arrest matters."

Every such case is chosen with the utmost care and is meticulously worked up. No indictment is sought unless the FBI has been able to provide evidence so conclusive as to be called incontrovertible and to line up a superabundance of witnesses whose testimony has been checked by every available means. Yet:

In twenty-one cases the grand jury failed to indict, and one indictment was dismissed on the Government's motion. There were five verdicts of guilty, five not guilty, and one nolo contendere.

To illustrate the difficulties that can beset civil rights prosecutions, Doar cites *United States v. William Rosencrans et al*, March 1964. This was a case in which six Florida Klansmen were indicted by a federal grand jury "in connection with the bombing of the home of a Jacksonville Negro whose son had recently entered a previously all-white school."

The defendants were indicted under Section 241, Title 18, for "conspiring to injure, oppress, threaten, and intimidate the victim"; and under Section 1509 for obstructing a federal court order enjoining interference with the rights of Negroes to attend integrated schools. One defendant, Rosencrans, pleaded guilty and was given a 7-year sentence. The jury acquitted one defendant on both counts and another on one count, and could not reach a verdict with respect to the other three. "Four of the five defendants were retried in November 1964 and acquitted."

This case was, incidentally—on the first round—the one that moved the National States Rights Party to author the headline which we quoted in Chapter XIX: "FBI CONSPIRACY TO FRAME JACKSONVILLE WHITES— ACCUSE FBI OF TERROR TACTICS!" The final outcome of it might be called par for the course. The whole history of federal prosecutions in the civil rights field has been marked by a vast discrepancy between the effort put forth and the convictions secured.

Thus, Carr reports, pp. 139–140, the outcome of a 1943 lynching case in Mississippi—*United States v. Luther Holder et al*—in which five men were indicted and all acquitted, including one who confessed to participation in the crime. In a packed courtroom where emotions ran high, the defense attorney told the jury, " 'The cause of white supremacy has been indicted' " and warned that a verdict of guilty would lead to " 'many more prosecutions when it meets the pleasure of those who seek to further centralize power in Washington.' " Various jurors told newsmen that the issue of states' rights, not the evidence presented, had determined their verdict.

Hoover has used a 1965 case that grew out of bombings in McComb, Mississippi, to illustrate the fact that local judges, like local juries, can be masters of the irrelevant. Joint efforts by the FBI and the Mississippi Highway Patrol had led to the arrest of nine white men on state charges. They were indicted, and all pleaded either guilty or nolo contendere.

The judge gave them a 30-minute lecture—and suspended their sentences, citing their "youth and good families . . . ," although four of the bombers were aged 44, 36, 35, and 33.[2]

The results of FBI investigations and federal prosecutions cannot, however, be measured solely by the convictions secured. Carr tells how the CRS learned to turn every conviction under Section 242—the police-brutality statute—into a lever with which to pry a further number of local law enforcement officers out of practices inimical to due process. Again, the number of lynchings declined abruptly in the 1940's as it became known that the FBI was tenaciously investigating such crimes.

Even acquittals can have an educative effect in cases where their glaring injustice revolts decent minds. As more and more minds have been thus revolted, juries have begun to bring in verdicts of guilty that would once have been unthinkable.

On the civil side, gains since 1957 have been striking in some areas and laggard in others; and no historian, we suspect, will ever be able to do an accurate job of apportioning credit for gains achieved. In the early 1960's, for example, civil rights workers undertook to break, by means of freedom rides and boycotts, the pattern of segregated transportation; but so, at the interstate level, did the Justice Department.

In 1961, at the department's request, the FBI conducted a survey of 294 cities in 17 states to determine whether or not interstate bus passengers were being subjected to segregationist practices. Evidence of segregation was found in 97 cities. Armed with this evidence, the department secured from the Interstate Commerce Commission a ruling to end such practices.

Similar investigations were made of railroad terminals, ferry boats that plied between two states, and 119 airports in

[2] *FBI 1967 Appropriation*, p. 79.

14 states, all of them used by regularly scheduled commercial flights. Since then, complaints in this area have, Mr. Doar indicates, declined sharply.

A like compounding of influences has been present in the field of voter registration. Here, civil rights workers have often exhibited an almost incredible measure of tenacity and courage. But federal authorities have also been on the job.

In 1961–1962, the FBI investigated alleged racial discrimination in voting in more than 100 counties, interviewed thousands of persons for evidence of discrimination that could be used in court, and photographed hundreds of thousands of voting records to be analyzed and compared with population statistics. By October 1962, Justice, on the basis of these data, had filed 30 suits in five states. The advances thus secured in Negro registration were notable—particularly in East Carroll Parish, Louisiana, and Macom and Bullock counties, Alabama.

By 1965, Doar writes, a "gratifying" degree of compliance had been achieved with regard to the rights of Negroes to equal use and enjoyment of public facilities and accommodations. Here again the contribution of courage made by civil rights workers is a matter of dramatic record. But Doar reports a fact not visible to the public eye: namely, that the mere starting of an FBI investigation "sufficed to bring compliance" in most instances. "Only a minority of cases have required litigation."

To turn from a report like that of John Doar to almost any one of the columns and articles which brand as deplorable the FBI's record in the civil rights field is to realize how little can be learned from the latter about the specifics of federal law. We have not found even one such piece that has based its charges on well-authenticated discrepancies between the FBI's assignment, as defined by law and departmental policy, and its performance. The preferred practice seems to be for the critic to set up a standard of his own by which the Bureau is to be judged—and then to denounce it for falling short.

In Chapter XV, we spoke of Wechsler's article, "The FBI's Failure in the South": the one in which he declares it to be "utterly clear" that all federal law enforcement work related to civil rights should be taken out of the hands of the FBI—because it does not provide personal protection for those who are involved in "the social revolution of our time." We return to it here to note the manner in which Wechsler provides for his argument what looks like a solid documentary base—and does so with exactly no reference to the precise terms of any civil rights statute.

His source is one that deservedly commands respect: the 1947 report of President Truman's Committee on Civil Rights, which was published under the title *To Secure These Rights*. To illustrate what this Committee said "about the 'dependence' of the Civil Rights Section of the Justice Department on the FBI in its investigative work," he quotes four full paragraphs:

The FBI handles virtually all the investigative work in Federal civil rights cases. It is unnecessary to comment on the remarkably successful record of the FBI in the general field of law enforcement. In the civil rights field there are many cases where high caliber investigative work has been done by the Bureau. However, there are also indications that upon occasion investigations in this very difficult and highly specialized area have not measured up to the Bureau's high standard in the handling of other types of cases.

There is evidence in the civil rights case files in the Department of Justice that the Bureau has sometimes felt that it was burdensome and difficult to undertake as many specific civil rights investigations as are requested. Moreover, investigations have not always been as full as the needs of the situation would warrant. Such shortcomings should be remedied by streamlining the somewhat cumbersome administrative relationships among the Civil Rights Section, the Criminal Division of the Department of Justice, the office of the Attorney General, and the Federal Bureau of Investigation.

The tendency of FBI agents to work in close cooperation with local police officers has sometimes been detrimental to the handling of civil rights investigations. At times, these local officers are themselves under suspicion. Even where this is not so, the victims or witnesses in civil rights cases are apt to be weak and frightened people who are not encouraged to tell their stories freely to Federal agents where the latter are working closely with the local police. Having in general established such a wholly sound relationship, it is sometimes difficult for the FBI agent to break the relationship and to work without, or even against, the local police when a civil rights case comes along.

A second difficulty which explains investigative shortcomings in some civil rights cases is the fact that the FBI agent must be trained broadly in law enforcement work and must be active on a wide front in enforcing the great variety of Federal criminal statutes which now exist. Accordingly, the agent is not always prepared to cope with the elusive and difficult aspects of a civil rights case. More highly specialized training of agents in this field would overcome some of the occasional shortcomings which are now present in the Bureau's work in cases of this type.[3]

Perhaps Wechsler realizes that so temperate a spelling out of problems and recommendations does not really point toward the drastic action which he is preparing to call necessary. In 1947, he says, it was "an open secret in Washington" that a much more critical version was toned down in the course of "bitter behind-the-scenes controversy."

Open secrets in Washington come a dime a dozen. They tend to be about as accurate as Bob Richards' version of what is "axiomatic among newsmen" with regard to the FBI's *Most Wanted* program. As evidence, their value is nil. But to round out the long quotation, Wechsler writes:

The year 1963 is not 1947; yet the same words still essentially characterize the ambiguous—and ambivalent—posture of the FBI

---

[3] *To Secure These Rights: Report of the President's Committee on Civil Rights* (U.S. Government Printing Office, 1947), pp. 122–123.

in a time when tensions are far deeper, when racist violence is far more widespread, and when the Negro's sense of alienation from the FBI has steadily grown rather than declined.

This description of the present situation goes undocumented.

The way the four paragraphs are presented makes it seem that the FBI was singled out for criticism because of its inadequate performance. The passage, however, is from a section of the report, pp. 114 ff., in which the Committee is making across-the-board recommendations for improving "the federal civil rights enforcement machinery."

Its criticisms and suggestions cover "statutory tools," the personnel resource of the CRS, the type of cooperation given to the CRS by United States Attorneys, the FBI's investigations, and the administrative setup of the Justice Department. Unsurprisingly, the Committee did not find perfection anywhere along the line, and it was no more critical of the FBI than of all the other parts of the "machinery."

Thus, declaring the intelligent and sympathetic cooperation of United States Attorneys to be "crucial to effective federal enforcement of the civil rights laws," it said:

Many United States Attorneys extend such cooperation. However, a staff survey of a random selection of the Section's case files disclosed serious shortcomings in the work of some United States Attorneys.

Noting that such Attorneys are "local lawyers" who have been appointed to their federal posts for four-year terms, the Committee went on to observe that while some have taken a courageous stand against "the ingrained prejudices and mores" of their communities, others have tried to avoid having to do so.

To be consistent, Wechsler would have to urge that United States Attorneys be dissociated from all federal civil rights work. For that matter, he would have practically to dismantle the Justice Department. But to be fair, he would have to quote the Committee as saying also that the Civil Rights Section, the FBI, and the United States Attorneys "deserve the highest praise for the imagination and courage they have often shown."[4]

Actually, no 1947 estimate of the FBI's work in the civil rights field can serve as a measure of its present performance. During the 1930's, Bureau agents had little chance to acquire skill in "this very difficult and highly specialized area"—because the Department was more passive than active in relation to civil rights. Then, just seven months after Attorney General Murphy created the CRS, World War II broke out—and the Bureau was plunged into a second new, difficult, and "highly specialized" area: that of national security and intelligence. Still further, the agent force was more than doubled between 1939 and 1945, so that the ratio of experienced agents to inexperienced was inordinately high.

Yet because of Wechsler's implications, we, too, shall go back to 1947. Robert Carr, we would recall, was not only the author of *Federal Protection of Civil Rights*, published in that year, but also Executive Secretary of the President's Committee and, broadly speaking, the author of *To Secure These Rights*.

We shall quote from his own book—*Federal Protection of Civil Rights*—for two reasons. First, it contains a wealth of detail about cases that is not to be found in the official document; and second, we doubt that even Wechsler would contend that Carr, as a private author, would be responsive to behind-the-scenes pressures. Certainly, no pressure in behalf of the FBI would have been exerted upon him by Cornell University, which published his book as one of its *Studies in Civil Liberty*.

On pp. 152–153, Carr discusses a 1940 police-brutality case in Atlanta which served to clarify "the working relationship

[4] *op. cit.*, p. 114.

between the CRS and the FBI." When the Bureau was first asked to investigate third-degree methods allegedly used by the police, it was reluctant to "endanger its good relations with the police departments of Atlanta, and other cities, which it had gone to great lengths to build."

Higher authorities in the Department "were inclined to side with the FBI." But after considerable "intradepartmental bickering," the investigations were ordered, "and the FBI did a thorough job of obtaining evidence for the prosecution." This was one of the first important cases handled by the CRS: *United States v. W. F. Sutherland.* From then on, "the two agencies, on the whole, have worked together reasonably well."

This passage comes closer than does any other in Carr's book to criticizing the FBI. Yet it reports only a disagreement that was ironed out. It would have provided real cause for concern if the Bureau, having been ordered to make the investigation, had grudgingly delivered second-rate results. But it did "a thorough job."

Many disagreements about policy marked the early years of the CRS—and did not prove anyone to be a villain. Some of them related to the problem of how the CRS was to learn about violations of rights. Carr reports, p. 142, that Assistant Attorney General John Rogge, head of the Criminal Division, wanted the CRS to have its own field offices, but that Attorney General Robert H. Jackson was opposed to the idea.

In the end, the CRS went about developing channels, private and public, through which it could receive information. Among the private, the NAACP became one of the most useful channels. "By far the most important public sources of complaint [were] the FBI field offices and the United States Attorneys."

On p. 154, Carr tells of a 1942 police-brutality case in Arkansas: *United States v. Culp.* Reports had reached the CRS that Culp, a deputy sheriff, was operating a "kangaroo court" in which persons whom he had jailed on trumped-up charges were "sentenced" to buy back their freedom. The FBI "made a series of very thorough studies." Armed with these, the CRS prosecuted the case, and three men were convicted.

On p. 172, he says that in a 1943 lynching case in Illinois a state grand jury "refused to indict anyone, because of lack of evidence." But "The FBI and the United States Attorney continued to investigate the case from the federal angle, with the aid of Frank Coleman of the CRS." Thirteen persons were eventually indicted by a federal grand jury.

On pp. 180–181, he uses a successfully prosecuted anti-peonage case, *United States v. Johnson,* to illustrate the extreme care with which a civil rights case must be prepared. "The FBI was extremely thorough in its investigations and did such an excellent job of assembling evidence against Johnson that he had little choice but to plead guilty . . . ."

While Carr gives various other such examples, he gives not even one example of a half-hearted or slipshod investigation—nor even one example of the FBI's holding back from any form of work that it was properly instructed to do. Speaking of certain 1946 lynchings at Monroe, Georgia, he says, p. 209, that "extensive but belated federal investigations could produce no evidence leading to an indictment of the culprits." He attributes the belatedness, however, not to the FBI, but to clumsy administrative arrangements.

In the years covered by both Carr's book and the report of the Committee—the years 1939–1946—federal *initiative* in the civil rights field was a new thing under the sun; the CRS was feeling its way toward an adequate policy and program; and FBI agents were having to "learn by doing" what they had not previously been called upon to do.

Since then, the new Civil Rights Acts have been passed; the CRS has matured into the Civil Rights Division; and the

FBI has not only built up a sizeable body of specialists in civil rights matters but also developed a policy of giving all agents basic training in this field. In brief, the key recommendations made by the President's Committee have either been met or are well on the way to being met.

Since we have followed Wechsler back to 1947, however, we wish to note that he and Carr represent strikingly different standards of judgment—just as do he and John Doar. Within Carr's frame of reference, there would be no room for "an open secret in Washington" that posed as evidence. There would be ample room for the complexities of problems, but none for stereotyped oversimplifications. There would be room for many disagreements about policy, but none for an arbitrary casting of those who disagreed as heroes and villains.

Carr does not by any means regard the FBI with what Cook calls "almost slavish adulation." But he judges it by the quality of the performance it turns in when it has been given a job to do—by federal law and appropriate authorities. It seems to us that this is the only proper standard by which it can be judged, and when this standard is applied, the Bureau's contribution to the cause of civil rights turns out to have been, and to be at this time, a very solid one.

TWENTY-FOUR

THE WHAT AND HOW OF ORGANIZED CRIME

SINCE 1957—the year when the Mafia leaders gathered at Apalachin, New York, and when the McClellan Committee on racketeering began hearings that continued until 1960—the available store of information about organized crime has swiftly expanded. Chapter 7 of *The Challenge of Crime in a Free Society* provides an admirably concise and readable account of what a crime syndicate is and of how it consolidates and uses its power.[1]

Organized crime—"a society that seeks to operate outside the control of the American people and their governments"—

involves thousands of criminals, working within structures as complex as those of any large corporation, subject to laws more rigidly enforced than those of legitimate governments.

Yet because a crime syndicate "desperately preserves its invisibility," most people are unaware of being affected by

[1] U.S. Government Printing Office, Washington, D.C.

347

it. "The price of a loaf of bread may go up one cent as the result of an organized crime conspiracy, but the housewife has no way of knowing why she is paying more."

The one-cent rise is too small to make probable any concerted protest or investigation. But:

It is organized crime's accumulation of money, not the individual transactions by which the money is accumulated, that has a great and threatening impact on American life. A quarter in a jukebox means nothing . . . . But millions of quarters in thousands of jukeboxes can provide both a strong motive for murder and the means to commit murder with impunity. Organized crime exists by virtue of the power it purchases with its money.

In sucking funds from the general public, the syndicate contrives in multiple ways to make what is "nothing" in itself add up to the kind of money with which it can purchase power:

The millions of dollars it can invest in narcotics or use for layoff money give it power over the lives of thousands of people and over the quality of life in whole communities. The millions of dollars it can throw into the legitimate economic system give it power to manipulate the price of shares on the stock market, to raise or lower the price of retail merchandise, to determine whether entire industries are union or non-union, to make it easier or harder for businessmen to continue in business.

The millions of dollars it can spend on corrupting public officials may give it power to maim or murder people inside or outside the organization with impunity, to conduct businesses in such fields as liquor, meat, or drugs without regard to administrative regulations, to avoid payment of income tax, or to secure public works contracts without competitive bidding.

The crime network is national and international. Yet, "Neutralizing local law enforcement is central to organized crime's operations." The syndicates cannot do business where they cannot buy protection—from members of the police force or from political office holders.

The number one source of wealth of today's crime bosses is gambling; and their enormous profits from it reach them

through channels so complex that even persons who work in the betting operation do not know or cannot prove the identity of the leader.

Next in order of importance comes loan-sharking. Interest rates vary from 1 to 150 percent a week; and

force, or threats of force of the most brutal kind, are used to effect interest collection, eliminate protest when interest rates are raised, and prevent the beleaguered borrower from reporting the activity to enforcement officials . . . .

In May 1968, the Smathers Committee—the Senate Subcommittee on Small Business and Business Loans—conducted hearings on loan-sharking. One witness testified that he had been bankrupted by sharks who had terrorized him into paying $14,000 in return for an original loan of $1,900.[1]

Among the money-makers, narcotics come third, with the Mafia controlling some 80 percent of the heroin sold in the United States, and the bosses realizing an annual profit of around $21,000,000. Because of the many hands through which the drug must pass to reach the corner peddler, the annual cost to addicts is estimated to be $350,000,000.[2]

As sources of wealth for the crime bosses, prostitution and bootlegging have lost their one-time importance. They now "play a small and declining role."

In contrast, the infiltration of legitimate business has become increasingly important. It provides a respectable front and a source of income on which "just enough taxes can be paid to avoid income tax prosecution." To gain control of businesses—and "exact illegal profits from the

[1] *Washington Post*, May 16, 1968.

[2] Figures provided by George H. Gaffney, Special Assistant to the Director of the Bureau of Narcotics and Dangerous Drugs.

public"—syndicate leaders employ "monopolization, terrorism, extortion, tax evasion."

Labor racketeering has enabled criminal forces to control strategic sectors of labor, steal from union funds, borrow from pension systems to underwrite illicit enterprises, and extort money from employers by threats of labor strife.

La Cosa Nostra—the Mafia—now dominates the underworld. The limits of its power are, indeed, almost impossible to determine, for other crime syndicates that appear to act independently are often tied in with it as lesser allies—or as vassals. Or they exist on sufferance—because they do not invade areas, geographical or operational, that the Mafia has staked out as its own. The wages of trying to compete with La Cosa Nostra, like those of informing on its activities, are death.

In 1963–1964, the Senate Permanent Subcommittee on Investigations, chaired by Senator McClellan, held hearings on *Organized Crime and Illicit Traffic in Narcotics*. Testifying on October 10, 1963, George C. Edwards, Police Commissioner of Detroit, presented a record of known gang murders in that area from 1927 to 1963. Their annual rate, he said, has declined since the Mafia has been trying to establish a respectable front. But the organization's "principal product" is still fear:

The Mafia front men are characterized by the smile, the glad hand, the tuxedo, and the ticket to the charity ball. But the basic Mafia tools are still money, murder, and corruption.

Its trademarks are still "the lime, the garrote, and the dead pig"—the last, to warn that "squealers" die. "Its slogan could still be Bodies by Mafia."[3]

Often, now, it might be "Missing Persons by Mafia." Sophisticated bosses prefer to have a victim "dis-

[3] *Hearings*, Part II, p. 409.

appear"—thus depriving the law of a corpse with which to substantiate its conviction that murder has been committed. But openly or in disguise the murders go on: 45 in the Boston area alone during the past six years. Whoever cannot be controlled *to whatever extent the bosses' purposes require* must be "whacked out."

Gang murders, we must note, are at the opposite extreme from murders of impulse. Each of them is a calculated act of discipline and intimidation. La Cosa Nostra is an outlaw body that cannot afford to tolerate any slightest infringement of its own laws. By its standards, the murders it commits are acts of law enforcement.

Its power to gain its ends by means of "money, murder, and corruption" derives from its tight hierarchical structure and its code: which are those of "the Mafia groups that have operated for almost a century on the Island of Sicily." Most of the top leaders are Sicilian. All members are Italian by birth or background.

The membership, estimated to be around 5,000 in this country, is divided into 24 "families," each headed by a "boss" whose authority over it is absolute. Supreme authority is vested in a "commission" controlled by the most successful bosses.

Below each boss are two men of equal status: the "underboss" or deputy; and the *consigliere,* or counselor—usually a semi-retired elder statesman. Below these two, the "buffer" layers begin: the layers of personnel that make it unnecessary for those at the top ever to communicate directly with low-ranking members, and that "insulate" them from the law.

The highest buffer layer is made up of the *caporegeme,* or "chiefs of operating units"; the lowest within the family structure of *soldati,* or soldiers. A soldier may operate an illicit enterprise on a commission basis or "own" it and pay for the right to operate with a percentage of his profits.

Below the *soldati* are non-family employees and commission agents. They need not be Italian and their total number may embrace the whole membership of lesser ethnic gangs. Their chores range from answering the telephone to taking bets and selling narcotics. No buffers protect them from the law.

The Mafia code specifies that subordinates must never interfere with the bosses' affairs or question the tasks assigned them. They carry out orders—and go to prison so that the men at the top can amass fortunes:

Loyalty, honor, respect, absolute obedience—these are inculcated in family members through ritualistic initiation and customs . . . , through material rewards and through violence . . . .

A "boss can order the execution of any family member for any reason"—and his pervasive informant system is designed to insure that no sufficient reason will escape his notice.

The first person to testify at the 1963 hearings—on September 25th—was Attorney General Robert Kennedy. On the basis of intelligence data, he explained how a boss's will to have somebody "knocked off" is implemented. The boss merely speaks to somebody of his wish to have the individual in question removed. That somebody "will speak to somebody else who will speak to somebody else and order it." The gunman who commits the murder does not know the original source of the order.

Thus, even if he is arrested, and even if he wants to strike a bargain with the police, he has nothing to tell that could threaten the boss. As for those who have knowledge:

. . . the usual reply of a convicted hoodlum in a position to give information is that he doesn't want to trade a jail cell for a hearse.[4]

Obviously, no law enforcement body could launch an effective campaign against La Cosa Nostra without knowing

---

[4] *Hearings*, Part I, p. 15.

more about it than its bosses want to have known. If there is to be in the end a well-planned counter-offensive, there must be in the beginning—and all along the way—*strategic intelligence*.

As we study the hearings, the Commission's report, and related documents, we realize that striking successes have been chalked up on the intelligence front. Broadly speaking, the Mafia's well-guarded secrets are no longer secret. Its impenetrable structure has been penetrated. The "insulation" which the bosses have provided for themselves has not prevented their being identified; and, with them, their close associates in the top layers of the structure.

Having defined *strategic intelligence* as "information regarding the capabilities, intentions, and vulnerabilities" of a group that is to be opposed, the President's Commission states:

For example, the body of knowledge built up by the FBI concerning the structure, membership, activities, and purposes of La Cosa Nostra is significant strategic intelligence.

The scope of such knowledge is suggested by charts and detailed reports included in the 5-volume text of the 1963–1964 hearings.

According to the Commission, the FBI began in 1961 to supply Justice's Organized Crime and Racketeering Section "with regular intelligence reports on 400 of the Nation's crime figures." Its ability to do so was not acquired over night. In 1944, the Bureau had inaugurated a fieldwide crime survey program under which each field office sent in to Washington headquarters, twice a year, detailed reports on organized gangs and individual racketeers, gambling, criminal control of unions, tieups between the underworld and local police and politicians, and related matters.[5]

As the law then stood, relatively few of the criminal activities reported came under the FBI's jurisdiction; but many

[5] *FBI 1968 Appropriation*, pp. 88–89.

leads were provided to local police departments and to other federal agencies—the Internal Revenue Service, and Federal Bureau of Narcotics, the Post Office Department, and the Customs Bureau. The extent of the FBI's intelligence-gathering activity is indicated by the materials it contributed to the McClellan Committee during its 1957–1960 hearings on racketeering.

The Bureau is not, of course, the only contributor to the Government's store of strategic intelligence. When, in 1963, Attorney General Kennedy testified that the FBI was "penetrating deeply into the operation and structure of the rackets," he paid tribute likewise to the work of many other agencies. Federal investigators as a group were, he said, "pooling information" on 1,100 racketeers.

As an opponent of La Cosa Nostra's "invisibility," however, the FBI has certain advantages over any one of the more narrowly specialized investigative units. Its diversified jurisdictional field impinges broadly upon the Mafia's diversified field of operations. It is an old hand at developing informant systems within would-be secret conspiracies. And, not least, having handled domestic intelligence in the national-security field since 1939, it has a sizeable body of long-term agents who have the basic skills that intelligence work requires.

We stress the Bureau's advantages in order to prevent a statement made by the Presidents' Commission from sounding like an implied criticism of other agencies. Speaking of La Cosa Nostra's twenty-four families, the Commission said, "To date, only the Federal Bureau of Investigation has been able to document fully the national scope of these groups."

It is an odd experience to turn from the hearings and the Commission's *Report* to Fred Cook's article, "The FBI and Organized Crime," in the May 1965 issue of *Ramparts*. Cook charges the FBI with having been both unwilling and unable to penetrate the Mafia. Like Turner, he declares

Hoover to be reluctant either to tangle with this underworld giant or to let anyone else do so; and he asks:

Is there more to this reluctance than meets the eye? That is the hardest question of all to answer. There can be no doubt that mob money exerts tremendous leverage in politics.

Acknowledging that he has no evidence with which to support such a thesis, he proceeds, then, to imply that the FBI Director may be under Mafia influence.

We are chiefly interested, however, in another of his theses. In part, he declares, the Bureau's "failure" is attributable to Hoover's "fetish for clean-scrubbed, 100 percent American types with college degrees":

... when it comes to infiltrating underworld rings, the hard-boiled local detective or narcotics agent, capable of looking as if he had just rolled out of a rumpled bed after a hard night with a bottle and a blonde, is often more effective.

We can only ask: *Effective to what end?*

Only rarely, we would assume, and for some singular reason, would an FBI Special Agent be given a long-term undercover assignment in an outlaw body. The Bureau's success in infiltrating both criminal and subversive groups has rested upon what we might call a division of labor between agents and informants.

We do not doubt that agents can look and act as "hard-boiled" as their assignments require. But the Bureau's intelligence job is not to get a trickle of information about a nationwide conspiracy from a few points of penetration. It is to insure maximum coverage—in all parts of the country, and from top to bottom of the conspiratorial structure. One of the most effective ways to achieve such coverage is to enlist the services of persons who are already on the inside.

The FBI agent's work begins, we might say, where that of the informant leaves off. His job is to follow investigative leads; to check and recheck for accuracy the data received; and so to correlate seemingly disparate items that the overall pattern of conspiratorial activity can be determined.

Demonstrably, the FBI agents have had what it takes to locate persons whose allegiance to a conspiracy has begun to waver; and then, *acting in their own role*, to convert such waverers into defector-informants. Demonstrably, also, they have had what it takes to win, and keep, the confidence of individuals who put their lives in daily jeopardy by informing.

Quite apart from such considerations, however, Cook's statement brings into question his knowledge of the makeup and policy of La Cosa Nostra. For an agent to infiltrate this conspiratorial body on any level above that of the expendable hirelings who have little information to give, he would have to qualify for family membership.

Traditionally, the Mafia required that each candidate for membership be known to have killed at least one person. This extreme requirement no longer holds—not in the United States, at least. But no one is admitted who does not have enough of a criminal record to assure the bosses that he will not boggle at what is demanded of him and that he will have a strong personal reason not to "squeal." The FBI is *a law enforcement body*. Who would want its agents to qualify for Mafia membership?

Beyond all this is the fact that Cook's tough-guy investigator would stand exactly no chance of penetrating the Mafia hierarchy at the level where plans are made and knowledge of the body's diverse operations is hoarded. And that is where the criminals are that the Government wants to reach.

Commissioner Edwards testified that when the Detroit Police Department first created, in the 1930's, a special squad to deal with "an already apparent threat of the Mafia," that outlaw body was made up of obvious gangsters who preyed chiefly upon their fellow Sicilians.

Today many of these very same criminals . . . are executives in well-tailored suits residing in expensive homes and directing racketeering enterprises of national and international scope.

In like vein, Commissioner Michael J. Murphy of the New York City Police Department declared the old marks of the gangster, including the ever-present "blonde," to be "20 years out of date:

Sophistication is so advanced that public relations policies are laid down . . . . The top echelon frowns on those who create a bad image. The air of respectability, the quiet life in the residential neighborhood, . . . is the order of the day.[6]

Those who want to keep tab on Mafia activities *at the level that counts* cannot act, today, as though they were operating in the 1930's—or in the pages of pulp fiction.

What access, for example, would Cook's disheveled character have to a John Montana—whose career was outlined at the hearings by Michael A. Amico, head of the Criminal Intelligence Division of the Buffalo, New York, Police Department?

In the 1930's, Amico testified, Montana began developing a taxicab company which, by the 1950's, was the largest in western New York. Along the way, it had absorbed various other companies—and had established a monopoly hold on "preferred taxi locations" in and around Buffalo.

During the same span of years, he had become deeply involved in city politics, business, and civic and charitable associations. "To list Montana's legitimate associates would be to list the who's who of Buffalo . . . ." In 1956, he was named Buffalo's "Man of the Year"—for his success in business, his services on the city council and zoning board, his multiple charities, and his "espousal of good government."

Meanwhile, his alleged Mafia associates constituted a Who's Who of the underworld. Amico named among them

[6] *Hearings*, Part I, p. 45.

Joseph Barbara, Sr., Stafano Magaddino, Fred Tandaccio, James La Duca, Sam Pietei, and others. At one time, Amico stated, he had been closely associated with Joe DiCarlo, a labor racketeer and "former Buffalo public enemy No. 1." In 1957, he was among those present at the gathering of Mafia leaders at the home of Joseph Barbara, Sr., at Apalachin, New York.

Together with nineteen others who were present, he was later indicted by a federal grand jury on charges of conspiring to obstruct justice, and was convicted—as were the others—in the United States District Court. Among the defendants, Montana was, it would seem, the only one who did not invoke his right not to incriminate himself. He said that he had, in effect, gone to Apalachin with Antonio Magaddino just for the ride—and for a visit with Barbara. While evidence seemed to establish his being a "trusted lieutenant" of Stafano Magaddino, allegedly La Cosa Nostra boss of western New York and Ontario, he disclaimed any knowledge of Magaddino's criminal activities.[7]

The Apalachin convictions—for reasons that we shall note in the next chapter—were reversed on appeal. From that time until his death in 1964, at the age of 70, Montana, according to Amico, had only rare contacts in public with his former underworld friends.

We have no knowledge of whether or not FBI agents have had any purposeful contact with Montana as an individual. But he illustrates a type of person in relation to whom these "clean-scrubbed" agents with law degrees can practice a kind of surveillance that requires no concealing of their identity—and a kind that would be impossible for a tough-guy detective.

When the bosses began to infiltrate the world of legitimate business and community affairs, they began to enter situations in which FBI agents could have quite normal contacts with them. In view of Montana's activity on the city

[7] *Hearings*, Part II, p. 501 ff.

council and his "espousal of good government," the Special Agent in Charge of the Buffalo field office could even have arranged, if he wished, to meet with him and discuss the problem posed by organized crime.

Indubitably, the FBI has developed informants within the leadership ranks of La Cosa Nostra. It knows in abundance what could not have been learned by any amount of infiltration of the lower buffer layers or of the layer of non-family hirelings. Attorney General Kennedy testified, in fact, that information about "what happened at Apalachin" had come from "an inside source."

In some instances, we suppose, this phrase might be used to refer to an electronic "source": a bugging device. But, on the record, the FBI did not have advance knowledge of the Apalachin gathering. The fact that it was taking place was brought to light by a New York State Trooper, Edgar Crosswell, who had been pursuing Barbara for thirteen years— according to Circuit Judge Clark in a separate but concurring opinion in *United States v. Russell A. Buffalino et al*—"in all possible ways (including tapping his telephone)" in an unsuccessful effort to get "evidence of illegality."

We cannot say how any high-echelon informant has been moved toward a shift of allegiance. We would guess the most common pattern to have been that of a wavering commitment that was encouraged by *someone* to become a firm commitment-in-reverse. Considering the hazards with which such an informant would be electing to live, and the investment of faith he would have to make in this persuasive *someone*, we doubt that the latter would look as though he had "just rolled out of a rumpled bed after a hard night with a bottle and a blonde."

TWENTY-FIVE

ELEMENTS OF A
COUNTER-OFFENSIVE

W HEN ROBERT KENNEDY said that "what happened at Apalachin" had been learned from "an
inside source," he added, "But we could not produce a witness who would tell you what happened." This addendum
points to the reason why intelligence cannot readily be
translated into convictions of Mafia bosses and their
lieutenants. To borrow a phrase from T. S. Eliot, between the
informing and the testifying "Falls the Shadow"—in this
case, the shadow of terrorism.

It may be fairly easy to convict a Mafia underling who has
committed a crime on order. But to trace the line back to
the man who started the order on its way down through the
buffer layers is, as Attorney General Kennedy testified, often
impossible.

Moreover, if every person involved in the order's transmission is identified, Justice may still not have even one witness
to put on the stand. After those with nothing to tell, those
who will not talk, and those who will talk only as confiden-

tial informants have been subtracted, there may be nobody left.

Information is not testimony; and under our system, a defendant has a right to be confronted by his accuser. What has most of all made difficult the conviction of bosses and their lieutenants has been the likelihood of an accuser's becoming a "Body by Mafia."

To secure witnesses against high-ranking criminals, Kennedy said, Justice must be able to grant immunity from self-incrimination, so that testimony can be required, and to provide protection from the vengeance of the Mafia. Asked by Senator Muskie how such protection could be provided, he answered:

We have taken steps, Senator, to even move people out of the country.

We have provided them positions and work where nobody would really have contact with them. We have arranged to move their families and have their names changed.[1]

Defendants, moreover, whom the bosses see as potential "squealers" may sign their own death warrants when they exercise their right to be released on bond. After twenty-four members of an international heroin ring had been indicted in New York, through the efforts of the Federal Bureau of Narcotics,

(t)he body of one defendant was found in the Bronx, full of bullet holes . . . . The badly burned body of a second defendant was found in a field near Rochester, New York.

Yet convictions of high-echelon criminals are multiplying. In cases investigated in whole or in part by the FBI, 281 convictions of organized crime figures were secured in fiscal 1968; and at the year's end, some 675 persons who had been indicted were awaiting trial. Attorney General Ramsey Clark has reported a sharp rise in 1968. A few examples from

[1] *Hearings*, Part I, p. 25.

the 1967 and 1968 lists can be taken to illustrate many more.

On May 9, 1967, Sam Battaglia, acting boss of the Chicago "family" of La Cosa Nostra, and one of his chief lieutenants, Joseph Amabile, were convicted on extortion charges, and each was sentenced to a 15-year prison term.

On November 9th, rackets boss John Dioguardi and two associates were convicted in New York City on charges of having worked a "planned bankruptcy" scheme.

In January 1968, "reported Philadelphia La Cosa Nostra 'captain' Pasquale Massi was convicted and subsequently sentenced to prison for attempting to bribe a witness and committing a crime on a Government reservation in Arkansas."

In May 1968, another reputed "captain," Carmine Persico, and three of his associates were convicted in New York city for the highjacking of $15,000 worth of textiles from a Brooklyn truck terminal.[2]

We can stare at the power structure of La Cosa Nostra until we become transfixed by it, but its vulnerabilities are as real as its strengths. It is vulnerable to anything that reduces the "invincibility" of the boss in the eyes of his underlings, that makes terrorism backfire, that penetrates or splits the organization, or that weakens the binding power of the code.

Like all totalitarian bodies, La Cosa Nostra needs to appear to be all strength and no weakness. Thus, it can be harmed in extraordinary measure by what would scarcely dent a more flexible and open organization. The Government's counter-offensive must capitalize this fact with consummate skill.

The conviction of a Mafia boss is, for example, an event with by-product consequences. It reports to those on every buffer layer that an individual in whom they have invested a life-and-death confidence is not actually "insulated" against the law. Also, it can close some important source of wealth.

If it leads to a long prison term, it can easily spark a struggle among would-be successors. And it can create a replacement problem—as it did in the Battaglia case.

Battaglia was acting as boss in place of Sam Giancana, who had fled to Latin America and gone into hiding. When Battaglia and Amabile were convicted, two retired members, Paul Rica and Anthony Accordo, were reputedly forced back into service—to handle the syndicate's affairs in the Chicago area.

Further, when Mafia leaders feel threatened, they often respond in a way that provides the Government with new opportunities for action. As we have noted, the "impenetrable" structure has been penetrated—in depth. The President's Commission reports a surprising result: chiefly because of the bosses' anxiety about infiltration, many of the families have, for several years, admitted no new members.

When family membership becomes static, the securing of convictions against its *soldati* takes on a new importance. For the duration of their sentences, imprisoned *soldati* represent an irreplaceable loss. A multiplying of convictions makes necessary a multiplying of non-member hirelings to carry on the work; and they are held in line only by fear and self-interest—not by the Mafia code.

Again, the bosses, when they feel threatened, tend to step up their use of terrorism; and terrorism *can* backfire. If a member knows, as Joseph Valachi did, or if he even suspects, that he is marked for liquidation, he can begin to see a jail cell, with maximum security, as a welcome alternative to a hearse. Thus, he can become ready to talk, and even to testify, in return for whatever protection the law can give.

Gang warfare has usually been the result of a struggle for succession; and such a struggle can result either from the death of a boss or from his long imprisonment. Once it has started, such a war is a murderous affair.

At this writing, a war for control of the family of former boss Joseph Bonanno has been going on in Brooklyn, New York, for more than three years. Constant investigative pressure by the FBI has made it into a 3-faction struggle and has prevented any contender's being able to reconsolidate the membership under his own control.[3] Within a period of weeks in the spring of 1968, there were four murders which the police attributed to this gang war; and one victim was a former underboss.[4]

A prolonged war of succession seriously reduces the power of a La Cosa Nostra family to carry on business as usual—and thus reduces its wealth. Also, and more important, as "Bodies by Mafia" multiply, so do informants—and witnesses.

The President's Commission indicates that, in addition to the above types of vulnerability, new types are being added by the effort of the bosses to live in two worlds at once. Having invaded the world of legitimate business, they need the services of experts who cannot be found in the family ranks; and these experts cannot be offered the role of expendable hirelings.

They demand both status and enough authority to issue orders that the bosses would be unqualified to tell them to issue. As the requisite authority is delegated, decentralization sets in; problems of discipline multiply; and new reasons for internal discontent are bred.

For the first time in the long history of the Mafia, loyal but unskilled *soldati* are finding that outsiders are being put above them in rank. Not only are their own roads to advancement being blocked, but they are being deprived of their reason to feel fiercely proud of their family membership—even on the lowest level of the structure.

The President's Commission regards internal rebellion as a distinct possibility; and it "would not take the form of strikes and picketing." It would usher in a wave of violence; and since rebellion at the bottom, unlike a war of succession at the top, would challenge the validity of the code, the vio-

[3] *FBI 1969 Appropriation*, p. 83.
[4] *Washington Post*, April 20, 1968.

lence, before it ended, could jeopardize both the old authority and the new respectability of the bosses.

Meanwhile, the bosses and their associates are involved in
complex relationships not provided for in the Mafia tradition. When investigative pressure makes it impossible for a
high-level member of La Cosa Nostra any longer to stand
with one foot in the world of 100-year-old Sicilian Mafia and
the other in that of 20th century America, with all its economic, social, and community involvements, which foot does
he move?

One imponderable that could influence his decision is well
worth noting. In an effort to provide themselves with an
inside source of expertness, many Mafia bosses have sent
their sons to top-level law schools and schools of business.
We have been told, but can offer the statement only as hearsay supported by logic, that the sons often decline, in the
end, to dedicate their lives to La Cosa Nostra. A boss might
well hesitate to jeopardize a son's legitimate career.

When it comes to talking to a Mafia leader who is confronted by obstacles that will not yield to "money, murder,
and corruption," an FBI agent has three assets. He has intelligence data to lay on the line, so that the leader knows how
unsecret his "secret" activities are. He is skilled in imple-
menting the Bureau's policy of helping persons who are
self-trapped in blind alleys to find new openings to the
future. And he has the traits that distinguish him from the
type of tough-guy operative who is, in the world of the
Mafia, too common to be impressive.

Cook speaks of these FBI traits as the product of a
Hoover "fetish." But it was Attorney General Harlan Fiske
Stone who laid down the principle that agents should be
"gentlemen." Only by being gentlemen, we would suppose,
could they command enough respect to be able to develop
informants among those who operate on the upper layers of
the syndicate structure.

Edwin Arlington Robinson once observed, "Nothing is
ever the same when time has been there." We might add,

"Not even the Mafia." Its machinery of terror is a fearsome thing. The underworld's annual take is reputed to be around $20,000,000,000. A host of law enforcement officers and public officials have been corrupted. But not even the Mafia has been able to intimidate or to buy off the forces of change.

Precisely because the organization is marked, now, by both old vulnerabilities and new, this is the strategic time for the Government—and concerned local governments—to put on the pressure and *keep it on*. Too often, back through the years, both federal and local campaigns against organized crime have been sporadic, not sustained, affairs. After each of them, the Mafia has enjoyed an interval of comparative freedom from pressure in which to regroup its forces—and extend its power.

During the past decade, law enforcement efforts in relation to the crime syndicates have become more consistent, and more knowledgeable, than ever before. Enough has been accomplished to provide considerable evidence as to what works—in terms of convictions secured and illicit enterprises broken up. The key elements that must go into a strong counter-offensive have, in significant measure, been identified.

Since laws cannot be enforced until they have been enacted, the first element is a battery of federal statutes precisely geared to the problems to be solved. No sector of the crime syndicates' wealth-gathering enterprises should be allowed to remain unreachable. Ideally, federal, state, and local laws should form a dovetailed whole.

The record indicates that both the Federal Bureau of Narcotics and the Internal Revenue Service are veterans of a long war against organized crime. But it also indicates that each of them has had, within its own area, a long-established, well-defined license to act.

This situation has not held with regard to the number one and number two sources of criminal wealth: large-scale interstate gambling and loan-sharking. Not until 1961 was the FBI given a statutory permit to take the offensive against the former; and the first federal law directed against the latter—the *Truth in Lending Act*—was passed by Congress on May 22, 1968.

No loan-shark has yet, at this writing, been prosecuted under this act; but at least two arrests have been made by the FBI. The first arrest under the new extortionist credit law took place in New York City, on October 3, 1968. The suspect was Alcides Parez, who was charged with having made a loan at usurious rates to a Brooklyn meat market owner, and then threatening the latter with violence if he did not keep up his high-interest payments—and this even after he had gone bankrupt. The second arrest was made in Chicago on October 8th. Here the suspect was Michael L. Biancofieri, who was charged with extorting exorbitant payments from a Schiller Park business man.[5]

The 1961 anti-gambling laws have more than proved their utility. During the first six months of 1963, Attorney General Kennedy testified, 160 racketeers were convicted, as against 35 in the same period in 1960; and the number has continued to rise. Two examples will illustrate what can be done under these laws that no federal agency could do prior to 1961.

In 1965, William Marfeo opened an independent gambling place in the Federal Hills district of Providence, Rhode Island: a district "owned" by Raymond Patriarca, allegedly Mafia boss of New England. Marfeo was told to close his place. He did not do so. On July 13, 1963, he was shot to death by a gunman who walked into the Korner Kitchen Restaurant where he was eating with friends.

Prior to 1961, the FBI would have had no jurisdiction over any aspect of this crime. In 1966, however, it had authority to trace the line back from the murder to the point where it was planned—not in Rhode Island, but in Massachusetts.

On March 8, 1968, Patriarca and two codefendants were

[5] *New York Daily News*, October 4, 1968; *Chicago Tribune*, Oct. 9, 1968.

convicted both of violating and of conspiring to violate Section 1952, Title 18, U.S. Code: *Interstate and foreign travel or transportation in aid of racketeering.* Subsection (a) of Section 1952 makes it a federal crime to travel "in interstate or foreign commerce" or to use "any facility in interstate or foreign commerce" with the intent to commit any crime of violence to further any unlawful activity.[6]

Prior to the passage of the above law, Patriarca could quite safely have relied upon the standard Mafia practice of ordering a murder to be committed—and letting someone else use the murder weapon, while he remained at a distance, in another state. The tactic is no longer reliable.

Our second example is of a quite different order. Among the persons convicted in 1967 was an international gambler named Gilbert Lee Beckley. His gambling network illustrates the type of operation which could, prior to 1961, take a continent as its province while having to contend only with state laws and local law enforcement officers. An FBI map shows that the Beckley network, with headquarters in Miami, Florida, embraced four Canadian cities—Vancouver, Calgary, Winnipeg, and Montreal—and, in this country, twenty cities in nineteen different states. Only Nevada held two of the cities: Reno and Las Vegas.[7]

A second element in a counter-offensive must be the improvement of local police forces, to make them more competent and less corruptible. Here, the 1968 *Omnibus Crime Control and Safe Streets Act* should have a landmark importance. It provides for a nationwide, federally sponsored effort to raise the applicant and training levels, and the salary scale, of local police departments.

On the training side, Title I, Section 404 authorizes the FBI Director, acting under the Attorney General, too

(1) establish and conduct training programs at the Federal Bureau of Investigation National Academy at Quantico, Virginia,

[6] *U.S. Code Annotated*, Title 18, Sections 1691–3000, Cumulative Pocket Part, p. 45.
[7] *FBI 1969 Appropriation*, p. 84.

to provide, at the request of a State or unit of local government training for State and local law enforcement personnel;

(2) develop new and improved approaches, techniques, systems, equipment, and devices to improve and strengthen law enforcement; and

(3) assist in conducting, at the request of a State or unit of local government, local and regional training programs for the training of State and local law enforcement personnel . . . .[8]

Many local police departments have, on their own, achieved high professional standards; but many have lacked both resources to do so and a supportive public opinion. The above training effort is not, of course, relevant only to the war on organized crime. Every area of law enforcement should benefit by it.

A third element must be the stimulating of community interest. Citizens at the grassroots must provide both intolerance of police laxity and corruption and a supportive appreciation of a high-level performance. Here we must again quote from Attorney General Kennedy's 1968 testimony:

Regardless of new laws or old, regardless of resourceful and dedicated Federal investigative efforts, and regardless of how well rounded a picture of organized crime our intelligence helps us to secure, the only force that can conquer organized crime is the vigilance of citizens in every community . . . .

The recurrent theme we have found in case after case is that where there is little public interest, the cash registers of organized crime clang loudly. Where public interest is aroused—and stays aroused—racketeers are driven into bankruptcy or prison.[9]

Turner, in his *Nation* article, declares that Mr. Hoover stands "almost alone" in regarding organized crime as a local problem. This is nonsense: we have found no one who has intimately studied or worked with the problem who has not put heavy stress upon the need for community action.

[8] *Public Law 90-351*, 90th Congress, H.R. 5037, July 19, 1968, p. 7.

[9] *Hearings*, Part I, p. 9.

The crimes that fill the coffers of the syndicates require a continuity of organization. Therefore, they require protection—from local politicians and law officers. No federal agency can appoint local office holders or determine the character of the policeman on the beat. For a continuity of crime to have a continuity of protection, there must be a continuity of public indifference at the community level.

When, in our culture, we speak of community action, we think of voluntary associations and *ad hoc* committees and movements. We think, in brief, of citizens learning and acting together. Organized crime is, now, a subject that imperatively calls for joint study and activity.

Finally, a strong counter-offensive demands, at the federal level, the existence of a body that can both stimulate inter-agency collaboration and use its results. The Organized Crime and Racketeering Section of Justice—now staffed with 70 legal specialists—seems admirably to serve this function.

While it was created in the mid-1950's, this Section did not achieve real importance until 1961. When, after the Apalachin gathering of Mafia chiefs in 1957, Attorney General Rogers found himself on the receiving end of clamorous public demands for action against the crime syndicates, he bypassed the department's Section altogether and formed the Special Group on Organized Crime—as a two-year experiment.

It was headed up by Milton R. Wessel of New York, and his Deputy Chief was Gerald L. Goettel. Richard Ogilvie was in charge of the Chicago headquarters. Its most publicized effort was directed against twenty of the persons present at Apalachin: it secured, on a charge of conspiracy to obstruct justice, convictions that were reversed on appeal.

When Robert Kennedy became Attorney General, he did not continue the Special Group. Instead, he reorganized and enlarged the Organized Crime and Racketeering Section. In this, we think he acted wisely; and what he thus started has been further developed by Attorneys General Katzenbach and Clark.

A strange mythology with regard to the Special Group on Organized Crime has been authored by anti-FBI propagandists, particularly by Turner and Cook. According to this mythology, the Group's record shows it to have been exactly what was needed to spearhead a successful attack on the crime syndicates; but to have been, *for just this reason*, anathema to Mr. Hoover—whose ego was allegedly affronted by its success.

To support this myth, the FBI's record in relation to organized crime is labeled as one of failure and inaction, while the Group's record is presented as one of dedication and accomplishment in the face of bureaucratic lassitude and hostility. Cook, in his *Ramparts* article, declares its "conviction of some twenty of the Apalachin conspirators and of Tony Accardo for income tax evasion" to have been "its two most notable successes."

He mentions the fact that both were "reversed on appeal" but does not indicate the bases for the reversals. These reasons, in the Apalachin case, at least, would seem to justify rather than impugn Hoover's lack of enthusiasm for the Special Group.

One reason why he was unenthusiastic was that he feared that its "fishing expeditions" would take it outside the law. Another was that he has always feared that a national police force might come into being by way of some hastily conceived effort, in a time of dramatically publicized crisis, to make our "disunified" system a match for a totalitarian opponent by unifying its law enforcement efforts—from the top down. We think that the handling of the Apalachin case shows his anxieties to have been justified.

Our conclusion derives from three documents. One is an article by the Group's Deputy Chief, Gerald L. Goettel, in the November 1960 *Harper's*, "Why the Crime Syndicates

Can't Be Touched." The second is the ruling handed down by Chief Judge Lumbard of the Court of Appeals, Second Circuit, reversing the Apalachin convictions.[10] The third, published with the second, is a separate but concurring opinion by Circuit Judge Clark. We take our account of events at Apalachin from the Court's ruling.

The gathering took place on November 14, 1957, at the home of Joseph Barbara, Sr.—an estate of 130 acres at the end of a dirt road. New York State Trooper Edgar Crosswell, accompanied by two agents of Treasury's Alcohol and Tobacco Tax Division, made a car check in Barbara's parking lot. The three men then set up a roadblock half a mile from the house.

At this roadblock, 58 persons were stopped on their way out from Barbara's place and were asked to identify themselves; 38 were questioned, without warrants or the making of any charge, about the reason for their presence and the purpose of the meeting. When it began to rain, some 20 of them were taken to the State Police barracks for questioning—still without legal warrant.

Of those questioned, only 27 gave any explanation of why they had been at Barbara's; and their answers were diverse. The most common answer "was that the purpose of the visit was to call upon a sick friend or to accompany someone doing so." Barbara had, in fact, been ill for some time. Two men, who lived nearby, said that they had frequently visited him during his illness. One said that he had accompanied a relative "who wanted to see Barbara to discuss a similar heart condition." Two said they had been invited to a party. Several gave business reasons.

The chief product of their being questioned was a wave of intense and persistent "nationwide publicity"—which Crosswell appears to have encouraged. In brief, a public demand for action against the Mafia was stimulated into being.

---

[10] *United States v. Russell A. Bulfalino et al*, No. 357, Docket 26194, U.S. Court of Appeals, Second Circuit, November 28, 1960. 285 *Federal Reporter*, 2nd Series, pp. 408 ff.

The FBI made a thorough investigation and, in line with established policy, submitted its findings to the United States Attorney of the region. Although many of the persons present were known to have criminal records on other counts, he found no proof that the *meeting* had a purpose which violated any federal law. Hence, no prosecutions were undertaken.

The public clamor continued; and, in due course, the Special Group on Organized Crime was formed. According to Goettel's article, it set about finding some basis on which the "Apalachin conspirators" could be prosecuted.

He writes that the Group spent eight months collecting data "which produced no indictments." It then decided to seek evidence by means of a grand jury investigation "of the Apalachin meeting itself." This investigation, which focused on the purpose of the gathering, brought to light nothing for which anyone could be prosecuted.

Goettel continues:

Gradually I realized that we were on the wrong track in seeking individual indictments. A conspiracy was preventing us from learning its secrets—a conspiracy to obstruct justice. Hence, I felt that our only chance was in a sweeping conspiracy charge. Our attack need not be directed at the conspirators' "business" about which our knowledge was meager and inconclusive, but rather at their actions in thwarting the many investigations . . . .

Twenty persons were finally indicted and brought to trial. At no point, according to the later ruling of the Court of Appeals, did the prosecution claim to know the purpose of the Apalachin meeting. Yet it contended that both refusals to answer questions and the giving of diverse answers, no one of which was proved to be false, constituted an obstruction of justice: in effect, a failure to acknowledge a purpose which was hypothesized to be illegal.

Goettel, in his article, writes that the Special Group had, without success, asked for copies of the FBI's investigative reports. The United States District Court ordered the Bureau's agents to testify. Ironically, their testimony—which had not been judged to be sufficient to warrant a prosecution—appears to have had decisive weight for the jury: the trial ended with a verdict of mass guilt.

The Court of Appeals made very plain its opinion that the entire performance, from the questioning at the roadblock to the final verdict, had been a travesty upon due process. Our concept of justice, it declared, could not be served by

a shotgun conspiracy charge aimed at everyone who gave an explanation inconsistent with the government's suspicion of the purpose of the meeting.

Indubitably, many of Barbara's guests were "bad people." But

their conviction for a crime which the government could not prove, on inferences no more valid than others equally supported by reason and experience and on evidence which a jury could not properly assess, cannot be permitted to stand.

Circuit Judge Clark, concurring, said that a prosecution "framed on such a doubtful basis" should not have been initiated in the first place, nor allowed to proceed so far:

For in America we still respect the dignity of the individual, and even an unsavory character is not to be imprisoned except on definite proof of a specific crime.

We want the Government to secure as many legitimate convictions as it can against organized crime figures. But to praise these Apalachin convictions as a "notable success" is to confuse rather than clarify the issue of what *is* legitimate under our system of law. Confusion is further compounded when, as in Cook's article, the FBI Director is sharply criticized for being meticulously law-bound and for not letting Bureau agents enter cases without a clear jurisdictional right to do so.

TWENTY-SIX

THE FBI AND THE CONCERNED CITIZEN

I S IT IN the nature of free institutions that they must be overthrown because of the very freedoms they sustain?" In a 1966 memorandum, Freedom House, New York, posed this question. Events of the two years since then have given it an even more pressing relevance than it had when the memorandum was issued.

We are bringing this book to a close at the end of September 1968—at a mid-point between the Democratic National Convention in Chicago, in late August, and the November Presidential election. Not a day goes by without thunder on the Left and the Right—with each extreme profiting by the other's manifestation of its will to demolish what it cannot control.

On September 21st, for example, the *Washington Post* carried an editorial headed "Spirit of Chicago." It reported that Rennie Davis, Tom Hayden, and Abbie Hoffman—"the three radicals who did such a nifty job at the Democratic National Convention"—had announced their plans for what they called "an 'election offensive' in the Chicago spirit."

The "spirit of Chicago," so the announcement went, would be "carried forward" to disrupt all meetings at which a Presidential candidate was to speak. Further, a "vote strike" would be held in November; and there would be "a massive demonstration in Washington on Inauguration Day." The Chicago spirit was said to be one of "defiance and resistance" *against the government*—because of the war in Vietnam.

The guerrilla strategists do not expect to prevent the election or inauguration of a President. They expect to capitalize on a series of occasions when a vast number of Americans will have a common focus of attention. Their aim will be—as they boast of its having been in Chicago—to harass law enforcement officials into types of action that will, when publicized in the press and on TV, win sympathy for the demonstrators and their alleged commitment to peace.

The measure of their success will be the number of "idealists" whose latent anti-authority feelings are made stronger and more nearly overt. But the real victors will be the extremists of the Right. Their chances of getting repressive statutes on the federal books and of downgrading our legal structure will be improved. Our minds turn back to 1919: the bomb-throwers produced, not a Government in collapse, but the xenophobic anti-radicalism of the "Red raids."

All this is preliminary to our emphasizing a fact that is too often overlooked: namely, that an open society, far from being one that almost runs itself, is the most demanding of all types. "We have got, I think, to maintain a balance," Hoover told the Warren Commission; and his words express the essence of freedom's drama and dilemma.

Elihu Root once declared that "every sovereign state has the right to protect itself by preventing a condition of affairs in which it will be too late to protect itself." The overwhelming majority of Americans, we feel sure, would agree. But they would not agree as to when the danger point was being reached; and no one has an infallible power to identify such a point.

In a recent article, "The American Commitment to Dissent," Alpheus T. Mason, from whose biography of Harold Fiske Stone we have quoted earlier, wrote that all the distinctive features of our system—its separation of powers, federalism, Bill of Rights, judicial review, and the rest—"were designed to maintain heritage and heresy in creative tension."[1]

To agree with this statement is one thing. But to recognize the point at which the tension between heritage and heresy is becoming so implacably hostile that it is destructive, not creative, is quite another thing.

The always-present problem of maintaining a balance becomes infinitely more complex in a period of crisis or acute social unrest—*because the number of persons who do not want it to be maintained is sharply increased.* Both the Right and the Left are overcrowded now with individuals and organizations that have, in effect, revised Voltaire. Their tactics proclaim, "I disagree utterly with what you say, and I will oppose to the death your right to say it."

Students of American history have frequently noted the odd fact that our Federal Government, which the framers of the Constitution saw as the most likely source of encroachment upon individual rights, has become their protector. To serve this function, it must be committed to the preservation of balance.

Here, the FBI performs a double role. On the intelligence front, it keeps accurate enough track of what is being done and planned by those who seek to destroy the structure of our rights that it knows when they cross the line between legitimate dissent and law-breaking. On the federal law enforcement front, it takes action against those who cross this line.

[1] *University: A Princeton Quarterly,* Summer 1968, p. 3.

Throughout this book, we have tried to define what we have a right to expect of the FBI—because of the strategic position it holds, for better or worse, within our open society. In the light of what we have said above, it seems appropriate, here at the end, to reverse the direction of our inquiry and ask what it has a right to expect of us.

The first item is rudimentary—and indispensable. It should be able to expect that if we want the benefits of liberty under law, we will neither claim the special privilege of being a law-breaker nor try to become a law-changer except by duly provided means that are within the law.

It should be able to expect that we will put behind us our immature tendency to regard the criminal as almost a hero—or as an underdog. A criminal, no matter how appalling his record, has rights that we must respect. If they are denied him, we are obligated to intervene in his behalf. But the right to be romanticized is not among them.

Addressing the South Carolina Chamber of Commerce, on January 11, 1968, Assistant to the Director C.D. De Loach spoke of a growing public awareness that a rising crime rate "represents not merely an increase in the number of crimes *committed,* but *an increase in the number of victims . . . .*"[2]

De Loach's point of view is a healthy development. Certain categories of victims—of poverty, racism, police brutality, emotionally destructive home conditions—have, quite rightly, been recipients of our concern and compassion. Victims of crime have not been so in comparable measure. It has almost seemed, at times, that our will to view the criminal as a victim of circumstances has militated against our extending our attention to those whom he has victimized.

Again, when the FBI has offered the public a clue as to how it could help reduce the incidence of one or another type of crime, it should be able to expect some responsive

[2] Assistant to the Director C. D. De Loach, *Respect for Law and Order* (FBI, Washington, D.C.), p. 9.

action. The simple matter of not leaving our car unlocked, or with the key in the ignition, is a case in point.

On a very different front, it ought to have a right to expect that when we hear charges that it has either over-stepped the bounds of law or held back from difficult assignments, we will not help to spread the charge further, by repeating it to all and sundry, until we have made some effort to check on how accurate it is—or at least to appraise its plausibility. To the FBI, and to every other agency of our Government, we owe, in this time of irresponsible and calculated rumor-mongering, a gift of silence: the exercise of freedom does not require that we make haste to pass along to others every unchecked derogation that we have read or heard.

Not least, as the Bureau shoulders, under the Omnibus Crime Bill, an increasingly heavy load of responsibility for the training of local police officers, it should be able to count on a supportive community interest.

Sixty years have passed since Attorney General Bona-parte, in January 1909, wrote to President Theodore Roose-velt about his problem of recruiting first-rate, well-educated men for his new investigative body, now the FBI. Such men, he said, were not inclined toward detective work because of the low pay and the low esteem in which it was generally held; and it was held in low esteem because such men were not taking it on.

In a host of communities, today, a Chief of Police who would like to build a truly professional force is trapped in the very type of vicious circle that Bonaparte was trying to break out of in 1909. The Government can help—through FBI training programs, and by making possible a salary scale that high-quality men will find attractive. But the community must provide for such men respect and admira-tion—and a renewed dedication to liberty under law.

On August 8, 1965, the press reported the findings of a

Gallup poll relating to the FBI. One question was, "If you had a son who decided to become an FBI agent, would you be pleased or displeased?" More than three persons out of four—77 percent—said they would be pleased.

So far as the Bureau is concerned, in brief, the problem of "esteem" has been solved—for as long a time as its current standards are maintained. When we think of how incredible the above type of response to *any* investigative body would have been in Bonaparte's day, it does not seem unrealistic to hope that the level of esteem in which police forces are held can be made to go up, as standards are raised, in community after community.

There will be problems to overcome. Not the least of them will be that the Chief of Police must himself be given professional status and made immune to political control. But as the rewards of raised standards become more and more apparent, the achievement of them should become more and more readily possible.

Before we end this chapter, and the book, we wish to take stock of the FBI's role in relation to applicants for federal posts. In the course of many conversations, in many parts of the country, we have discovered that this role is widely deplored—and widely misunderstood.

The first fact to pin down is that the principle of checks and balances, so indispensable to our system, covers the use of the Bureau's files—or, as various critics prefer to call them, with police-state overtones, the "dossiers." The fixed policy is that *those who investigate must not evaluate*. Hoover has repeatedly stressed the dangers that would result from this policy's being flouted or discarded; and we have found no evidence of a departure from it in the field of national security investigations.

The terms of the national security program are beyond the reach of the FBI to alter or abolish. They are products of two executive orders. As clear an explanation as we have found of how the operation is carried on is in an article by Hoover called "Role of the FBI in the Federal Employee Security Program." First published in the July-August 1954 issue of *Northwestern University Law Review*, this was revised and brought up to date in December 1961.

On March 21, 1947, President Truman instituted the Federal Employee Loyalty Program, by means of Executive Order 9835. This provided that "every civilian employee or applicant for employment in the executive branch of the government was subject to an investigation for loyalty."

On April 27, 1953, President Eisenhower replaced this program by the Federal Employee Security Program, by means of Executive Order 10450. This Order carried forward the earlier requirements but broadened them to take account of factors other than loyalty that might have a derogatory influence upon an employee's performance. Among these factors were alcoholism, drug addiction, mental or physical disability of a type which competent medical authority rated as likely to impair judgment, the making of false statements on the applicant form, sexual perversion, a criminal record, and anything that might make the applicant subject to blackmail.

Executive Order 10450 instructs each departmental or agency head to designate as "sensitive" all positions under him in which a disloyal occupant could exert "a material adverse effect on the national security"; and it specifies that each position thus designated "shall be filled or occupied by a person with respect to whom a full field investigation has been conducted." It also defines a minimal investigative procedure to be followed with employees or applicants for non-sensitive posts.

In all this, the primary investigative responsibility rests, not with the FBI, but with the employing agency, "unless the person is in the competitive service"—in which case it rests with the Civil Service Commission. Agencies that lack investigative facilities use those of the Civil Service. Except where it *is* the employing agency, the FBI enters the picture only in response to requests made and data provided by other federal bodies; and only to perform tasks spelled out in the executive order.

One minimal procedure required is a fingerprint check—to determine whether or not the individual has a record of arrests. Hence, all federal agencies forward to the FBI the prints on which they want a report. It makes the requisite search of its fingerprint files and transmits to the requesting agency, *without evaluation or recommendation*, a factual report on its findings.

This fingerprint check, which is often attributed to Hoover's "relentless" will to punish people for past mistakes, is a routine prescribed by an executive order. "As of October 31, 1961," Hoover writes, "a total of 2,696,443 sets of fingerprints have been processed under the present program, of which 182,222 or 6.76 percent have been identified with previous arrest data."

All this does not mean that everyone with a record of arrest is fired or denied employment, but only that the employing agency or the Civil Service Commission has a basis for looking further into his case and making an appropriate decision. Any individual who feels a decision with respect to him to be unjust has the right of appeal. Far from overemphasizing past mistakes, the program brings relief to those who can establish that such mistakes belong to their past; not their present: it lets them slough off the burden of secrecy and accompanying fear.

Also, it protects the Government, and the taxpayer, against the perennial criminal. Thus, one man admitted to a single arrest, "but neglected to mention an extensive criminal record dating back to 1932, including, among other things, arrests for grand larceny, forgery, hit-and-run driving, [and] burglary . . . ."

The minimal procedure also calls for a name check. The employing agency furnishes the FBI with a standard form that has been filled out and signed by the applicant or employee and that holds enough identifying data to enable the Bureau to search its investigative files. One type of form is used by those who hold, have been appointed to, or are applying for a "sensitive" post; and in each such case, the FBI must make a full field investigation. A different form is used by all other employees, appointees, and applicants.

"As of October 31, 1961, a total of 2,419,954 forms had been processed under Executive Order 10450, of which 2,303,174 were returned with appropriate notations revealing no derogatory information." Such a notation is not a *clearance*. It signifies only that the FBI files, as of that date, contain "no derogatory information, either subversive or nonsubversive, within the provisions of Executive Order 10450 . . . ." For the FBI to give *clearance* would be for it to arrogate to itself an evaluative—almost a judicial—function.

If the files reveal *nonsubversive* derogatory information, this is "immediately furnished, without comment or recommendation, to the Civil Service Commission for appropriate action and transmittal to the employing agency." What happens in consequence depends upon this agency. The FBI conducts no investigation.

But if the files reveal *subversive* information, the Bureau must, under the Executive order, make a full field investigation "to either prove or disprove the available derogatory data." This wording is crucial. The FBI's task is neither to clear the individual nor to prove him guilty, but only to determine whether specific allegations that are on file are true or false.

"In one instance, for example," Hoover reports, "information was received that a government employee was a member of the Communist Party. Moreover, a letter received at an FBI field office alleged that he appeared to be strongly in favor of Communism." And someone with his name was known to have signed various Communist nominating petitions.

The FBI investigation, however, proved both the original and the second allegation to be false. "Moreover, it was determined that none of the signatures on the nominating petition were written by the employee."

In another case, however, where a government employee was investigated because the files showed that he had been reported as a member of the Communist Party, the fact of his having been so for at least six years was established. "A Communist Party registration card for this person was located for two successive years, giving the Communist Party branches to which he had been assigned." These facts, without editorial comment, were transmitted to the employing agency.

Robert Frost once wrote, "The fact is the sweetest dream that labor knows"; and the fact might well serve as a text for FBI investigations. Painstakingly to assemble facts and transmit them, unedited and unevaluated, to whoever must interpret them as a basis for federal action: this is the proper and *limited* role of the FBI.

One insistent criticism is that the "dossiers" are as receptive to malicious falsehood and deliberately planted rumor as to accurate data. This is literally true. But what alternative would be more just, in the long run, to everyone concerned? How could the FBI be *selectively* hospitable to materials provided by citizens and multiple agencies without, in effect, substituting for investigation some "intuitive" method of separating fact from falsehood?

What is received becomes just so much inert matter in the file unless or until there is a specific reason, dictated by some federal law, to make a checkup on its truth or falsity. Data so glaringly fanciful that they could safely be dismissed as "out of this world" are not likely to weigh against anyone after an investigation.

For a moment, here, we must assume a "guinea pig" role; for we have had to decide how we intend to think and feel about the catch-all character of the FBI files. The fact is that we know, in more than a few cases, what has been sent in about us. No one has "leaked" information. But Far Right individuals and groups that have written to program chairmen or issued leaflets to warn against our "nefarious" influence have frequently added a notation: "Copy to the FBI."

As we have read some of the more extraordinary of these, we have been tempted to feel that if the FBI were of sound mind it would drop its copies into the wastebasket. Yet *we would hate to have it do so*. If its policies allowed it to do so, we would begin to fear it as a threat to our freedoms.

Very emphatically, we do not want the FBI, on our behalf or that of anyone else, to set up shop as an evaluating body. We want it to do its limited, neutral job of fact-finding—and *to stay in its place*. We want this bureau, of all bureaus, to operate on the level of the prosy and slogging; and to do so, it must treat all leads as potentially equal.

Testifying before the Warren Commission, Hoover made plain his awareness that many allegations received belong in the nonsense category. No lead that could conceivably have yielded new evidence was ignored in the FBI's investigation of the assassination of President Kennedy. But often the agent who followed a lead arrived at a person who had identified the assassin by "psychic vibrations" or who admitted that what he had written to the Bureau was "an entire falsehood."

In such a case, the agent's task is not to tell off the unbalanced, irresponsible, or malicious person who has wasted his time. It is the prosy one of getting a signed acknowledgement of the "psychic" or false character of the allegation. This signed statement joins the original letter in the file.

The FBI's obligation to act as a neutral recipient of proffered data is a chief reason, however, why its files *must* remain confidential. Any one of them, in the hands of a person activated by malice, or simply untrained to interpret such a miscellany, could become, as Hoover has emphasized, "a dangerous instrument of injustice."

In an article called "The Confidential Nature of FBI Reports," in the Fall 1956 issue of *Syracuse Law Review*, he explored this subject in careful detail. In doing so, he quoted from a letter which Attorney General Robert H. Jackson had sent, on April 30, 1941, to the Chairman of the House Committee on Naval Affairs—declining to furnish FBI reports to this Committee:

Disclosure of information contained in the reports might . . . be the grossest kind of injustice to innocent individuals. Investigative reports include leads and suspicions, and sometimes even the statements of malicious and misinformed people. Even though later and more complete reports exonerate the individuals, the use of particular or selected reports might constitute the gravest injustice, and we all know that a correction never catches up with an accusation.

Those who deplore the "secrecy" of the files and the readiness of Justice to drop a prosecution rather than deliver to *anyone* the full contents of any file, need to rethink their stance.

When President Truman instituted the Federal Employee Loyalty Program, there was no way to estimate how many persons had, through the years, made their way into federal employment for reasons inimical to our national welfare. On four counts at least, the time was ripe for a checkup.

World War II had brought a vast, sudden buildup of federal personnel. Also, it had created a manpower shortage that made it difficult to maintain exacting standards of employment. We were unexpectedly involved in a Cold War for which the Soviet Union had been preparing while we still called it an ally. And since no one knew how many subversives might have made their way into the Government, anyone could put into circulation whatever estimate his temperament or ideology might dictate.

The time was ripe, moreover, for a *continuing* program of checkup on applicants. We had burned behind us the bridges of isolationism. There was exactly no chance that we could again retreat from world involvements. Thus, it was predictable that diverse nations and ideological bodies would, as time went on, try to plant within our Government persons who would channel to them data which they had no right to possess.

From the outset, the Program was denounced as a gigantic "witch-hunt" authored by Hoover as part of his "relentless" war on liberals and dissenters. Thus, it seems relevant to recall certain facts and figures.

When the Program was three years old, Morris Ernst, Counsel for the American Civil Liberties Union, included his findings with respect to it in his article "Why I No Longer Fear the FBI."

He had "personally checked" about one hundred complaints that agents used improper methods of gathering data, and had found no convincing evidence to support them. The same was true, "in spite of alarms and outcries," or charges that the files were being used to hound innocent people out of their jobs.

"It surprised me," he wrote, "to learn that, of 2,873,180 employees whose records were examined by the FBI, all but 12,825 were promptly cleared." After further investigation "only 230 employees were finally dismissed"; and 163 of these successfully appealed their dismissal. In short, there were 67 persons out of 2,873,180—or one out of every 42,835—whose dismissals were confirmed. And "1474 resigned before their cases came up." Ernst remarks wryly that when he was writing his article, the FBI was under fire both for conducting a "witch-hunt" and for not finding as many subversives as it should.

We will end on this note. If there is one thing of which we have become aware in the course of this study, it is that the work of the FBI is far less melodramatic than it is often made to appear and far more quietly dramatic than is commonly realized. The drama stems from its relationship to freedom's enterprise.

INDEX

Abel, Rudolf, 187

Accordo, Anthony, 363

ACLU, *see* American Civil Liberties Union

Act to exclude and expel from the United States aliens who are members of the anarchistic classes, An (1918), 40–41

Afro-American, 169

Agents, procedures followed by Federal Bureau of Investigation, 117–18

Aguici, Vito, 142

Akerman, Amos T., 12–14

Alcohol and Tobacco Tax Unit, Treasury Department, 77, 189

Aliens, 318
   as advocates of revolutionary violence, 42
   1918 act on, 40–41
   Palmer on, 44–46, 116
   Post on, 45

Amabile, Joseph, 362–63

American Civil Liberties Union (ACLU), 136–37, 323

"American Commitment to Dissent, The" (Mason), 377

American Communism and Soviet Russia (Draper), 42n

American Foreign Policy and the Cold War (Aptheker), 179–80

American National Bookstore News, 271–72

American Nazi Party, *see* National Socialist White People's Party

"American OGPU, An" (*The New Republic*), 247–48

American Opinion, 248, 275, 278

American Political Science Review, 212

American Protective League (APL), 36–37, 38, 40

Amico, Michael A., 357–58

Anarchists, 40–41

Andrews, Mark, 280

Anti-Communist Christian Association, 285–87, 291–92

Anti-racketeering Act (1934), 77
   amendment to, 79

Anti-radicalism, post World War I, 40–43

APL, *see* American Protective League

Aptheker, Herbert, 179–80

Attorneys General
   approval of eavesdropping by, 122, 127
   on checks and controls in FBI, 102, 113, 114
   pre-FBI history of, 11–20
   See also Ackerman; Bonaparte; Brewster; Clark; Cummings; Daugherty; Devens; Gregory; Harmon; Jackson; Katzenbach; R. Kennedy; McGrath; McReynolds; W. H. H. Miller; W. Mitchell; Moody; F. Murphy; Palmer; Randolph; Rogers; Stone; Wickersham; Williams

Baldwin, Roger, 137

Bank robbery, 105, 256–57

Barbara, Joseph, Sr., 259, 358, 372

388